CHARTERS AND CUSTUMALS
OF THE ABBEY OF
HOLY TRINITY
CAEN

Part 2
The French Estates

Charter 1. British Library, Add. Ch. 15279

RECORDS OF SOCIAL AND ECONOMIC HISTORY
NEW SERIES 22

CHARTERS AND CUSTUMALS OF THE ABBEY OF HOLY TRINITY CAEN

Part 2
The French Estates

EDITED BY
JOHN WALMSLEY

Published for THE BRITISH ACADEMY
by OXFORD UNIVERSITY PRESS

Oxford University Press, Walton Street, Oxford OX2 6DP
Oxford New York Toronto
Delhi Bombay Calcutta Madras Karachi
Kuala Lumpur Singapore Hong Kong Tokyo
Nairobi Dar es Salaam Cape Town
Melbourne Auckland Madrid
and associated companies in
Berlin Ibadan

Published in the United States
by Oxford University Press Inc., New York

British Library Cataloguing in Publication Data
Data available

ISBN 0–19–726137–X

Typeset by J&L Composition Ltd, Filey, North Yorkshire
Printed in Great Britain
on acid-free paper by
The Cromwell Press,
Melksham, Wiltshire

TO MY MOTHER
EDITH URSULA WALMSLEY

Foreword

With the publication of this volume scholarly justice has been done and a longstanding academic obligation fulfilled: Dr. Walmsley's meticulous documentation of the French estates of the Abbey of Caen can now be studied in juxtaposition with their English counterparts, edited by Dr. Marjorie Chibnall and published in 1982 as Volume V in the present series. Medievalists will appreciate the synergy created between the two volumes.

Dr. Walmsley considers it probable that the separation of England and Normandy in 1204 prompted a review of the landholdings and diverse other privileges enjoyed by an Abbey with extensive assets in both regions. The main documentary basis for the volume consists of two surveys, 60–70 years apart. Detailed internal detective work comparing the two sets of data elucidates the 'real' from the 'ideal' in the surveys, with some entries for the same property helping to confirm both surveys, but others compounding the difficulties of interpreting each. More widely the documents open a window onto the structure and function of local society (particularly for the vavassor and sub-vavassor groups) revealing a picture of great diversity and flexibility over time. Much insight is also offered into local economic and social conditions; together with glimpses of intriguing detail—such as the flourishing Norman vineyards, bacon and cheese imports from England, farm gates with locks and manorial officials lining their own pockets at the Abbey's expense.

April 1994

Peter Mathias
*Chairman, Records of Social and
Economic History Committee*

Contents

LIST OF ILLUSTRATIONS   viii

PREFACE   ix

ORIGINAL SOURCES   x

ABBREVIATED REFERENCES   x

EARLY ABBESSES OF CAEN   xii

INTRODUCTION   1
     1. The Cartulary   1
     2. The Estates 1066 – c. 1113   4
     3. The Estates at the Time of the Surveys c. 1113 – c. 1180   12
     4. Surveys A and B Compared   14
     5. The Administration of the French Properties   20
     6. Social Classes   23
     7. The Cartulary Documents   26
     8. The Original Charters   28
     9. The 1257 Survey of Abbess Juliana de Saint-Sernin   31
     10. Note on the Editing   32

NOTE ON CURRENCY, LAND MEASURES AND DRY MEASURES   33

ORIGINAL CHARTERS 1–21   35

SURVEYS   53
First Series, A   53
Second Series, B: 61
     Carpiquet   61
     Saulques   70
     La Rouelle   72
     Juvigny-sur-Seulles   74
     Vaux-sur-Seulles   75
     Sallen   77
     Grainville-sur-Odon   79
     Escanneville   82
     Gonneville   87
     Beauvoir   87
     Bougy   89
     Auberville-sur-Mer   89
     Bavent   92

Montbouin   94
Tassilly   96
Ranville   99
Villons-les-Buissons   103
Amblie   107
Graye-sur-Mer   109

CARTULARY DOCUMENTS 1–27   112

GLOSSARY   138

ADDENDA AND CORRIGENDA IN PART 1   141

INDEX OF PERSONS AND PLACES   143

INDEX OF SUBJECTS   157

List of Illustrations

Charter 1. British Library, Add. Ch. 15279   *Frontispiece*

Map: The Estates of the Abbey of Holy Trinity, Caen, in Central
Normandy   5

Preface

The publication of the French charters and surveys of the abbey of Holy Trinity, Caen, represents the filling of a small but important lacuna in Anglo-Norman historical records. It is also a publication that seems to have been 'on the agenda' for a long time, and it might appear presumptuous for one domiciled on the other side of the globe to take on a task more prudently left to someone better versed in and physically closer to Normandy and its history. Any reluctance I may have had in this regard, however, was overcome by the generous encouragement and advice of Dr. Marjorie Chibnall, who published the English material relating to Holy Trinity in volume V of this series. My indebtedness to her and to Professor Lucien Musset of Caen is evident in many of the pages of this work.

Over a number of years I have received the cooperation of staff at the Archives départementales du Calvados, the Bibliothèque nationale in Paris, and the British Library. I have also received generous study leave and financial support from Macquarie University, Sydney, and in 1991 a research grant from the Australia Research Council. My thanks are extended to all these institutions and to the individuals associated with them.

I should also like to express my particular thanks to Dr. Cicely Howell of Western Australia and Dr. Howard Clarke of University College, Dublin, for reading and commenting on drafts of this work.

John Walmsley
Macquarie University
New South Wales
Australia

April, 1994

Original Sources

Caen, Archives du Calvados:
  H, Trinité de Caen (uncatalogued),
  Original charters, cartons 25, 26, 65, 73,105
  Cartulaire de l'Abbaye Sainte Trinité de Caen (carton 86)

Paris, Bibliothèque nationale:
  MS lat. 5650

London, British Library:
  Add. Ch. 15279

Abbreviated References

Abbayes caennaises	*Les actes de Guillaume le Conquérant et de la reine Mathilde pour les abbayes caennaises*, ed. L. Musset, Mémoires de la société des antiquaires de Normandie, xxxvii, Caen, 1967.
AN	*Annales de Normandie.*
Birdsall, *La Trinité*	Birdsall, 'The Abbey of La Trinité at Caen in the 11th and 12th Centuries', unpublished Ph.D. thesis, Harvard University, 1925.
Boussard, *Henri II*	J. Boussard, *Le gouvernement d'Henri II Plantagenêt*, Paris, 1956.
BSAN	*Bulletin de la société des antiquaires de Normandie.*
Carabie, *Propriété foncière*	R. Carabie, *La propriété foncière dans le très ancien droit normand (xie–xiiie siècles)*, Caen, 1943
Charters and Custumals	*Charters and Custumals of the Abbey of Holy Trinity Caen*, ed. M. Chibnall, Records of Social and Economic History, n.s., v, London, 1982.
David, *Curthose*	C.W. David, *Robert Curthose, Duke of Normandy*, Cambridge, Mass., 1920.
Delisle/Berger	L. Delisle and M. Elie Berger, *Recueil des actes de Henri II*, 4 vols. Chartes et diplômes relatifs à l'histoire de France, 1909–27.

Delisle, *Etudes*	L. Delisle, *Etudes sur la condition de la classe agricole et l'état de l'agriculture en Normandie*, Evreux, 1851.
EHR	*English Historical Review.*
Génestal, *Rôle des monastères*	R. Génestal, *Rôle des monastères comme établissements de crédit, étudié en Normandie du xie à la fin du xiiie siècle*, Paris, 1901.
Haskins, *Institutions*	C.H. Haskins, *Norman Institutions*, Cambridge, Mass., 1925.
Hippeau, *Dictionnaire*	C. Hippeau, *Dictionnaire topographique du département du Calvados*, Brionne, 1883.
Johnson, *Monastic Profession*	P.D. Johnson, *Equal in Monastic Profession: Religious Women in Medieval France*, Chicago, 1991.
Léchaudé d'Anisy, *Extraits*	A.L. Léchaudé d'Anisy, *Extraits des chartes et autres actes normands et anglo-normands qui se trouvent dans les Archives du Calvados*, Mémoires de la société des antiquaires de Normandie, vol. viii, pt. ii, Caen, 1834. Supplemented with an Atlas of seals by G. Mancel.
Legras, *Bourgage de Caen*	H. Legras, *Le bourgage de Caen: tenure à cens et tenure à rente (xie–xve siècles)*, Paris, 1911.
Ord. Vit. (ed. Chibnall)	*The Ecclesiastical History of Orderic Vitalis*, ed. M. Chibnall. 6 vols. Oxford, 1969–80.
Regesta	*Regesta Regum Anglo-Normannorum*, ed. H.W.C. Davis, C. Johnson, H.A. Cronne, and R.H.C. Davis. 4 vols. Oxford, 1913–69.
RHD	*Revue historique de droit français et étranger.*
Round, *CDF*	*Calendar of Documents preserved in France, 918–1216*, ed. J.H. Round, London, 1899.
Strayer, *Administration*	J.R. Strayer, *The Administration of Normandy*, Cambridge, Mass., 1932.
TAC	*Le très ancien coutumier de Normandie (texte latine)*, ed. E.-J. Tardif, Rouen, 1881.
Tabuteau, *Transfers of Property*	E.Z. Tabuteau, *The Transfers of Property in Eleventh-Century Norman Law*, Chapel Hill/London, 1988.
Valin, *Le duc de Normandie*	L. Valin, *Le duc de Normandie et sa cour (912–1204): étude d'histoire juridique*, Paris, 1909.
1257 Survey	L. Musset, 'Reconstitution de la jurée de 1257', unpublished typescript.

Early Abbesses of Caen[1]

Matilda, 1059 – 6 July, 1113
Cecilia, 1113 – 13 July, 1127
Isabel, *c.* 1127
Beatrice of Hugueville, after 1128, died before 1135[2]
Alicia, occurs for some years before and after 1135. Possibly the same
  person as
Adeliz, fl. *c.* 1142 × 1152.[3]
Dametta, occurs in 1150s and 1160s
Johanna, occurs from 1180s to 1227/8
Isabella de Crèvecoeur, 17 July, 1230 – *c.* 1237
Juliana de Saint-Sernin, 4 October, 1237 – *c.* 1266

[1] Based on *Charters and Custumals*, 139–40, except where indicated in footnotes.
[2] *Ord. Vit.* (ed. Chibnall), II, 130, n. 1.
[3] B.L., Add. Ch. 15279 (Charter 1).

Introduction

Little justification needs to be made for the publication of the twelfth-century surveys of the French estates of the Benedictine abbey of Holy Trinity, Caen. It is a matter of regret that these surveys were not published in 1982 alongside those for the English estates,[1] perhaps even that the complete contents of the abbey's famous cartulary have not appeared in a single volume, as promised long ago by Léopold Delisle and René-Norbert Sauvage.[2]

The principal purpose of this small volume, therefore, is to publish the two series of French surveys and other documents in the Caen Cartulary relating to the abbey's French property, with the exception of those already published by Lucien Musset[3] and with the exception of the extremely damaged late-thirteenth-century material at folios 89–95. In addition, and with the same purpose as Marjorie Chibnall's volume in this series, a selection of original charters relating to the abbey's early history has been included on the grounds that their chronology runs parallel with the principal contents of the cartulary. The *terminus ad quem* for the charters is *c.* 1230, a date that marks the end of the long abbacy of Johanna, or possibly two Johannas, from *c.* 1180 to *c.* 1227/8.[4] It also marks a notable division between two periods of documentation, the earlier one being thin and patchy, the later one from the 1230s to the 1290s being relatively abundant.[5]

1 The Cartulary

There is little to be added to what has already been said about the nature of the main cartulary of Holy Trinity, Caen.[6] Most of the cartulary is

---

[1] *Charters and Custumals of the Abbey of Holy Trinity Caen*, Records of Social and Economic History, new series, v, ed. M. Chibnall (Oxford, 1982).
[2] Paris, Bibliothèque nationale, MS lat. 5650. L. Delisle, *Etudes sur la condition de la classe agricole et l'état de l'agriculture en Normandie* (Evreux, 1851), xxix; J. Yver, review of Carabie, *Propriété foncière* in *RHD* (1943), 105, n. 1.
[3] *Les actes de Guillaume le conquérant et de la reine Mathilde pour les abbayes caennaises*, ed. L. Musset (Mémoires de la société des antiquaires de Normandie, xxxvii, Caen, 1967), nos. 2, 8, 11, 12, 16, 17, 21, 22, 29.
[4] *Charters and Custumals*, 140.
[5] Cf. R.-N. Sauvage, *L'Abbaye de Saint-Martin de Troarn au diocèse de Bayeux, des origines au seizième siècle* (Caen, 1911), xxxvi–xxxvii, and H. Legras, *Le bourgage de Caen: tenure à cens et tenure à rente (xie–xve siècles)* (Paris, 1911), 25. See also *infra*, 'The Original Charters'.
[6] *Abbayes caennaises*, 22–3; *Charters and Custumals*, xxii–xxiv.

written in a late-twelfth- or very early-thirteenth-century charter-hand, which has a rather more careful appearance to it in the earlier folios than in the later folios.[1] At any rate, mistakes—omissions, erasures, alterations, and superscriptions—become more frequent towards the end of the document, as possibly the scribe tired of the task. Although the cartulary may be seen as part of the general transition from the 'age of charters' to the 'age of registers',[2] part of a general movement towards a tidier, more legalistic approach to the keeping of important records at all levels of society, it probably also reflects a heightened concern by the abbey for the integrity of its property in England, France and the Channel Islands after the separation of England and Normandy in 1204. In any event, it is important to see the cartulary as a whole, rather than simply as the source of two early series of surveys, for in this way it becomes easier to account for some of the apparent omissions from the surveys, especially the omission of urban property

The following is a list of those parts of the cartulary published here:

ff.13v–15r	Notice of a final concord, 20 January 1183 (Document 1)
ff.20r–23v	First survey of French estates, *c.* 1107×1113 (Survey A)
ff.23v–24r	Ouistreham rental, n.d. (Document 2)
f.23v	Ouistreham fish-market and shipwreck rights, 1230 (Document 3)
ff.24r–25r	Purchases of vineyards, urban property, and tithes, 1083×1084 (Document 4)
f.25r–v	Memorandum of land of Ralph, *pretor* of Villons-les-Buissons, n.d (Document 5)
f.31r–v	Sale of land at Sallen to which the abbey was made heir, late 11th/early 12th century (Document 6)
ff.31v–32r	Charter of Turold Papillon granting tithes to the abbey, before 1109–1113 (Document 7)
f.32r–v	Charter of Hawisa, wife of Robert Marmion, granting land to the abbey, 1106 (Document 8)
f.32v	Charter of Wiger of Sainte-Mère-Eglise granting land at Mortefemme in the Cotentin to the abbey, before 1082 (Document 9)

[1] Cf. Birdsall, 'The Abbey of La Trinité at Caen in the 11th and 12th Centuries', (unpublished Ph.D. thesis, Harvard University, 1925), 256, who describes the hand as 'the miniscule with rounded forms characteristic of the second half of the twelfth century'.

[2] T. Foulds, 'Medieval Cartularies', *Archives*, 18 (1987), 16. See also D. Walker, 'The Organization of Material in Medieval Cartularies' in D.A. Bullough and R.L. Storey (eds), *The Study of Medieval Records: Essays in Honour of Kathleen Major* (Oxford, 1971), 132–50, for the development of an 'archive sense' in the twelfth and thirteenth centuries.

ff.32v–33r — Farm of the abbey's property in Jersey, 1066–1113 (Document 10)

f.33r — Grant by the abbess of 6 acres, 4 fields, and a house in Colleville to Boso, late 11th/early 12th century (Document 11)

ff.33r–34r — Notification by Abbess Dametta that Robert of Calix has made the abbey heir to his property in Calix, Caen, c. 1152 – c. 1178 (Document 12)

f.34r–v — Charter of Robert Curthose, 1087–94 (Document 13)

f.38r–v — Ouistreham survey, n.d. (Document 14)

ff.39v–40v — Account of the spoliation of the abbey's estates after the death of William I, 1087–1100 (Document 15)

ff.60v–87r — Second survey of French estates, c. 1175–80 (Survey B) Carpiquet (ff.60v–64v) Saulques (f.65) La Rouelle (ff.66r–67r) Juvigny-sur-Seulles (f.67) Vaux-sur-Seulles (ff.67v–68r) Sallen (ff.68v–69v) Grainville-sur-Odon (ff.69v–71v) Escanneville (ff.71v–73r) Gonneville (f.73r) Beauvoir (ff.73v–74r) Bougy (f.74r) Auberville-sur-Mer (ff.74r–76r) Bavent (ff.76r–77r) Montbouin (ff.77r–78v) Tassilly (ff.78v–80r) Ranville (80r–82r) Villons-les-Buissons (ff.82r–84v) Amblie (ff.84v–85v) Graye-sur-Mer (ff.85v–87r)

f.87r — Notification that Abbess Johanna proved her legal right to a dwelling in Caen, 1183 (Document 16)

f.87r — Grant of a house in Caen by William of Calix, late 12th century (Document 17)

f.87v — Notification of a dispute over the advowson of the Church at Carpiquet, 1185 (Document 18)

f.88r — Notification that Godfrey of Tourlaville inherited his grandfather's messuage in Caen with the obligation of bleeding the abbey's oxen changed to payment of one pound of pepper, late 12th century (Document 19)

f.88r — Charter of Abbess Cecilia granting permission to move the abbey's mill, 1113–1127 (Document 20)

f.88r — Charter of Abbess Alicia granting a field in fee in return for wood for mill repairs, c. 1135 (Document 21)

f.88v — Record of judgement made at the Exchequer at Falaise concerning eleven sesters of grain from a mill in Caen, Easter 1217 (Document 22)

2   *The Estates 1066 – c. 1113*

Before turning to a consideration of the twelfth-century surveys incorporated in the abbey's principal cartulary it is worth reviewing the range
of the estates as revealed in the series of charters issued during the lifetimes
of the abbey's founders and initial benefactors.

   The consecration of the abbey of Holy Trinity by Maurilius, archbishop
of Rouen, on 18 June 1066 provided the natural opportunity to compile a
single comprehensive document on the extent of the abbey's estates, its
liberties and privileges. This took the form of a *pancarte*, or confirmation
charter, whose dispositive section consists mainly of summaries of earlier
grants, even to the extent of incorporating their witness lists.[1] Duke
William's personal contribution, together with that of his wife, does not
appear to have been conspicuously generous. At this stage its main
elements were the two relatively distant estates (*villae*) of Barges and
Chauffour, near Exmes in the *département* of Orne, 240 acres of arable
and eight acres of meadow in Caen, and a wide variety of tithes, some as
far afield as Jersey. Duchess Matilda's contribution consisted principally
of purchases made at a cost of more than 160 *livres* and one mark of gold,
and involved a greater proportion of property in the vicinity of the abbey:
for example in Caen itself, Vaucelles, Bénouville, Amblie, and Escanneville.
The balance of the property came largely from families whose women had
entered Holy Trinity as nuns. Adelaide, the daughter of Thurstan Haldup,
founder of Lessay Abbey in the Cotentin, brought with her a widely
dispersed estate with interests in Carpiquet, *Puteus*,[2] Feugeurolles, Eterville,
Démouville, Cuverville, Cornières, Rucqueville,[3] Ingouville, and Cauville.
Others contributed more modest assets, principally in the form of churches,
at Falaise, Guibray, Sallen, Vaux-sur-Seulles, and Foulbec. Matilda, the
founding abbess, purchased an unspecified amount of land at Hérouville,
to the north-east of the abbey, for 100s, but this was probably acquired
with abbey funds rather than through her own family's resources.[4]

   Although the foundation charter was mainly concerned with grants of
landed property and its associated revenue, it concludes with two sets of
special liberties and privileges. With the consent of Duke William,
Maurilius, archbishop of Rouen, Odo, bishop of Bayeux, Hugh, bishop of
Lisieux, John, bishop of Evreux, and four nobles, virtually all who were

---

[1] *Abbayes caennaises*, no. 2; *ibid.*, 25–41, 'notes de diplomatique'.
[2] *Puteus* seems to have been closely associated with Carpiquet here and in later references.
Cf. Charter 16: *puce fondre*; Carpiquet B, **21** and f. 64r, *De puteo effundre*. There is a field
called *La Pièce Fondrée* 2 km west of Carpiquet.
[3] The one ploughland at Rucqueville escaped Musset's notice: *Abbayes caennaises*, no. 2, 56
[4] *Abbayes caennaises*, no. 2, 55.

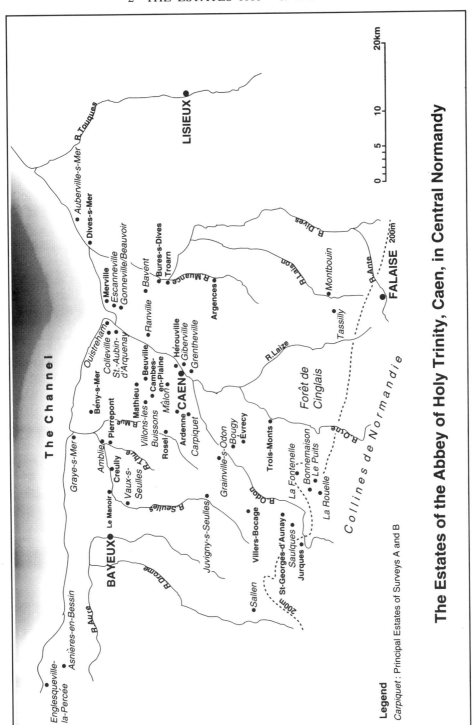

The Estates of the Abbey of Holy Trinity, Caen, in Central Normandy

Legend

Carpiquet : Principal Estates of Surveys A and B

associated with the abbey church of Holy Trinity, from the abbess and the nuns to their clergy and household servants (*famuli*), were declared exempt from all episcopal financial obligations except those relating to divine correction. Secondly, at the instigation of the bishop of Bayeux, citizens of Caen could elect to be buried at the abbey without their parish priests exacting compensatory sepulture fees.[1]

At this stage, six or seven years after its foundation in *c.* 1059, the abbey's material possessions had a very scattered, untidy look about them. Only four *villae* appear in their entirety in the list of donations, and three of these were situated more than thirty kilometres from Caen.[2] The remainder of the estates consisted of fractions of villages, unspecified amounts of land, churches and half-churches, mills, a total of six plough-lands in Jersey, Bures-sur-Dives, Caen, Cornières, Rucqueville, and Vaux-sur-Seulles, a total of 751 acres of arable and eight acres of meadow, woodland near Sallen, and an assortment of tithes from woodland, churches, tolls, fish, whales, salt, and rights of stewardship in the region of Bavent and Dives-sur-Mer in Calvados and in Gacé and Ecouché in Orne. As yet, of course, there was no question of property in England.

In 1082 another *pancarte* was issued by William and Matilda.[3] It is clear from either of the complete versions of this charter that the complement of estates belonging to the abbey had grown enormously, extending, within Normandy, beyond Calvados and Orne to the other *départements* of Manche, Eure, and Seine-Maritime. If the length of the 1082 charter and the number of place-names recorded in it are any guide—a crude but the only available measure—the abbey's estates had at least doubled since 1066.[4] All the estates mentioned in the consecration charter of 1066 are confirmed directly and specifically, with the exception of one ploughland at Bures-sur-Dives and the 240 acres of arable and eight acres of meadow at Caen.[5] More significantly, eight vills (*villae*), rather than four as in 1066,

---

[1] *Abbayes caennaises*, no. 2, 56. Notwithstanding later claims, from the late twelfth- to the eighteenth-century, the abbey was not granted total exemption from episcopal jurisdiction. It was simply granted freedom from financial *debitum* not freedom from jurisdictional *consuetudo*. Cf. J.-F. Lemarignier, *Etude sur les privilèges d'exemption et de juridiction ecclésiastique des abbayes normandes depuis les origines jusqu'en 1140* (Archives de la France monastique, xliv, Paris, 1937), 170–2. For the granting of identical rights in relation to the parish church of St. Giles see *Abbayes caennaises*, no. 8, 88–9, and Charter 5.

[2] Barges and Chauffour (*dép.* Orne), and Sallen in western Calvados. The fourth, Escanneville, lay 15 km north-east of Caen.

[3] *Abbayes caennaises*, no. 8.

[4] About ninety place-names are recorded, compared with less than forty in the charter of 1066.

[5] The land in Caen, however, may be represented by the grant of Calix (*villam quę vocatur Caluiz*): *Abbayes caennaises*, no. 8, 83.

seem to be held in their entirety, including estates that were to play a key role in the abbey's economy, such as Ouistreham at the mouth of the River Orne, Carpiquet, a few kilometres west of Caen, Auberville-sur-Mer, Sallen, and the *villa* of Calix. The donation of additional tithes, mills, meadow, arable, woodland, vineyards, and numerous unspecified amounts of land[1] gives an even more haphazard look to the abbey's possessions, but a few interesting features do emerge.

One of these seems to have been the development of an interest in viticulture. Queen Matilda purchased the agreement of Robert fitz Hamo to the addition of sixty arpents of vineyards at Chouain and Ducy-Sainte-Marguerite on the River Seulles.[2] She was also responsible for the acquisition of seven arpents at Argences, fifteen kilometres south-west of Caen, and a total of thirteen arpents at Léry, Aubevoye, and Vernon on the left bank of the Seine in the region between Rouen and Mantes. Abbess Matilda, too, was involved in purchasing vineyards: in three separate transactions in 1083/4 she bought a total of three arpents in Argences and Exmes at a cost of 27 *livres* and 10 *sous*.[3] The complete absence of evidence from later periods suggests that this viticultural activity was shortlived.[4]

The second development of note is that the 1082 charter contains evidence of a deliberate policy of consolidation through purchase and exchange. Two properties at Le Fresne-Camilly, near Creully, and *Maisnile Urselli* (unidentified, but probably in the same vicinity), which had been donated by Adelaide, daughter of Thurstan Haldup, were exchanged for three churches and their tithes in Caen, namely St. Stephen the Elder, St. Martin, and St. George (the castle church). The most significant single acquisition in this period, however, concerns the manor of Carpiquet. In 1066 only half of Carpiquet was in the abbey's possession as a result of the abovementioned Adelaide's entry to the religious profession. By 1082 the other half had been purchased for the abbey by the queen from Odo, Adelaide's brother, and Ranulf, *vicomte* of Bayeux. Until her death in 1083 Queen Matilda devoted a considerable amount of energy and cash to buying property for the abbey. Many of the donations of laymen, for example, could not be completed without payment from either the queen or the abbess to gain the assent of overlords or relatives whose honour, fee, or inheritance might be affected.[5]

---

[1] About a quarter of donations fall into the unspecified category.
[2] This purchase appears only in version II of the 1082 *pancarte*: *Abbayes caennaises*, no. 8, 88.
[3] Document 4.
[4] According to Delisle, *Etudes*, ch. 15, Norman viticulture reached its peak in the late eleventh and early twelfth centuries.
[5] Mention of these payments is a distinctive feature of the 1082 charter rather than the 1066 charter.

Undoubtedly one of the reasons for the haphazard appearance of the abbey's early endowment was that it consisted of numerous grants occasioned by the taking of the veil by female relatives of landholders throughout Lower Normandy. The 1066 and 1082 *pancartes* make direct reference to sixteen such donations. In association with other evidence, including a summary of the donations of founding members and the mortuary roll of Abbess Matilda, we have knowledge of more than thirty inmates from the early period of the abbey's history.[1] The range of their social origins is wide with a bias, especially at this stage of the abbey's development, towards the aristocracy, creating a community consisting largely of widowed and unmarried noble women. At one end of the scale there is Cecilia, one of the daughters of William and Matilda and a future abbess, and the daughters of Ranulf, *vicomte* of Bayeux, and of Thurstan Haldup; at the other end, there is the sister of William Bacco, whose dotation consisted of two-thirds of the tithes of Blay (twelve kilometres west of Bayeux) together with one villein (*rusticus*), and the daughter of Richard of Roullours, who brought with her an annual rent of one muid (*modius*) of wheat at Rosel, nine kilometres west of Caen.

The end of the first half-century of the abbey's existence is conveniently marked by the survival of yet a third version of the 1082 *pancarte*, which includes additions to the period 1105–9.[2] This version, which is known only through a copy made by the Abbé Gervais de la Rue in the early nineteenth century, is virtually identical in its early stages (preamble and dispositive) to the longer version of the 1082 charter (Version II), except that it furnishes information on the tenantry at Mortefemme in the Cotentin.[3] There follows a series of twenty-two donations, especially from families of new recruits, additional purchases and acquisitions, particularly in the Cotentin, some of which may have been omitted from the 1082 *pancarte*, but some of which are clearly post-1082 and even post-1105. This series of grants, donations and purchases is followed by a record of the abbey's enfeoffment of Humphrey of Adeville, dated 30 June 1109, *per tale servitium quale miles facere debet*.[4]

Apart from a certain preoccupation with the Cotentin, the most striking

---

[1] *Abbayes caennaises*, 47–8. There are twenty-nine nuns in Musset's list, to which should be added Aubrey (*Abbayes caennaises*, no. 22), another Aubrey, daughter of Fulk (*Abbayes caennaises*, nos. 8 and 22), Gisla, daughter of Thurstan (*Abbayes caennaises*, nos. 8 and 22), and an unnamed relative of William of Giberville (*Abbayes caennaises*, no. 27).

[2] *Abbayes caennaises*, no. 27.

[3] There were four free men and twelve customary tenants (*hospites*). Cf. Document 9.

[4] Adeville, four kilometres north of Carentan in the Cotentin, was held for 'knight service' and escort duty within and beyond Normandy. The abbey itself was exempt from knight service.

feature of the new acquisitions is the wider range of urban interests. Cecilia, not yet abbess but generally acting with or in the place of the ageing Matilda, was involved in two purchases of land in Calix; Gamul and his daughter gave the abbey sixty acres in the vicinity of Bayeux (*in territorio Baiocensi*) and a messuage in the city itself (*civitate*); and King William gave the abbey a messuage in Rouen to accommodate the abbess on her visits to the archdiocesan centre (*ad hospitandam abbatissam quando Rothomagum veniret*) and a messuage in Barfleur in the Cotentin to facilitate the receipt of rents from the English estates (*ad recipiendum redditus abbatię Sancte Trinitatis . . . portarentur illuc de Anglia*).[1]

The abbey's possession of the *burgum* of Quettehou (ten kilometres south of Barfleur), which had been granted by William and Matilda in the early 1080s,[2] was also confirmed in this early twelfth-century *pancarte*. Although the earliest reference to the *burgum* of Quettehou is in a charter of uncertain origin, which includes the donation of the two English manors of Great Baddow in Essex and Umberleigh in Devon,[3] it was further confirmed, along with two houses in England and a variety of English-made vessels, vestments and other gifts, probably in 1083.[4] Quettehou almost certainly served a similar function to that of the port of Barfleur mentioned above. Likewise, the grant of Le Homme (the modern Sainte-Mère-Eglise), twenty kilometres south of Quettehou, would have served a useful purpose in the transportation of goods from Barfleur or Quettehou to Caen.[5]

From the very beginning the abbey's urban interests in Caen itself were considerable. The consecration charter of 1066 records an initial endowment of 240 acres of (arable) land and eight acres of meadow in Caen. To this was added (in the second *pancarte*) the *villa* of Calix immediately to the south and east of the abbey. The same *pancarte* of 1082 records further additions in Caen, such as fifty acres purchased from Waleran, the son of Ranulf a successful local moneyer,[6] a mill within the borough of Caen granted by Ranulf, *vicomte* of Bayeux, unspecified lands which had belonged to Godfrey *iuvenis*, Roger the constable, and a William Patric,

---

[1] *Abbayes caennaises*, no. 27, 139. It is not clear whether William I or II is meant.

[2] *Abbayes caennaises*, no. 15.

[3] *Abbayes caennaises*, no. 15. See also *Charters and Custumals*, xxv-xxvi.

[4] *Abbayes caennaises*, no. 16.

[5] *Abbayes caennaises*, no. 8, refers to the *burgum de Hulmo*; no. 21 refers to *castrum quod dicitur Hulme*. Quettehou would fall into L. Musset's category of *bourgs portuaires*, which were characteristic of the Cotentin: 'Peuplement en bourgage et bourgs ruraux en Normandie du Xᵉ au XIIIᵉ siècle', *Cahiers de civilisation médiévale*, ix, no. 2 (1966), 186.

[6] For a discussion of Ranulf see L. Musset, 'A-t-il existé en Normandie au XIᵉ siècle une aristocratie d'argent?', *AN*, 9 (1959), 292–4. The same fifty acres are referred to as one ploughland in the Caen Cartulary, cf. ff. 2r and 11r (*Abbayes caennaises*, 55 and 87).

and the tithes of one mill and of the ducal ovens. An incomplete *pancarte* of 1066–83 makes reference to a few of the additions mentioned above, albeit in slightly different terms.[1] For example, it is very likely that the 240 acres of the 1066 charter are represented by land for three ploughs in the later charter.[2] The abbey was also granted the right to a road and two-thirds of the tithe of the provostship of Caen. The 'obedientary' charter of c. 1082–3 refers to the tithe of malt and bread, which formed part of the revenue of the provostship of Caen, land for two ploughs, ten acres of meadow and one and a half mills *ad victum sanctimonialium*.[3] The only additional urban property in Caen mentioned in the *pancarte* of 1109–13 is the land and houses that Fulchod, the queen's chamberlain, held, and two purchases of land in Calix. By the 1080s it is clear that the Calix area was becoming the focus of the abbey's expanding urban interests. In 1083–4 more than twelve *livres* of the abbey's 'works money' (*nummis operis*) was spent in obtaining land there.[4] Calix was, in effect, forming the eastern part of what was to be known as the *Bourg-l'Abbesse*, as opposed to the *Bourg-l'Abbé* and the *Bourg-le-Roi*.[5]

Further afield, but connected to Caen by the very navigable Orne, the large manor of Ouistreham was emerging as a market of note. Robert Curthose's charter of 1087–1094, confirming the abbey's rights in the borough of Caen from the castle wall to the abbey church and over all dwellings in Vaugueux to the wall in one direction and the Orne in the other, as well as all fishing rights, concludes with the first reference to the market and tolls of Ouistreham.[6]

There can be little doubt that the rule of Robert Curthose as duke of Normandy (1087–1106) witnessed inroads into the wealth and prosperity of the abbey of Holy Trinity. The main evidence for this is the long list of dispossessions recorded in the principal Caen Cartulary.[7] The account is lengthy and in places graphic. Total losses seem to have occurred at Tassilly, Montbouin, and Le Homme (Cotentin); unspecified amounts of land were seized at Quatrepuits, Cierney, and Doumaisnil, meadow at Graye-sur-Mer and Thiéville, woodland at Sallen, annual rents of more than 124 *livres roumois*, livestock, including more than sixty oxen, eight horses, twenty sheep and an unspecified number of pigs. Grain rents were

---

[1] *Abbayes caennaises*, no. 11.
[2] See 'Note on Currency, Land Measures and Dry Measures'.
[3] *Abbayes caennaises*, no. 12.
[4] See Document 4. The urban purchases are misleadingly incorporated in a section headed *De vineis Argentiarum*.
[5] Legras, *Bourgage de Caen*, 28–31.
[6] Document 13.
[7] Document 15. Cf. Haskins, *Institutions*, 63–4.

seized, woodland, vineyards and saltpits taken over, and their produce confiscated. There were beatings, killings, and incarceration of the abbey's men, some of whom were even forced to work on Count Henry's castles in the Cotentin, which had been placed under his control in 1088.[1]

Drastic as this picture may seem, it is notable that, for the most part, these losses were suffered on estates that were peripheral geographically if not economically. This is especially true of property in the Cotentin.[2] Similar losses of a peripheral kind occurred at Gacé (Orne), Hénouville (Seine-Maritime), Vernon and Foulbec (Eure). Furthermore, within the *département* of Calvados itself the most serious damage was inflicted on the relatively distant estates of Tassilly, Montbouin, Sallen, Auberville-sur-Mer, Grandcamps-les-Bains, Asnières-en-Bessin, and Englesqueville-la-Percée.

Moreover, some losses seem to have had more to do with second generation changes of mind and heart than with the misrule of Curthose, as heirs and even original donors attempted to retrieve what they or their forefathers had alienated. 'The family that gave was often the family that took away'.[3] Richard, son of Herluin, having been paid for his land at Tassilly and Montbouin,[4] had apparently taken back both properties into his own hands. The tithes of Hénouville (canton Duclair, near Rouen) granted by Aubrey, who had become a nun with the consent of her sons, Hugh and Roger, were appropriated by a William chamberlain, the son of Roger de Candos and possibly the grandson of Aubrey.[5] More directly and incontestably, whereas Robert Bertran had granted the abbey two free men and their tithes in Colombelles near Caen and his sister had donated all her interests there, for which the priest of Colombelles paid 5s annually to Holy Trinity,[6] a successor, William Bertran, is included in the list of despoilers for depriving the nuns of two vavassors (probably the two free men), their tithes, and 5s annual rent in the same parish.[7] Richard de Courcy, who was a witness to the settlement of a dispute between Holy Trinity and the abbey of St. Stephen in 1083,[8] is accused in this list of taking four *livres* and twenty sheep from the nuns, and, in association with

---

[1] *Ord. Vit.* (ed. Chibnall), IV, 120–1.

[2] It is possible that the losses or at least the difficulties at Barfleur and Quettehou in the Cotentin led directly to the development of Ouistreham as the main port for English goods.

[3] P.D. Johnson, *Equal in Monastic Profession: Religious Women in Medieval France* (Chicago, 1991), 47. Cf. M. Chibnall, *The World of Orderic Vitalis* (Oxford, 1984), 58–9.

[4] *Abbayes caennaises*, no. 11, 94.

[5] *Abbayes caennaises*, no. 8, 87.

[6] *Abbayes caennaises*, no. 8, 88.

[7] *Regesta*, I, no. 168 (1079–82): Robert and William Bertran appear together in a charter of William I to St. Stephen's Abbey in Caen.

[8] *Abbayes caennaises*, no. 17.

Ranulf, *vicomte* of the Bessin, of seizing a further fifteen *livres* from the abbey's property at Grandcamps-les-Bains.

Although circumstances in Normandy may have encouraged much of the above activity,[1] the nuns' list of complaints should be tempered by the fact that Holy Trinity was a favoured ducal foundation and that it received special attention from both Robert Curthose and William Rufus.[2] Nor should it be forgotten that by this time the abbey would have been receiving the considerable benefits of property acquired in England.[3] In any event, the building programme of the abbey church does not reflect any shortage of funds in the period *c*. 1090 to *c*. 1120.[4]

3 *The Estates at the Time of the Surveys c. 1113 – c. 1180*

The well-known surveys of the estates of Holy Trinity, Caen, constitute the bulk of the contents of the Caen Cartulary and provide the main evidence for a history of the abbey's estates in the twelfth century. There are two series of surveys for the English and French estates alike, conventionally referred to as A and B in chronological order. Unfortunately they are not identical in format in the way that, for example, those for Burton Abbey in England are, and to a lesser extent, even those for Shaftesbury Abbey.[5] The Caen surveys, however, do have at least one thing in common with the Shaftesbury surveys in that they fall either side of the reign of Stephen.[6]

By way of contrast with the series of eleventh- and early-twelfth-century *pancartes* both series of surveys of the Caen estates reveal a very circumscribed group of properties. Survey A of *c*. 1113 provides information on barely two dozen places; Survey B of *c*. 1175 – *c*. 1180 on only

---

[1] *Ord. Vit.* (ed. Chibnall), IV, 146–8, *et passim*.

[2] C.W. David, *Robert Curthose, Duke of Normandy* (Cambridge, Mass., 1920), 124–5, 219.

[3] L.Musset, 'Les conditions financières d'une réussite architecturale: les grandes églises romanes de Normandie' in *Mélanges offerts à René Crozet*, ed. P. Gallais and Y.-J. Riou (Poitiers, 1966), I, 309–10.

[4] M. Baylé, *La Trinité de Caen: sa place dans l'histoire de l'architecture et du décor romans* (Geneva, 1979), 17–18.

[5] B.L., MS Loan no. 30, ff. 28–36, printed in parallel in C.G.O. Bridgeman, 'The Burton Abbey Twelfth Century Surveys', *Staffordshire Historical Collections* (1916), 212–47; and B.L., MS Harley 61, ff. 37–52v and 54v–55 (first series), 55v–89 (second series).

[6] M. Postan, 'The Chronology of Labour Services' in *Essays in Medieval Agriculture and General Problems of the Medieval Economy* (Cambridge, 1973), 99–100; A. Williams, 'The Knights of Shaftesbury Abbey', *Anglo-Norman Studies*, 8 (1986), 214–5, who dates the main Shaftesbury surveys to *c*. 1130 and *c*. 1170. See also J.A. Raftis, *The Estates of Ramsey Abbey* (Toronto, 1957), 306, who argues that the earliest Ramsey surveys should be seen as a double set datable to *c*. 1135 and *c*. 1160.

nineteen. All of these estates were situated in the modern *département* of Calvados; all but three were situated in the diocese of Bayeux; and all but four within an area bounded by the Rivers Dives and Seulles to the east and west respectively and the hills of Swiss Normandy to the south—in short, the Caen Plain.[1]

Why the more distant properties in Normandy were excluded from the surveys is a matter for conjecture. None of the abbey's possessions in the Cotentin is mentioned, which, together with the omission from Survey A of Tassilly, Auberville-sur-Mer, Colombelles, Foulbec, Grandcamps-les-Bains, and Sallen, suggests that the dispossessions *tempore* Robert Curthose were not short-term,[2] and that the rubric introducing Survey A—*Hęc sunt reditiones honoris nostrę ęcclesię Sanctę Trinitatis Cadomi*—refers to the revenue expected at that time from the rural estates. So far as the cartularian was concerned the abbey's interests in Jersey might have been covered by the farm of the property there to Osmund of Canville,[3] and the abbey's urban interests were dealt with, at least to some degree, by the series of charters relating to Calix and Curthose's charter of 1087–94.[4] For the most part the surviving original charters of the twelfth and early thirteenth centuries (Charters 1–21) are also limited to the area encompassed by the surveys and give some support to the notion that the abbey's effective complement of estates in Normandy had become somewhat limited in the twelfth century.[5]

Claims to the original endowments, however, were not abandoned, as the confirmation charters sought from Henry II and Richard I testify.[6] And there is reason to believe that, after our period, many of these claims met with success.[7] There is the possibility that, just as English properties and revenue may have helped to compensate for losses in Normandy in the late eleventh century, so gains and/or restorations in Normandy in the first half of the thirteenth century helped to compensate for increasing difficulties in securing revenue from English properties after 1204.

[1] See Map, p. 5 above. Auberville-sur-Mer is in the diocese of Lisieux, and Montbouin and Tassilly are in the diocese of Sées. Englesqueville and Asnières-en-Bessin in Survey A and Sallen and Auberville-sur-Mer in Survey B lie slightly beyond the area bounded by the Dives and Seulles.
[2] Tassilly, Auberville-sur-Mer, and Sallen, however, were restored by the time of Survey B.
[3] Document 10.
[4] Documents 4, 13.
[5] The one exception is Charter 7.
[6] Cf. Delisle/Berger, II, 199–203, and Caen, Archives du Calvados, carton 25/1, liasse 'Rois'.
[7] *Infra*, 'The 1257 Survey of Abbess Juliana de Saint-Sernin', 31–2.

4 *Surveys A and B Compared[1]*

Survey A is undoubtedly the more problematic of the two series of surveys. It is very short and succinct and purports, as we have noted, to be no more than the *reditiones honoris nostrę ęcclesię Sanctę Trinitatis*. It certainly dates from the early twelfth century, yet after 1106, on the basis of a reference to the capture of Robert Curthose at the battle of Tinchebray. Indeed, the purpose of the exercise may well have been to review the abbey's main sources of income after the depredations suffered during the disorders of Curthose's reign. Equally, it may have been conducted to mark the transition from the rule of Matilda, the founding abbess, to Cecilia, who ruled from 1113 to 1127. It is largely for this reason that a date of *c.* 1113 is ascribed to Survey A.[2] In any event, Survey A certainly has a complete look about it in the context of both the English and the French estates.[3] In other words, it is possible that we are not dealing with a fragmentary or selective survey. On the other hand, we are dealing with a late-twelfth/early thirteenth-century copy of a record (or records) drawn up almost a century earlier, and the purpose of the copy at the later date was in all probability different from the purpose of the original exercise.

No greater precision is possible in the dating of the second series, Survey B, although it is clear that the main body of the survey comes from the period *c.* 1175 – *c.* 1180. There are two references to conditions and terms in the time of Abbess Dametta (Vaux-sur-Seulles B, **3**, second entry; Montbouin B, **6**), who probably ruled for most of the third quarter of the twelfth century. Furthermore, a number of the abbey's Survey B tenants appear in charters of the last quarter of the century. The reference to William du Hommet (Ranville B, **39**) without the title of constable, which he acquired in 1179, is suggestive of a time-frame in keeping with that argued by Chibnall for the English surveys.[4]

In the context of the debate on 'surveys'[5] Survey A falls firmly in the custumal/demesne survey classification, being concerned principally with rents, obligations and services owed by the peasantry and one or two 'farmers' to the nuns of Holy Trinity, and these are entered, for the most part, in very brief, and at times enigmatic, terms. It is probably concerned with what ought to have been rather than what was necessarily the case, the theoretical rather than the actual obligations, and is probably the work

---

[1] References to Survey B are followed by the marginal numbers in bold indicating tenants and tenements.

[2] See p. 53.

[3] Tabuteau, *Transfers of Property*, 307, n. 166.

[4] Cf. *Charters and Custumals*, xxxii.

[5] P.D.A. Harvey, *Manorial Records* (British Records Association, no. 5, 1984), 15–24.

of an abbey official who made the record from existing abbey documents, including charter evidence, as in the case of the farm of Mâlon, whose entry includes the witnesses of both parties to the original agreement.

By contrast the second series of surveys, Survey B, is far more detailed than A and with its greater emphasis on valuations of tenant land and of demesne produce and rents leans towards being 'extent' in character. Survey B was also more thoroughly and obviously investigative in character with panels of jurors consisting of a cross-section of the tenants, who attested the veracity of terms and conditions, and occasionally acknowledged that they lacked a complete knowledge of tenurial conditions.[1] A likely explanation for the preservation of the earlier brief surveys is that they may have been intended to serve as a yardstick on which to base and test the work of the later jurors—as an abbreviated form of earlier terms and conditions. Their very existence invites a comparison of the contents of the two series.

Such a comparison results in a wide range of correspondence. For a number of estates—Graye-sur-Mer, Juvigny, Grainville-sur-Odon, Bavent, and Villons-les-Buissons—the links between the two surveys are quite strong; for Carpiquet, Ranville, and Amblie, they are somewhat weaker; whilst for Vaux-sur-Seulles, Escanneville, Montbouin, and Bougy Survey A could have formed only the barest of guides to the compilers of Survey B. For the most part, however, it is clear that there is a positive comparative element between the two series of surveys, even if it is difficult to establish exactly what purpose they served.

The pairs of descriptions for Graye-sur-Mer and Juvigny are the most remarkably consistent. The earlier surveys could virtually stand as summaries of the later ones. At Graye-sur-Mer the two half-villeins of Survey A are represented by William de Mara and Ralph of Cambes-en-Plaine with ten and seven acres respectively for almost identical obligations in Survey B (Graye B, **10**, **12**); the ten *censarii* of Survey A by the nine tenants holding no more than an acre each *in vilanagio* and paying cash rents in Survey B (Graye B, **2**, **11**, **13–16**, **18**, **19**, **21**); the nine principal bordars in Survey A by eight tenants *in bordagium* and perhaps the one *in masuagio* in Survey B (Graye B, **1**, **3–6**, **8**, **9**, **25**, **26**); and the twelve vavassors of Survey A by the fourteen tenants *in vavasoria* of Survey B (Graye B, **15**, **27–34**, **36**, **38–41**). Henry of Sainte-Croix-sur-Mer with four acres *in vavasoria* in Survey B (Graye B, **39**) is undoubtedly the successor to William of Sainte-Croix with four acres in Survey A. Almost too neatly

---

[1] The names of the jurors are given only for Carpiquet of the French estates, and for Tilshead, Avening, and Horstead of the English estates, where they represented virtually all social levels. Cf. *Charters and Custumals*, 46, 48, 51 and 63; R. Lennard, 'Early Manorial Juries', *EHR*, 77 (1962), 511–18.

there remain ten tenants in both surveys: six bordars, a shepherd, a sower, a smith, and Harvey with one acre in Survey A, and several messuage-holders, fee-farmers, and one holding *in serganteria* in Survey B (Graye B, 7, 17, 20–24, 34, 35, 37). The total recorded population in Survey A is 46, with the possibility of some duplication; in B it is 41. A major omission from Survey B for Graye-sur-Mer is any reference to demesne, whereas Survey A records land for two ploughs in demesne, as well as the existence of a smith, whose responsibility was the maintenance of the plough-irons.That there was still involvement in demesne activity at the time of Survey B, however, may be inferred from the obligations (*summagium et servicia*) of all tenants *in bordagium* and *in vilanagio* and the boonworks and services (*precarias et servicia*) due from all vavassorial tenants. On the other hand, it may be significant that the principal change in the conditions of the successors of the two half-villeins in Survey A, William de Mara and Ralph of Cambes-en-Plaine, was from one acre of *corvées* to champart, a form of sharecropping arrangement.

In the case of Juvigny-sur-Seulles too there is a broad similarity in the subject matter of both surveys. Survey A records three vavassors, two of whom possessed thirty acres each and the third, five acres; Survey B records two tenants, each holding thirty acres *in vavasoria* (Juvigny B, 1–2). The three *villani* of Survey A are neatly represented by six tenants, each holding ten acres *in vilanagio* (a typical half-villein tenement) in Survey B (3–9), whose renders in cash, hens and bread are exactly half the quantities owed by their predecessors. On the other hand, their grain rents appear to have doubled from four mines of malt barley in Survey A to four sesters of mixed grain in Survey B. This may well have been the *quid pro quo* for relaxation of the *corvées*, which are detailed in Survey A but not in Survey B. Unlike Graye-sur-Mer, Survey B for Juvigny does include direct reference to demesne, which consisted of a modest five and a half acres and two vacant holdings worth all together two and a half sesters of wheat and three and a half sesters of barley, and about nine acres in the open fields (*in campania*).

Correlation between other pairs of surveys is far less neat than at Graye-sur-Mer and Juvigny. For example, at Bavent, although superficial comparisons may be made through the observation of totals, it is far more difficult to 'pair up' individual tenants and tenements. Thus, while total recorded population, acreage, and cash rents are 15, 51 acres (including ten in demesne), and 5s in Survey A, compared with 12, 40⅜ acres (with no mention of demesne), and 4s in Survey B, only with difficulty can individual successors of Survey A tenants be identified in Survey B. The most positive identification is Ranulf of Bavent (Bavent B, 3) as the likely successor to the *firmarius* of Survey A who rendered a total of four sesters of wheat, barley and oats. In Survey B an identical rent for a combination of wheat, barley and oats was due from two of the holdings of another Ranulf. Hugh de Gruchy of Survey B (Bavent B, **8**), who held a vavassoriate of ten acres may well have been the successor to the vavassor with twelve acres in Survey A. Jordan of Bavent (Bavent B, **9**) with duties to attend court may have been the successor to the serjeant with one acre of demesne in Survey A. As for the four bordars in Survey A, they may well be represented at least in part by three of the unspecified tenures of between ½ and 1½ acres held by Billeheut, Hawisa, and Ansgar in Survey B (Bavent B, **7, 4, 6**). Beyond this it is difficult to speculate: for example, the four tenants holding in fee-farm in Survey B (Bavent B, **1–3, 5**) could have been the successors of either the vavassors or the *mediatores* of Survey A.

Much the same kind of exercise can be conducted with Grainville-sur-Odon and Villons-les-Buissons. At Grainville there is a reasonable correspondence between Survey A's record of two vavassors, two half-villeins, and ten *inter bordarios et censarios* paying 22s 6d, and Survey B's record of four tenants *in vavasoria* with 15, 3½, 4, and 30 acres (Grainville B, **3–6**), three holdings *in vilanagio* containing 4, 9, and 9 acres (Grainville B, **7, 13/14, 15/16**), and a total of nine tenures *in mansura, in bordagium, in firma* and *in feodifirmam* involving about 12½ acres and 13s 9d in cash rents. A further 11½ acres were the subject of encroachment and 33 acres of demesne produced approximately 29½ sesters of grain rents. At Villons-les-Buissons there is also a large degree of agreement between the two surveys, even in the context of the demesne. The half-ploughland of demesne in Survey A is matched by the 49¾ acres identified in the opening section of Survey B, and worth according to the final entry five muids, or sixty sesters, of wheat (Villons B, **1, 35**). More interesting perhaps is the way in which the six vavassors of Survey A have given way to three holdings *in vavasoria* owing the standard obligation of horse-service (*servicium equi*) and four owing service on foot (*servicium peditis*) (Villons B, **2–4, 5–8**). The four full-villeins of Survey A are comfortably represented by four twenty-acre tenancies *in vilanagio* each of them held jointly in Survey B (Villons B, **6/14, 6/7, 15–18, 19–21**). There is very little correlation, however, between the four bordars of Survey A and the cluster of smallholders consisting of eight *in bordagium* (Villons B, **6, 22–8**), one *in masuagio* (Villons B, **10**), and six unspecified in Survey B (Villons B, **8, 9, 11–13, 29**).

At Amblie, which at an early date had been allocated to the almonry,[1] both surveys emphasise the importance of the mill as a source of grain

---

[1] *Abbayes caennaises*, no. 12 (1066–83), 97.

rent: nine muids at the time of Survey A; five muids at the time of Survey B (Amblie B, **15**), with a further three muids and ten sesters from the demesne, and two muids from tithes (Amblie B, **18–19**). There were three vavassors at the time of Survey A; two tenants, each with 24 acres *in vavasoria* and four others with a total of 7¼ acres *in vavasoria* in Survey B (Amblie B, **1–6, 9**). The three bordars in Survey A are followed by four tenants *in bordagium* in Survey B (Amblie B, **11–13**). And it is tempting to see Osmund the Wise with five acres in fee-farm at Pierrepont near Amblie for produce rents (Amblie B, **17**) as the successor to the *mediator* with six acres recorded in Survey A.

For Ranville Survey A records nine vavassors, four half-villeins, two *censarii*, one ploughland in demesne, and a mill worth six sesters of grain; Survey B records six tenants with a total of 162 acres *in vavasoria* (Ranville B, **1–6**), three tenants with eight acres each *in vilanagio* (Ranville B, **22, 10, 23**)—which corresponds well with Survey A's four half-villeins—and no less than fifteen tenants (Ranville B, **7–12, 14–21, 24**) holding a total of about thirty-one acres at fee-farm, principally for produce rents and boonworks. Leased demesne amounted to 49⅜ acres returning 57¼ sesters of grain and—for nine virgates of meadow—24s.

Most of Survey A's description of Carpiquet is taken up with the obligations of the *vilani*, who are described in almost as much detail as in Survey B. The principal difference between the two is that the later survey adds champart and boonworks to the standard list of dues, and spells out in greater detail the carting and *corvée* obligations. So far as numbers are concerned there is a total of 14½ *vilani* in Survey A as opposed to fifteen tenures *in vilanagio*, involving twenty-six tenants and co-tenants, in Survey B (Carpiquet B, **8–33**). Survey A records nine bordars, two oxherds, a forester, and a crier (*preco*); Survey B twelve tenures *in bordagium*. There is nothing, however, in Survey A on the vavassors, who are so prominent in Survey B (Carpiquet B, **1–7**), nor is there any hint of the large number of smallholders on the demesne (Carpiquet B, **55–89** *et al.*), many of whom had no doubt been attracted by the novel and favourable terms of burgage tenure.[1]

Both surveys for Vaux-sur-Seulles identify the mill, the church, and the two-thirds share of the tithes as the principal sources of wealth to the abbey. The mill alone in Survey B is valued at twenty-two muids of wheat and three muids two sesters of barley, with the miller himself responsible for a cash rent of 36s, 200 eels, 24 capons, 44 loaves and 400 eggs (Vaux B, **1**). The two-thirds share of tithes was worth five muids of grain; and the priest contributed 20s and candles at the feast of the Purification

---

[1] Carpiquet B, **53**. Cf. Legras, *Bourgage de Caen*, 37; Carabie, *Propriété foncière*, 161–2.

(Vaux B, **1**, **14**), as his predecessor had done at the time of Survey A. Survey A's one ploughland in demesne seems to have been largely leased out by the time of Survey B at a rate of about one sester per acre: 43 acres for 43 sesters of wheat, 23 acres for twenty sesters of barley and oats, and an unspecified amount of land (probably 1½ acres) for three mines of mixed grain (Vaux B, **2**). Apart from the priest no population is recorded in Survey A, whilst in Survey B two tenants *in vavasoria*, of whom the miller was one, and nine tenants *in bordagium* are recorded (Vaux B, **3–13**).

One of the most difficult of estates to reconcile is Escanneville. In Survey A it appears alone; in Survey B it appears as part of a complex that includes Gonneville and Beauvoir. Survey A records three vavassors; Survey B records six with 20½ acres at Escanneville and one with ten acres at Beauvoir. Three and a half villeins are recorded in Survey A with total rents of seven sesters of malt, 3s 6d, 4½ quarters of wheat, three and four ewes in alternate years, eleven hens, and 210 sheaves of mixed grain; whereas Survey B records seven villeins, six with four acres each and the seventh with five acres owing five quarters of oats, a half quarter of wheat, one goose, half a ewe (or 12d), 1½ hens, 10 eggs, 6d for carting wine, and 5d *cens*. As it happens, the thirteen *bordarii* of Escanneville A can be matched with a total of thirteen tenants *in bordagium* in Survey B (Escanneville B, **8–9**, **11–16**, Gonneville B, **5**, and Beauvoir B, **1–2**, **8–9**). There can be no question of the importance of the region as a source of salt supplies, but there are distinct difficulties about reconciling Survey A's one muid and two ambers of salt with Survey B's 34 *summae* or 204 bushels, and a further 19 *summae* from the count's tithe at Varaville.[1]

For those estates for which there is evidence in both series of surveys only Bougy and Montbouin defy all attempts at comparison. For these estates Survey A's evidence is cryptic in the extreme. Survey A's record of twenty acres and unspecified tithes at Montbouin may well be represented by the twenty-four acres and tithes allocated to the almonry in Survey B, but the considerable quantity of rents and other property in the later survey would have to be subsumed under Richard son of Herluin's land in Survey A. Likewise, Survey A's cryptic record of fifteen sesters of grain at Bougy is followed in Survey B by a total of forty-nine sesters of grain and other miscellaneous rents.

A handful of estates conclude with totals (*summae*) of produce and

---

[1] There are no references to salt at Escanneville in the early charters of endowment. Tithes of salt, however, were associated with Bavent and 'Divette' to the south of Escanneville (*Abbayes caennaises*, 55, 84, 94). During the troubled times of Robert Curthose William, count of Evreux, an important landholder in Bavent, expropriated the abbey's salt-works at Escanneville (Document 15).

cash rents,[1] but in most cases a gap of four to nine lines was left blank. Presumably the scribe intended to calculate these totals and insert them at a later date, for if the source of the surveys included totals it would have made more sense to have copied them at the same time as the main text. Only at Montbouin, where the *summae* are added in a different hand from that of the main text after space had been left for them, do we catch a glimpse of this process, especially in the case of the almonry's totals, which take into account the revised value of the tithes owing to the abbey (Montbouin B, **21**, **23**).

5   *The Administration of the French Properties*

The foundation charter of 1066 provides few clues as to the administration of the original endowment of the abbey. As noted above, a great deal of the early property granted to the abbey by the relatives of new recruits and by other donors was not conveniently located. Indeed one suspects that many grants to monasteries consisted of peripheral estates which would have been as difficult, if not more difficult, for their lay owners to manage as for the church with its far greater administrative resources. It was probably this accretion of surplus, distant and vulnerable property some distance from a nucleus of more significant estates of royal and ducal origin that made consolidation through exchange and purchase one of the first tasks of many administrations.[2] Rare indeed was a provision such as that of Thomas Bardulf's charter to the abbey allowing an exchange of distant for nearer and more convenient properties and rents if they became available.[3]

Even by 1082, and the time of the second of the great *pancartes*, there is little to indicate how the abbey could ensure that it benefited from its still very dispersed endowment. There is, however, a hint here and there.The royal grant of the services of Geoffrey Salomon and Helto the steward of Graye-sur-Mer probably involved the transference of their administrative functions from the king to the abbey.[4] The machinery for the collection of the tithe at Blay and Cairon is no doubt indicated by the inclusion of a villein (*unum rusticum*) to help in supervision and

---

[1] Viz. Escanneville, Gonneville, Beauvoir, Bavent and Ranville. The totals for Carpiquet appear in the middle of the survey.
[2] Cf. C. Holdsworth, *The Piper and the Tune: Medieval Patrons and Monks* (The 1990 Stenton Lecture, Reading, 1991), 21–4.
[3] Charter 3.
[4] *Abbayes caennaises*, no. 8, 87: *Ego Willelmus rex concessi servicium illud quod Goifridus Salomonis et Heltho dapifer reddebant mihi de Grai supradicte ęcclesię.*

collection.[1] The land, and presumably services, of two free men in Jersey may well have been given to aid in the collection of the tithe of five parishes and the sixth sheaf from one and a half parishes there.[2] In the same *pancarte* Robert Bertran specifically assigned two free men and his tithe at Colombelles near Caen to the abbey.[3]

By this time there seems to have been a rudimentary obedientiary system in place. An incomplete charter of 1066 × 1083,[4] which took into account the acquisition of property in England, allocated the bulk of the French estates together with the manor of Minchinhampton in England for the general maintenance of the nuns and for the needs of abbey guests. Likewise the dues from a recently established fair at Caen on the octave of Pentecost were assigned *ad victum monialium* to supplement tolls received from the Meadow Fair in October. The requirements of the abbatial chamber were met from the remainder of the English estates (Felsted, Tarrant, and Pinbury), the tithe from the queen's wool in England, and from gifts of clothing other than precious robes (*pallia*), which were reserved for the sacristy. The almonry's income consisted mainly of tithes from estates in Normandy, three-quarters of the manor of Villons-les-Buissons, ploughlands and mills at Amblie and Quettehou, forty acres at Englesqueville, land at Le Foc in Manche, and the tithe of all beasts, bacons and cheeses imported from England. The sacristy was maintained in general through altar oblations and gifts of gold or fine cloth, and more specifically from the altar gifts and sepulture proceeds from the churches of St. Stephen the Elder and St. Martin in Caen, profits from the church and mill at Vaucelles, and from the churches of Falaise, excluding their grain rents. Lighting for the dormitory was provided from the tithe of tolls at Ecouché, that of the infirmary from 40s rent paid by four tenants at Les Moutiers.[5]

By contrast with the English estates, all of which were farmed out at the time of Survey A either to individuals or groups of individuals,[6] the French estates were exploited more directly by the abbey and its officials. Small and isolated properties were held for fixed rents in cash and/or kind, but for the most part and certainly on the major estates of Ouistreham, Carpiquet, Graye-sur-Mer, Grainville-sur-Odon, Juvigny-sur-Seulles, Bavent, Escanneville, and Villons-les-Buissons the concern

---

[1] *ibid.*, 83, 86. Cf. R. Lennard, 'Peasant Tithe-Collectors in Norman England', *EHR*, 79 (1954), 580–96.
[2] *Abbayes caennaises*, no. 8, 84.
[3] *ibid.*
[4] *Abbayes caennaises*, no. 12.
[5] *Abbayes caennaises*, 168: Les Moutiers-en-Auge, cant. Morteaux-Coulibœuf, or Les Moutiers-en-Cinglais, cant. Bretteville-sur-Laize, or Les Moutiers. Hubert, cant. Livarot.
[6] *Charters and Custumals*, xl.

was to record the amount of land held in demesne and the obligations and services of the principal tenantry. Paradoxically these obligations and services are far less detailed than for the English estates. This may well be the result of a stronger tradition of survey making in pre- and early post-Conquest England.[1] Equally, however, a familiarity with what was expected of vavassors, villeins, *censarii* and bordars has left its mark with expressions such as *serviunt sicut debent* at Grainville and Bavent, *serviunt sicut vilani* at Escanneville, and *servientes sicut debent* at Villons.

Not surprisingly, in view of the correlation noted above, Survey B confirms a great deal of Survey A, but it does so in far greater detail. There seems to be a single administration concerned with recording peasant labour services and rents in cash and kind, the demesne in terms of mills, churches, and woodland, as well as demesne acreage and/or rents, for leasing of the demesne seems to have become far more pronounced than it had been in the early twelfth century. But the process had not been all one way. There is evidence that the abbey had experimented, perhaps to its cost, with farming out whole manors, as it had done in England. At Carpiquet Adam fitz Roger (Carpiquet B, **36**) had at some stage received the manor with the demesne buildings in good order, with a complete wall around one barn, another new barn, and gates with locks. According to the jurors of Survey B this was no longer the case. Furthermore Carpiquet was one of only two estates whose repairs were specified as the communal obligation of the tenants holding in villeinage.[2] Adam himself had become the most ubiquitous tenant at Carpiquet possessing no less than nine plots of land, most of it on the demesne and some of it with doubtful legality. In short, there is a strong parallel with Simon of Felsted, who used his position as farmer so well in England.[3] At Auberville-sur-Mer too there is the strong suggestion that William Moltun (or Montun) and Herbert de Bollevilla had been joint farmers (Auberville B, **1, 12**). They had received farming equipment, livestock, and grain at the commencement of their term from the abbess herself on one occasion and from Warin the priest on another. Stephen's reign, especially the early years, had undoubtedly been as disruptive in Normandy as in England.[4]

---

[1] This comment owes a great deal to H.B. Clarke, 'The Early Surveys of Evesham Abbey: an Investigation into the Problem of Continuity in Anglo Norman England' (unpublished Ph.D. thesis, University of Birmingham, 1978), esp. 326–34.

[2] Carpiquet B, ff. 61v-62r: *Omnes isti debent operari ad manerium reficendum*. The other instance was Villons-les-Buissons, f. 83v: . . . *reficiunt masuagia manerii et fosseta et ea quę ad manerium pertinent* (Villons B, **6/14**), where some sort of enquiry was made into the assarting activities of the bailiff (see Document 5).

[3] *Charters and Custumals*, xl–xlii.

[4] For evidence of the disruption in Normandy see *Ord. Vit.* (ed. Chibnall), vi, 454–51. More than half of Orderic's final book (his book xiii) is taken up with the distressed state of Normandy in the years 1135–41. See also R.H.C. Davis, *King Stephen* (3rd edn, London, 1990), 15–16, 24–6.

Other administrative arrangements included the establishing of four canons principally to conduct sacramental duties at the abbey.[1] They were provided with housing near the abbey (in the modern Rue des Chanoines) and were supported by forty acres and four free men in Caen, thirty acres in Blainville, half the church and half the tithes of Bénouville, half the tithes of Colleville and Cairon, the tithes of Périers-sur-le-Dan, two-thirds of the tithe of Blay, and two villeins attached to Cambes-en-Plaine. Significantly, the tithes at Colleville, Cairon, Blay, and Montbouin were accompanied by the services of one or more villeins (*rustici*), and in the case of Giberville, a bordar.[2] Finally, a church was built in honour of St. Giles where, appropriately, the poor could be buried in the presence of the almoner and the four canons.[3]

6 *Social Classes*

Both surveys, of course, provide valuable information on economic and social classes and their obligations to the abbey. In this respect the main terminological or linguistic difference between the two series is that, whereas Survey A categorises the tenants of land as *vavassores, villani, bordarii, censarii, mediatores, firmarii, aloers*, and the like,[4] and treats them as groups, Survey B eschews the classification of tenants in favour of classification of tenure; named individuals rather than groups are described as holding land *in vavasoria, in vilanagio, in bordagium,*[5] *in feodifirmam*, etc. Jean Yver's comment that 'C'est la catégorie de la terre qui qualifie l'homme, alors qu'un peu plus tôt, c'est la qualité sociale de l'homme qui avait entraîné la qualification de la terre' is applicable beyond the vavassorial class.[6] The earlier survey is characterised by an almost strict hierarchical structure reminiscent of early polyptyques and indeed of Domesday Book itself, and as such may obscure the nuances of the real situation, whereas the later survey presents a range of tenures, a variety of which could be held by a single individual.

---

[1] *Abbayes caennaises*, no. 12, 97. See also L. Musset, 'Recherches sur les communautés de clercs séculiers en Normandie au xie siècle', *BSAN*, 50 (1959), 5–38, esp. 12. Cf. Johnson, *Equal in Monastic Profession*, 191.

[2] The tithes of Montbouin and Giberville were part of the allocation to the almonry.

[3] *Abbayes caennaises*, no. 12, 98. Cf. Charter 5.

[4] There are also references to a *forestarius, preco, faber, bercarius, seminator*, and two *bubulci*.

[5] In the two instances where the term is given in full *in bordagium* is preferred to *in bordagio*: Vaux B, **5** and Sallen B, **15**.

[6] J. Yver, '*Vavassor*: note sur les premiers emplois du terme', *A.N.*, 40, no. 1 (1990), 45. Cf. A.L. Poole, *Obligations of Society in the XII and XIII Centuries* (Oxford, 1946), 3–4.

The most prominent of these classes in both surveys in terms of landholding and status were the vavassors, who in Normandy as a whole occupied a position somewhere between villein and knight.[1] Although clearly descendants of a powerful class with some of their number possessing forty to seventy acres of land, by the last quarter of the twelfth century almost half of the 96 tenants holding *in vavasoria* held ten acres or less; at Graye-sur-Mer eleven of the fifteen vavassors held considerably less than five acres each.[2] Despite this variation a set of common obligations is discernible: escort service with a horse (*servicium equi*), carting and carrying duties (*summagium*), often associated with oxen for the vinage, which was frequently commuted for 5d or 6d in addition to the traditional *regarda* of bread, hens, capons, and eggs. Nor did they escape boonworks.[3] Surprisingly, there are only three instances of commutation of the principal vavassorial services in a total of 96 tenures involving a little more than 1500 acres. Two of these are at Grainville, where Helias de Kemino rendered one sester of oats *pro servicio equi* and where Wimond paid 4s *pro servicio [equi?]* from four acres (Grainville B, **4, 5**); the third is at Auberville-sur-Mer where Thomas of Auberville paid 7s for four acres *in vavasoria* (Auberville B, **30**). One of the most interesting developments is the emergence at Villons of a small group of sub-vavassorial tenants owing service on foot (*servicium peditis*): this is all that may have been possible from their holdings of 2½, 1½, ¾, and ½ acre (Villons B, **5–8**).[4] At the other end of the scale two vavassors with holdings of 24 and 40 acres had acquired the soubriquet of *Le Chevalier* (Montbouin B, **7** and Tassilly B, **24**).

Another sub-vavassorial group consisted of those holding in fee-farm.

---

[1] The most recent works on vavassors from a non-Norman and Norman point of view are P.R. Coss, 'Literature and Social Terminology: the Vavasour in England' in T.H. Aston, P.R. Coss, C. Dyer, J. Thirsk (eds), *Social Relations and Ideas: Essays in Honour of R.H. Hilton* (Cambridge, 1983), 109–50, esp. 115–17, and J. Yver, *Vavassor*, 31–48, esp. 41–48. For earlier studies, especially on origins, see H. Navel, 'Les vavasories du Mont-Saint-Michel à Bretteville-sur-Odon et Verson (Calvados)', *BSAN*, 45 (1937), 137–65; H. Chanteux, 'Quelques notes sur les vavasseurs', *RHD*, 36 (1958), 630–1.

[2] L. Musset, 'Autour de la seigneurie rurale normande. Quelques problèmes d'évolution', *RHD*, 31 (1954), 161, distinguishes between vavassors on coastal estates with four acres on average and others with as much as eighty acres in the poorer parts of the Bocage.

[3] Boonworks are specified at Carpiquet, Grainville, Tassilly, Ranville, Villons and Graye, and may well be implied by the word *servicia* elsewhere. Coss's comment that 'They owed, in addition to homage and relief, a few light services and money rent, though never renders in kind or servile labour'. ('The Vavasour in England', 116) seems far from the mark in the context of Normandy.

[4] Cf. Yver, *Vavassor*, 47, n. 58: the *vavassores equites* and *vavassores pedites* at Jumièges. At Carpiquet two bordage tenures owed *servicium peditis* (Carpiquet B, **38–9**).

Like the vavassors in Survey B a few of these had holdings as large as 12, 20 and 24 acres, but for the most part they held much less: at Ranville seventeen held a total of thirty-one acres between them. Several tenancies in fee-farm, however, are virtually indistinguishable from vavassoriates. At Auberville Ralph Pigache held six acres at fee-farm for 6s rent, eight loaves, four capons, forty eggs, and *servicium equi* (Auberville B, **31**); and at Montbouin two fee-farmers jointly held twelve acres for grain rents and carting services to Caen (Montbouin B, **1/2**).[1] If there is a distinction, beyond that of origins[2] and, in most cases, the obligation to provide a horse, it is that fee-farmers tended to hold smaller parcels of land for which they paid in cash and grain.

For half of the estates recorded in Survey B there is no mention whatsoever of villeins or tenants *in vilanagio*;[3] instead, the landholding pattern is clearly divided between tenure *in vavasoria* and tenure *in bordagium*. On those estates where villeinage tenure is recorded there is a wide range of landholding and obligations similar to those observable among the vavassors. At Carpiquet and Villons-les-Buissons in particular substantial holdings *in vilanagio* had been kept intact albeit as multiple tenancies: fourteen holdings involving twenty-six tenants and 387 acres at Carpiquet, and four holdings involving eleven tenants and eighty acres at Villons. These tenures were still burdened with extremely heavy labour services and rents: *corvées*, champart, cash and grain rents, pannage, carting, and the *regarda* of eggs, poultry, and bread. At Juvigny-sur-Seulles, Grainville-sur-Odon, Ranville, and Escanneville there appears to have been some success in preserving fractions of villein tenements with blocks of ten-acre, nine-acre, eight-acre, and four-acre holdings respectively, but the obligations due from them were not as intensive as at Carpiquet and Villons, the abbey's principal supply manors. Finally at Auberville-sur-Mer and Graye-sur-Mer most of the tenants holding *in vilanagio* are indistinguishable from those holding *in bordagium*. Indeed at Graye-sur-Mer they are indiscriminately listed together. It is abundantly clear that what mattered on these two coastal estates was rent in cash and kind rather than category of tenure.

By far the most numerous of tenants were smallholders of a wide

---

[1] Cf. Montbouin B, **12**.

[2] M. de Biéville, 'Les fieffermes, mode de gestion du domaine normand de la couronne', *RHD*, 41 (1963), 551: 'Le terme de "fiefferme" apparaît en Normandie dès le debut du XIIe siècle pour désigner la concession à perpétuité d'un immeuble rural'. See also M. de Biéville, 'Les fieffermes, institution originale du droit normand', *RHD*, 45 (1967), 405–6.

[3] viz. Saulques, La Rouelle, Vaux-sur-Seulles, Sallen, Bougy, Bavent, Montbouin, Tassilly, and Amblie.

variety holding an acre or two at most.[1] Most of these are classified as tenants *in bordagium* holding for small cash rents, services that included carting and boonworks, grain renders including champart, and the *regarda* of eggs, hens, and capons.[2] Although those holding on bordage terms may have performed the servile and base obligations characteristic of such tenure it is clear that many were able to take advantage of their relatively unencumbered and flexible conditions.[3] At Carpiquet Adam son of Roger (Carpiquet B, **36**) was perhaps the most successful of such achievers. At Sallen demesne land held on champart terms by bordars is clearly distinguished from land held in bordage; and at La Rouelle nineteen bordage tenants held 70½ of their 82⅞ acres on champart terms. Other smallholders included those holding messuages, enclosures, curtilages, cottages, and small fractions of acres and virgates *in masuagio*, *in mansura* and the like,[4] for small cash and produce rents. Nor should we forget the numerous tenants on the demesne, especially at Carpiquet and Ranville where they rendered grain rents and at Auberville-sur-Mer where they paid cash.[5] Besides these there existed a number of encroachers on the demesne for whom neither services nor rents are specified.[6]

7 *The Cartulary Documents*

In this edition of the cartulary material the two principal surveys are followed by the remainder of the Cartulary Documents (Documents 1–22), excluding those already published by Musset and Chibnall. Six of these documents have been published in one form or another by Stapleton, Round, Delisle and Berger, Valin, and Haskins,[7] but it is worthwhile reprinting them here alongside the previously unpublished material not just in order to make the record complete, but to replace versions which are in some cases difficult to obtain, in other cases inadequate or inaccurate, and in most cases not annotated in any way.

---

[1] For all the estates they probably number between 250 and 300.

[2] No tenants *in bordagium* are recorded at Juvigny, Bougy, Auberville-sur-Mer, Bavent, and Ranville. On the remaining estates they total some 150 with about 275 acres.

[3] Cf. L. Musset, 'La tenure en bordage, aspects normands et manceaux', *RHD*, 28 (1950), 140.

[4] These number about fifty with a total of 43 acres.

[5] At Carpiquet 37 tenants held a total of 71 demesne acres for a little more than 140 sesters of wheat, at Ranville 17 held about 50 acres for 57¼ sesters of grain; and at Auberville 18 tenants paid 110s 7d for 94 acres of demesne.

[6] The main encroachments or purprestures are to be found in Auberville B, Grainville B, and Tassilly B.

[7] Documents 1, 13, 15, 16, 18, 20.

All but three of the Cartulary Documents are datable to within two or three decades. The exceptions are broadly speaking of a survey kind, viz. Documents 2, 5 and 14. Those relating to Ouistreham are the most enigmatic: a short rental and a general survey. The close association in the Cartulary of the rental (Document 2) and Survey A together with the association of Ouistreham with St. Aubin and Colleville, as in Survey A, gives some strength to the view that the rental and Survey are contemporaneous. There is no duplication of material; rather there is the possibility that the rental is an actual record of individual cash rents paid by the twenty-seven listed tenants in contrast with Survey A's record of twenty-nine villeins who were expected to pay a uniform 4s 6d each.[1] In the same document the ten principal rentpayers at St. Aubin and Colleville are called *censarios* and paid varying rents totalling 29s.

The second document relating to Ouistreham (Document 14) is even more enigmatic than the first. It can only be described as a broad overview of landholders at Ouistreham. Its place in the Cartulary between a charter of Henry I confirming the abbey's estates in England and two accounts of losses suffered by Holy Trinity in the early to mid-twelfth century may be the only clue as to its purpose and relationship, if any, to the main surveys, for it refers indirectly to some destruction in the context of two ruined tenements (*mansuras devastatas*) belonging to the demesne of a certain Adelaide. Beyond this it is difficult to go. For the record, it reveals a group of twenty tenants of virtually vavassorial standing holding some 604½ acres, and demesne, consisting of Adelaide's and 'the bishop's' portions, amounting to 179 acres.[2] The sub-tenantry consisted of 59 free men, 15 full-villeins, 11 half-villeins, and 111 bordars.

The third document in this 'survey' group of documents (Document 5) is a record of land belonging to Ralph, the bailiff of Villons-les-Buissons. If the term *frusta* indicates recent assart land, perhaps this *commemoratio* is an attempt to monitor the activities of one of the abbey's more important manorial officials, and may not be dissimilar in purpose from the record of the list of assarts attributed to Simon of Felsted in England.[3] The problem of self-aggrandizement of manorial officials was probably far greater for nunneries than for male monasteries.

The final group of Cartulary Documents (nos. 23–7) comes not from the Caen Cartulary at Paris but from a fourteenth-century cartulary at

---

[1] Document 2. One paid 6s, five paid 5s each, ten paid 4s each, six paid 3s each, and five paid 2s each.
[2] This description of the demesne adds to the puzzle of this document, for there is no other record of a bishop or an Adelaide holding land at Ouistreham.
[3] *Charters and Custumals*, 44–5.

Caen and concerns grants of wheat and cash rents to Holy Trinity.[1] The 1220s appears to mark the beginning of a long period of acquisition of grain rents (principally wheat, but also barley and oats), cash rents, and small quantities of land in the vicinity of Caen. Many of the original deeds relating to these transactions are to be found in the carton of French deeds (carton 26, see below) and in a number of uncatalogued dossiers and files in the Holy Trinity archive.[2] Inferior copies of a few of these, recording donations and purchases made for the benefit and maintenance of the altars of the abbey church, were probably made by the abbey's sacristan.

8   *The Original Charters*

Most of the surviving original charters from the twelfth and thirteenth centuries are to be found in two cartons in the Archives du Calvados at Caen,[3] and appear to have reached this convenient though uncatalogued form as a result of being extracted from larger files or dossiers containing much later material.[4] One of these cartons is marked 'Angleterre' (carton 25), but happens also to include a few deeds relating to Normandy and the Channel Islands and a file containing more than thirty papal bulls, the earliest of which was issued by Pope Lucius III in 1184.[5] The other carton (carton 26) is far more homogeneous in that it contains twenty-eight files

---

[1]   Caen, Archives du Calvados, H, Trinité de Caen, carton 86, Cartulaire de l'Abbaye Sainte Trinité, which is also entitled 'Recueil de Chartes Anglaises et Françaises jusqu'en M.CCC.VI.' It is, in fact, the result of joining together two cartularies, one of English deeds, the other of French deeds.

[2]   For the period 1230–97 there are more than sixty purchases of wheat rents among the deeds in the box of French charters (carton 26), in the Cartulaire de l'Abbaye Sainte Trinité de Caen (carton 86), and in a number of the larger files organised by estates and provisionally numbered (especially cartons 4, 72, 94). The abbey was clearly acting as a source of credit for tenants. Cf. Génestal, *Rôle des monastères*, esp. pt. ii, 'La rente'. There are considerably more of these purchases by Holy Trinity, Caen, than by any of the monasteries listed in Génestal, *loc. cit.*, 199–203.

[3]   Caen, Archives du Calvados, H. Trinité de Caen, cartons 25 and 26. The provisional numbering of cartons, dossiers, cartularies, and other material relating to the abbey of Holy Trinity was probably undertaken in 1963 in the move to the new Archive building, but there is no corresponding inventory. (*Guide des archives départementales du Calvados*, 188). In 1992 the contents of cartons 25 and 26 were re-arranged in cartons 25/1 and 25/2, and 26/1 and 26/2.

[4]   Many of the medieval charters were probably used as the starting-point to support property and other claims in the seventeenth and eighteenth centuries. Some evidence for this is provided by carton 97 (Tassilly). In a file relating to a recognition (*aveu*) dated 29 May 1781 there is a reference to three supporting charters (*pièces du parchemin*) of 1293, 1585 and 1609. Those for 1585 and 1609 are stilled attached to the file, whereas the 1293 charter has found its way to carton 26/2.

[5]   Charters 3, 5, 7, 8, 11.

identified by Norman place-names and in which there is a total of 164 charters. They are almost exclusively of the thirteenth century, but only eleven are pre-1230.[1] Among the larger dossiers from which these charters seem to have been culled there are a further forty or so thirteenth-century charters, the earliest of which are published here.[2]

Notwithstanding the fact that the abbey of Holy Trinity can boast 'One of the richest collections of documents in all Normandy',[3] there are very few original twelfth-century charters for England or France.[4] It has not been thought necessary to reproduce the confirmation charters of Henry II and Richard I.[5] Nor, of cartulary copies of charters, has it been thought necessary to reproduce the three pre-1230 charters relating to burgage tenements published in Legras' *Le bourgage de Caen*.[6] However, the well-known charter of Thomas Bardulf, granting the abbey a cash rent from a mill in England or an equivalent cash rent in Normandy, is published here since it is essentially a Norman charter with Anglo-Norman concerns.[7]

Of greatest importance and interest, perhaps, are the two earliest charters emanating from the abbey itself.[8] The earlier of the two is a grant by an Abbess Adeliz[9] of a complete dwelling in the Bourg-l'Abbesse in favour of the recently established Premonstratensian abbey at Ardenne.[10] It is difficult to be certain of prenominal terminology at this date, but it is a distinct possibility that the Abbess Adeliz of this charter of 1142 × c. 1152 is a different person from Abbess Alicia of Document 21. The second and slightly later charter was probably issued by Adeliz's successor, Abbess Dametta.[11] It is a notification by the abbess to Froger, bishop of Sées (1157–84), that she and the convent have canonically conferred the

---

[1] Charters 4, 6, 9, 10, 12–16, 18, 19. Most of the charters are summarised in Léchaudé's *Extraits des chartes et autres normands et anglo-normands qui se trouvent dans les Archives du Calvados* (Mémoires de la société des antiquaires de Normandie, vii and viii, Caen, 1834–5), together with an Atlas of seals compiled by G. Mancel.

[2] Charters 17, 20, 21. Poor copies of Charters 20 and 21 are to be found in the uncatalogued Cartulaire de l'Abbaye Sainte Trinité at the Archives du Calvados, Caen (Documents 25, 23).

[3] D. Matthew, *The Norman Monasteries and their English Possessions* (Oxford, 1962), 8.

[4] For England see *Charters and Custumals*, Charters 3, 4, 6–8, and possibly 9.

[5] Caen, Archives du Calvados, H, Trinité de Caen, carton 25/1, liasse 'Rois'. Henry II's charter is published in Delisle/Berger, II, no. DCI; Richard I's charter is virtually identical.

[6] Legras, *Bourgage de Caen*, Appendix, nos. 2, 3, 7.

[7] Charter 3.

[8] The earlier of the two, B.L. Add. Ch 15279, is mentioned in Legras, *Bourgage de Caen*, 24, but is dismissed as of no great importance. The second is attached to other papers (including an extract from the 1257 Survey of Abbess Juliana de Saint-Sernin) supporting the abbey's claims to the patronage of the church of Tassilly in 1632 (Caen, Archives du Calvados, H, Trinité de Caen, carton 105).

[9] The extension of *Adel'* to *Adeliz* is provided by an endorsement to the charter.

[10] Charter 1.

[11] Charter 2.

church of Tassilly on a priest called Nicholas. As such it stands in some contrast to two charters issued by a successor of Froger in 1208 and 1217 indicating that the bishop, Silvester, canonically conferred the churches of Barges and Falaise on their respective priests, after presentation by the abbess.[1]

In view of the drying up of donations of real estate to monastic institutions in the course of the twelfth and thirteenth centuries it is significant that one-third of the few surviving charters for the period 1150–1230 are concerned with the abbey's rights to tithes and churches.[2] There is the suggestion of lengthy litigation in secular and ecclesiastical courts before final settlements were reached, involving the diocesan court in the case of the tithes of Escanneville, involving papal nominees in the case of Holy Trinity's share of the tithe at Vaux-sur-Seulles, and settlement in a secular court over the two-thirds share of tithes from twelve acres in the same manor.[3]

Furthermore, in contrast with the first series of surveys the right of the abbey to the advowson (donatio) of churches is a marked feature of the second series, viz. at Carpiquet, Juvigny,[4] Vaux-sur-Seulles, Sallen, Grainville-sur-Odon, Auberville-sur-Mer, and Tassilly; and episcopal charters of the early thirteenth century confirm the abbey's rights to the advowson of churches at Barges and Falaise in the diocese of Sées.[5] As we have seen, as early as the third quarter of the twelfth century the abbess of Caen seems to have made a point of making her own nomination to the church of Tassilly and of notifying the bishop accordingly. A case that was brought to a secular court in accordance with Norman and English custom[6] concerned darrein presentment at Carpiquet in 1185, which seems to have been easily determined in favour of the abbess against Ralph fitz Eude.[7] Notwithstanding this judgment, however, it was still necessary for Ralph's successors at Carpiquet, Ivo of Ouistreham and William, his brother, to renounce their claim to the advowson of Carpiquet thirty-nine years later.[8]

Six of the surviving original charters are written in the same hand.[9]

---

[1] Charters 7, 8.

[2] Charters 7–9, 16, 17, 19. Cf. M.F. Soudet, 'Les seigneurs patrons des églises normandes au moyen âge', Travaux de la semaine d'histoire du droit normand 1923 (1925), 313–26.

[3] Charters 17, 19, 9, respectively.

[4] Juvigny B: Quarta pars presentationis ęcclesię.

[5] Charters 7, 8.

[6] TAC, cap. 23, 77; and Tractatus de legibus et consuetudinibus regni Anglie qui Glanvilla vocatur, ed. G.D.G. Hall (London, 1965), bk, IV, i-iii and bk. XIII, xviii-xx.

[7] Document 18. Cf. Boussard, Gouvernement d'Henri II, 291–2, who points out that the written proof of the charters obviated the need for a jury to make a decision.

[8] Charter 16.

[9] Charters 9, 11–14, 16, from the period 1218–24

Two of these (Charters 12 and 13) are grants of land by Abbess Johanna to tenants in return for grain rents; the other four appear to have been drawn up by the same scribe on behalf of tenants granting rights and property to the abbey. Another charter written up on behalf of the grantor of property to the abbey is clearly written in the same hand as the English charter of David, chaplain, in connection with property in London,[1] which suggests an integrated cross-Channel administration on the eve of the separation of 1204.

9   The 1257 Survey of Abbess Juliana de Saint-Sernin

Limited comparative use has been made of a reconstituted survey of 1257.[2] The original has not survived but much of it was summarised in French and small sections of it translated from Latin into French in a *Bref Mémoire des Chartes et Antiquités* in 1622, which included references to the original foliation.[3] Ten years later Philip le Bret, the abbey's procurator, copied extracts in Latin from the same survey, principally in connection with the Escanneville group of estates. These extracts include the title and date of the survey and the lists of jurors for Ouistreham and Tassilly.[4] Together with other even more fragmentary material from the still unclassified abbey records at the Archives du Calvados, these later sources have enabled Musset to reconstruct the outlines of the original survey.[5]

Judging from its original length of a least 150 folios and the detailed descriptions for Escanneville, Gonneville, Varaville, and Beauvoir,[6] the survey of 1257 must have been the most wide-ranging of the abbey's known surveys. It seems to have been conducted along the same lines as the twelfth-century Survey B, commencing with lists of jurors, followed by descriptions of demesne produce and cash renders, and tenant holdings

---

[1] Charter 4; *Charters and Custumals*, Charter 9.

[2] I am indebted to Professor Lucien Musset of the University of Caen for a typescript copy of his 'Reconstitution de la jurée de 1257'.

[3] Caen, Archives du Calvados, H, Trinité de Caen, unclassified, 284ff.

[4] Caen, Musée des Beaux Arts, Collection Mancel, MS 74, ff. 144–50, and Archives du Calvados, H. Trinité, dossier Tassilly, Clauses 1 and 2: *In isto libro continentur terre, obventiones, redditus, proventus, et jura spectantia ad monasterium Sancte Trinitatis de Cadomo.*
Hec est iurata facta ex provisione religiose domine Juliana de Sancto Serenico, Dei gratia abbatisse Sancte Trinitatis de Cadomo, anno Domini millesimo ducentesimo quinquagesimo septimo, et omnes jurate alie subsequentes.

[5] e.g. Caen, Archives du Calvados, H, Trinité de Caen, dossiers for Varaville, Saulques, and Asnelles.

[6] Survey 1257, ff. 46–53; copy in Caen, Musée des Beaux Arts, Collection Mancel, MS. 74, ff. 144v–50r.

under the familiar groupings of fee-farms, vavassoriates, villeinages, and bordages, and closing with *summae*. By contrast with the twelfth-century surveys, however, the 1257 Survey was not limited to the Calvados region, and even in its very abbreviated seventeenth-century form touches upon properties, rents, and rights in almost one hundred locations, including the Channel Islands[1] and the Cotentin, but excluding England.

10   *Note on the Editing*

In this edition the original charters are referred to as Charters (1–21), the custumals or surveys as A and B preceded by the name of the estate, and the cartulary material from both the Paris and Caen cartularies as Documents (1–27). Marginal numbers in Survey B refer to paragraphs, or to individual tenants or tenements for ease of reference. Likewise in Survey B English headings in square brackets indicate category of tenure. A blank line indicates the end of such entries and/or a MS indication of a new paragraph.

In keeping with Chibnall's edition of the English *Charters and Custumals*, where an original charter has survived the punctuation and capitals of the original have been retained. Square brackets are used for doubtful readings, extensions, and, in Charters 1 and 13, supplied words; suspensions are left where there is considerable doubt about the ending intended by the scribe. Only medieval endorsements to charters have been given.

In the case of the Surveys and the Cartulary Documents capitals and punctuation have been modernised and some necessary editorial licence applied. The scribe seems to have been uncertain of some of the documents and has produced a number of passages whose meaning is clear but whose grammar is not. In particular there is no consistency in the case used with the preposition *pro* where it is used in connection with rents: sometimes it is used with the accusative, at other times with the ablative. Modern practice has been followed in printing *u* and *v* and *j* and *i*. In transcribing the Latinized form of the English name Alveredus has been preferred to Aluered, and the diphthong ę has been retained throughout.

---

[1] *Abbayes caennaises*, 52, n. 1.

Note on Currency, Land Measures and Dry Measures

Currency

In Survey A and in other documents of the first half of the twelfth century the currency is Norman, based on the mints of Rouen and Bayeux.[1] In Survey B and other documents of the second half of the twelfth century the currency is exclusively Angevin,[2] which replaced *le denier normand* until the introduction of the Touraine currency after 1204.[3] The three currencies—Norman, Angevin, and Tournois—seem to have been valued at par. Stability and control were the determining factors in the change from the one to the other. The neighbouring currency of Maine was valued twice as highly, and that of England fourfold.[4]

Land Measures

The virgate (*virga* or *virgata*) in Normandy was one quarter of an acre, and not a multiple of acres (usually about thirty) as in England.

The Norman acre seems to have been much larger than, sometimes twice as large as, the English acre. Consequently the Norman ploughland (*terra unius carruce*) tends to consist of fewer acres than its English counterpart: about sixty acres according to Delisle.[5]

Dry Measures

For most estates, especially those in Survey B, the following grain measures applied:

---

[1] Cf. Document 15, *tempore* Robert Curthose.

[2] Cf. Document 12 (*c.* 1152 – *c.* 1178).

[3] Cf. Charters 11 (1221), 14 (1223).

[4] F. Dumas, 'Les monnaies normandes (X^e–XIIe siècles)', *Revue numismatique*, 6th ser., 21 (1979), 84–137, esp. 87–101.

[5] Delisle, *Etudes*, 298–301; H. Navel, *Recherches sur les anciennes mesures agraires normandes: acres, vergées et perches* (Société des antiquaries de Normandie, Caen, 1932).

3 bushels   =   1 quarter
2 quarters =   1 mine
2 mines   =   1 sester
12 sesters =   1 muid

At Escanneville there is the suggestion of a muid composed of 16 sesters.[1] It has to be remembered, however, that most if not all estates had measures of varying capacity. This is specifically stated in charters for Bény-sur-Mer, Rosel, Bougy, and Mathieu, and in Survey B for Carpiquet, Sallen, Juvigny, Montbouin, Villons-les-Buissons, and Amblie. At Villons no fewer than three grain measures are recorded: the measure of Caen, the measure of the almonry, and the measure of Villons itself.[2]

Salt measures occur in Escanneville A and B. Survey A refers to one muid (*modius*) and two ambers (*ambros*) of salt; Survey B refers to bushels and cartloads (*summae*), from which it is clear that six bushels equalled one cartload.

The 1257 Survey for Escanneville introduces two additional terms: a *pesella* (O.F. *peise*) of twelve bushels and an *asquez*, which was probably one or two bushels. A total of 202 *aquets* of salt were due from Escanneville and Varaville in 1436/7, according to the accounts for that year.[3]

[1] Escanneville B, **56**.
[2] Villons B, **9**, **6/14**, **35**.
[3] Caen, Archives du Calvados, H, Trinité de Caen, Comptes 1436/7, ff. 35r–41r. Cf. Escanneville B, **56**.

Original Charters

1 *Charter of Adeliz, abbess of Holy Trinity, Caen, to the Premonstratensian canons of St. Mary, Ardenne (founded c. 1138), granting them the whole messuage of Guimar, the Breton, in the Bourg-l'Abbesse, Caen.*

[1142 × 1152]

Original charter, British Library, Add. Ch. 15279.

[Omnibus][1] Sancte matris ecclesie filiis Adel[iz][2] Sancte trinitatis cad' abbatissa et totius eiusdem ecclesie conventus salutem. Notum sit vobis omnibus quod nos in communi capitulo concessimus deo et sancte marie et canonicis de ardena totam masuram Guimar britonis que est in burgo nostro . sicut de vico ad vicum protenditur liberam et quietam ab omni consuetudine et redditu ad ecclesiam Sancte trinitatis pertinente . omnia eis in predicta masura dantes et concedentes que ad manum domini pervenire poterunt vel in teloneo seu consuetudine vel alia qualibet causa rationabili . Teste philippo baiocensis episcopo[3] . Vmfredo capellano suo . Richerio clerico . Radulfo de capella . Radulfo de cainneio[4] . Hug[one] pasturel . Willelmo filio Rogeri . Fulchered[o] oger . Roberto filio bernardi.[5]

Endorsement: *Adeliz abbatisse Sancte Trinitatis de Cadomo* (12th/13th cent.).
Size: 8.5 × 17.25 cm.
Seal: missing.
NOTES
[1] MS damaged; word supplied.
[2] This may well be Abbess Alicia (*Aalisa* in *Charters and Custumals*, 47 and 139, but, the endorsement notwithstanding, *Adel'* could stand for Adela or Adelaide, in which case this would represent an hitherto unknown abbess of Caen. Dametta was probably abbess by 1152 (*Charters and Custumals*, 139, n. 7). In any event this is the earliest extant charter emanating from the abbey of Holy Trinity, Caen.
[3] Philip de Harcourt, bishop of Bayeux 1142–63.
[4] Probably Cagny, canton Troarn, 8 km south-west of Caen.
[5] Cf. *Regesta*, III, no. 22 (April–Dec. 1154), Round, *CDF*, no. 516 (1152–4), writ of Henry as duke of Normandy and of Aquitaine and count of the Angevins to Robert son of Bernard and the men of Caen to ensure that the prior of Ardenne freely hold his house in Caen. This suggests that Robert was already the *prévôt* of Caen. Cf. Haskins, *Institutions*, 167.

2 *Notification by the abbess of Holy Trinity, Caen, to Froger, bishop of Sées, that she has canonically conferred the church of Tassilly on Nicholas, the priest.*

[1157 × 1184]

Original charter, Caen, Archives du Calvados, H, Trinité de Caen, carton 105 (Tassilly).

Frog[ero] gratia dei Sagiensi episcopo[1] et omnibus prelatis sanctę dei ecclesię tam presentibus quam futuris Domina Sancte Trinitatis de cadomo abbatissa[2] et totus conventus eiusdem ęcclesię salutem. Quoniam vita hominum brevis est . et eorum etiam memoria labilis . ideo per hoc scriptum notificari volumus vobis . quod nos concessimus huic clerico nomine nicholao . canonice ęcclesiam de tasilleio in perpetuam elemosinam. Testes sunt Radulfus de capella[3] . Benedictus[4] . Johannes[5] . et Robertus brito[6] . Bernadus de gardineio[7] . Radulfus de herruvilla[8] . Robertus filius Renaudi . et herneis presbiter . nicholaus de vescavilla[9] . Durandus et multi alii.

Endorsement: *quaedam littera presentationis ecclesie de tassilleyo* (13th/14th cent.).
Size: 7.5 × 18.5/20.5 cm.
Seal: missing.
NOTES
[1] Froger, bishop of Sées 1157–84.
[2] Probably Abbess Dametta.
[3] Witness to Charter 1 and Document 12.
[4] Benedict *capellanus* of Document 12.
[5] John *capellanus* of Document 12.
[6] Cf. Saulques B, **27**, Robert the Breton, vavassor. He was also a witness to a charter of Abbess Johanna, probably in the early 1180s (Legras, *Bourgage de Caen*, appendix, charter no. 2).
[7] Bernard *clericus* of Document 12; possibly related to William *de Gardigno*, Tassilly B, **16**.
[8] Hérouville, north-east of Caen.
[9] Vesqueville, part of La Hoguette, 4 km south-east of Falaise.

3 *Charter of Thomas Bardulf granting to the abbey of Holy Trinity, Caen, an annual rent of 30s sterling from a mill in Elvaston (Derbyshire), after Matilda, his daughter, had been received as a nun at Holy Trinity. Half of this rent had been allocated by Rohaisia, Matilda's mother, for her daughter's religious education for life, after which the whole sum was to be received by the abbey. Provision is also made for an exchange of the rent for an equivalent in Anjou currency if Thomas benefits from escheats in Normandy.* [1178 × 1182]

Original charter, Caen, Archives du Calvados, H, Trinité de Caen, carton 25/1, liasse 'Biens sis en Angleterre'.
Round, *CDF*, no. 435 [1170–87].
Léchaudé d'Anisy, *Extraits*, no. 8.

Universis Sancte matris ecclesie filiis ad quos presens carta pervenerit . Thomas Bardul[1] salutem. Sciatis me dedisse et concessisse . et hac presenti carta mea confirmasse . abbatie sancte Trinitatis de Cadomo .xxx. solidos Stelling[orum] in Anglia . annuatim reddendos ad Festum sancti Michaelis in molendino meo de Elwadeston' qui sedet super Derwente in perpetuam elemosinam cum Mathilde filia mea ibidem monacha facta concessu et voluntate Rohaisie uxoris mee matris eiusdem Mathilde de cuius hereditate molendinus (*sic*) erat. Quia ita eadem Rohaisia uxor mea precepit in vita sua ut prenominatus redditus daretur prefate Mathildi filie sue ad eam consulendam in religione *?* ita quod prefata filia mea habebit inde .xv. solidos quandiu vixerit annuatim . et post eius decessum remanebunt integre prefatei (*sic*) .xxx. solidi Stelling[orum] prefate abbatie.[2] Quare volo et firmiter precipio quod predicta abbatia habeat et teneat prenominatum redditum . bene et in pace integre et honorifice in perpetuam elemosinam . cum prenominata filia mea datum. Et si forte aliqua Escaeta contingeret mihi in Normannia que eidem abbatie esset propinqua et assidua excambirem prenominatum redditum in Andeg' ad valentiam Stelling[orum] . eidem abbatie . vel heres meus. Ita quod mihi redderet hanc cartam vel heredi meo et haberet novam cartam de excambio . et mea res de Anglia mihi remaneret quieta et heredibus meis quando prefata abbatia excambium suum haberet ad graantum suum in Normannia. Testibus his . Willelmo filio Radulfi senescallo tunc Normannie[3] . et Henrico filio Radulfi . Ricardo de Cardif . Eudone de Fontanis et Rogero . Jordano de Landa . Rogero de Arre Radulfo de Wall[ano]monte[4] . Paride clerico . Willelmo de Caluz . Jordano de Grendon' . Balduino de Toene . Roberto le nevo . Willelmo de Logevilla . Osberto capellano . Ansquitillo clerico[5] . Willelmo clerico de Argent' . cum multis aliis.

Endorsement: *littera Thome Balduf de Anglia de xxx s. stellingorum* (13th/14th cent.).
Size: 20.5/21 × 21/22 cm.
Seal: missing.
NOTES
[1] Cf. Delisle/Berger, Introduction, 'notes bibliographiques', 463; Boussard, *Henri II*, 557, n. 4; and *Charters and Custumals*, xxi, n. 3. Thomas Bardulf's gift is included in the confirmation charter of Henry II to the abbey, 1180–1182: Round, *CDF*, no. 439, Delisle/Berger, II, 203, no. DCI.
[2] The earmarking of donations to professed relatives is discussed in Johnson, *Monastic Profession*, 41–2, 107–12.
[3] Cf. J. Le Patourel, 'Guillaume Fils-Raoul, sénéchal de Normandie, 1178–1200', *AN*, 30 (1980), 321–2. William fitz Ralph, Jordan de Landa, Roger of Arry, and William of Calix appear in Documents 16 [1183] and 18 [1185].
[4] Cf. Documents 17, 18 [1185].
[5] Osbert, chaplain, and Anquetil, clerk, are witnesses to Document 18.

4 *Charter of John de Soligny granting Johanna, abbess, and the convent of Holy Trinity, Caen, six portions of land totalling 17¼ virgates in*

Bény-sur-Mer (cant. Creully) for the abbey's acceptance of Margaret, his grand-daughter, as a nun.   [late twelfth century, probably *c.* 1180]

Original charter, Caen, Archives du Calvados, H, Trinité de Caen, carton 26/1, liasse 'Bény'.

Omnibus sancte matris Ecclesie filiis tam presentibus quam futuris ad quos presens scriptum pervenerit.[?] Johannes de solign[eio].[1] salutem in domino. Quoniam .J.[ohanna] dei gratia abbatissa sancte Trinitatis de Cadomo Et Eiusdem Ecclesie Conventus ad petitionem meam susceperunt .M.[argaretam][2] neptem meam filiam Hacol[ii] . filii mei in monialem suam.[?] volui gr[ati]am tanti honoris mei liberaliter inpensi.[?] Conpetenter Eis retribuere.[?] Et Congrua bonorum meorum prosequi largicione. Proinde noveritis universi me Cum assensu Et Concessione Hacol[ii] filii mei Concessisse et dedisse et presenti Carta Confirmasse predictis abbatisse et monialibus et Ecclesie sancte Trinitatis de Cadomo . in territorio de Ben[eio] . terras subscriptas et Carta presenti nominatas . videlicet tenendas Eis in perpetuam Elemosinam . liberas et quietas ab omni servitio et omni Consuetudine et ab omni talleia et omni redditu et Exactione . sicut aliqua Elemosina potest unquam et debet liberius et quietius teneri . videlicet . desubtus domum horosie .iii. virgatas terre . In Exsarto .iii. virgatas et dimidiam virgatam . Retro Gardign' .i. virgatam et dimidiam. Ad Caput vici .i. virgatam et dimidiam. Ad limitem de dowr' .iii. virgatas. In curceria vie de Cortiseign' .v. virgatas terre. Ut autem et predicta donacio a me facta et Concessio Hacol[ii] filii mei permaneat semper stabilis et firma.[?] Eam mea presenti Carta et sigillo meo Confirmavi. Et Hacol[ius] filius meus sigillum suum apposuit ad Eamdem Confirmandam. Testibus hiis . Jord[ano] de tribus montibus[3] . Roberto senescallo de Corcell'[4] . Willelmo Lachor' . Frogerio de Brakevill'[5] . Willelmo de Graeio Cum pluribus aliis.

Endorsement: *littera de Beni. Copia est in quaterno .C.* (13th/14th cent.).
Size: 18.5 × 14/14.5 cm.
Seals: missing; two parchment tags.
NOTES
[1] Cf. Delisle/Berger, Introduction, 'notes bibliographiques', 399.
[2] Charter 12 supplies the full name.
[3] See H. Legras. *Bourgage de Caen*, appendix, charters 2 (1173–83) and 3 (1165–98), to which Jordan of Trois Monts was a witness. He was also a witness to the charter of David, chaplain, in favour of Abbess Johanna (*Charters and Custumals*, no. 9), which is written in the same hand as the above charter and is datable to 1193 × 1220.
[4] Probably Courseulles-sur-Mer, 5 km north of Bény-sur-Mer.
[5] Bracqueville, 0.5 km south of Bény-sur-Mer.

5 *Charter of Pope Lucius III confirming the rights of the abbey of Holy Trinity, Caen, over the church of St. Giles, as granted by William the Conqueror with the assent of the bishop of Bayeux.*[1]   [13 November 1184]

Original charter, Caen, Archives du Calvados, H, Trinité de Caen, carton 25/2, liasse 'bulles'.
Printed in J. Ramackers (ed.), *Papsturkunden in Frankreich*, II, Normandie (Göttingen, 1937), no. 257.
Léchaudé d'Anisy, *Extraits*, no. 48.
Regesta Pontificum Romanorum, II, ed. P. Jaffé and G. Wattenbach (Leipzig, 1888), no. 15325.

LUCIUS episcopus . servus servorum dei . Dilectis in Christo filiabus . . Abbatisse et Conventui sancte Trinitatis de Cadomo salutem . et apostolicam benedictionem. Iustis petentium desideriis . dignum est nos facilem prebere consensum et vota que a rationis tramite non discordant effectu prosequente complere. Eapropter dilecte in Christo filie vestris iustis postulationibus grato concurrentes assensu . ecclesiam sancti Egidii cum omni iure . et pertinentiis suis sicut eam iuste et canonice possidetis . et libertates tam circa vos quam circa familiam vestram et circa clericos vestros vel ecclesie Beati Egidii servientes sicut per felicis memorie .W. regis (*sic*) Angl[orum] assensu Baiocensis episcopi rationabiliter sunt concesse et usque ad hec tempora per quadraginta annorum curricula inviolabiliter observate possessiones quoque universas quas predicto temporis spatio usque ad hec tempora pacifice possedistis, auctoritate vobis apostolica confirmamus et presentis scripti patrocinio communimus. Nulli ergo omnino hominum liceat hanc paginam nostre confirmationis infringere vel ei ausu temerario contraire. Siquis autem hoc attentare presumpserit indignationem omnipotentis dei et beatorum Petri et Pauli apostolicorum eius se noverit incursurum.
Datum Veronam Id. Novembris.

Endorsement: *confirmatio donationis facte a rege Anglorum.*
Size: 19 × 21.25 cm.
Seal: missing; fragment of silk cord in red and gold.
NOTE
[1] Cf. *Abbayes caennaises*, no. 8, 88–9: *Ad heç Baiocensis Odo episcopus, interveniente gratia et dilectione nostra, predictam Sanctę Trinitatis ęcclesiam cum atrio, abbatissam cum sanctimonialibus, omnem clerum in eodem loco servientem, universam familiam ejusdem ęcclesię cibo sustentatam, ab omni exactione pecunię episcopalium reddituum liberam esse concedit. Sed et ęcclesiam Beati Egidii cum atrio ipsius quo modo supradictam liberam et quietam et clericos ibidem servientes eo modo quo supra liberos esse permittit.*

6 *Charter of Philippa of Rosel granting the abbess and convent of Holy Trinity, Caen, six portions of land in Rosel (cant. Creully) for quittance of an annual rent of one muid of wheat.*[1]   [1202]

Original charter, Caen, Archives du Calvados, H, Trinité de Caen, carton 26/1, liasse 'Rosel'.
Léchaudé d'Anisy, *Extraits*, no. 57.

Notum sit omnibus tam presentibus quam futuris ad quos presens carta pervenerit. quod ego Philippa de Rosel² pro salute mea et antecessorum meorum concessi et dedi . et in perpetuam et puram . et quietam elemosinam assignavi ecclesie et abbatisse et conventui sancte trinitatis de cadomo terras subscriptas . de dominico meo de Rosel pro uno modio frumenti quem ego debebam annuatim et hereditarie predictis abbatisse et conventui et quem habuerant de me et antecessoribus meis annuatim . Videlicet campum de viis furcatis . campum de sirecamp' . campum de villeta . campum de virgatis . campum de valle desubtus limitem de lacon' . et campum de colle. Quamobrem volo et precipio quod predicte ecclesia et abbatissa et conventus teneant et possideant predictas terras integre et pacifice et libere et quiete in perpetuam et puram elemosinam . et quietam ab omni redditu et omni servicio et omne consuetudine . pro quitantia predicti modii frumenti. Et ego et heredes mei tenemur guarantizare predictas terras predictis abbatisse et conventui. Et si forte non possemus eas guarantizare. nos teneremur excambire eas competenter ad equalem valorem. Ut autem et predicta concessio et donatio mea permaneat semper stabilis et firma. eas mea presenti carta et sigillo meo confirmavi. Hoc autem factum est apud cadomum ad scacarium domini Regis . coram baronibus scacarii. Anno ab incarnatione domini .m.°cc.°ii.° Radulfo taxone senescallo Norm[annie].³

Endorsement: *copia est in quaterno .C.* (13th/14th cent.).
Size: 16 × 20 cm.
Seal: missing; cord tag.
NOTES
[1] Cf. Charter 13.
[2] Cf. Round, *CDF*, no. 517 [1176], charter of Philippa, daughter of Hugh Rosel to the abbey of St. Mary at Ardenne (BL, Add. Ch. 15278). By 1199 Philippa was already a widow (Round, *loc. cit.*, n. 1).
[3] Ralph Tesson, seneschal of Normandy, 1201–4(?).

7 *Notification of Silvester, bishop of Sées, that on the presentation of the abbess and nuns of Holy Trinity, Caen, he has canonically conferred the church of Barges (dép. Orne) on Samson of Avenelles.*   [1208]

Original charter, Caen, Archives du Calvados, H, Trinité de Caen, carton 25/2, liasse 'Evêques de'.
Léchaudé d'Anisy, *Extraits*, no. 58.

Universis Sancte matris Ecclesie filiis presentes litteras inspecturis? Silvester dei gratia Sagiensis Episcopus[1] salutem in domino; Noverit universitas vestra . nos ad presentationem . . abbatisse et monialium sancte trinitatis de Cadomo ad quas ius patronatus Ecclesie sancte marie de villa barge pertinere dinoscitur? Sansoni de Avesneles[2] clerico eamdem ecclesiam cum pertinentiis suis liberam et vacantem canonice contulisse. Actum Anno gratie .m.°cc.°viii.° valete.

Endorsement: *presentacio ecclesie beate marie de bauge* (13th/14th cent.).
Size: 4.75/5.4 × 16.6 cm.
Seal: missing; tag missing. Léchaudé d'Anisy, *Extraits*, records the existence of a broken seal.
NOTES
[1] Bishop of Sées, 1202–20.
[2] Avenelles, cant. Exmes.

8 *Notification of Silvester, bishop of Sées, that on the presentation of the abbess and nuns of Holy Trinity, Caen, he has canonically conferred the church of St. Gervase at Falaise on William Acarin.* [1217]

Original charter, Caen, Archives du Calvados, H, Trinité de Caen, carton 25, liasse 'Evêques de'.
Léchaudé d'Anisy, *Extraits*, no. 61b.

Universis Christi fidelibus ad quos presens Scriptum pervenerit? Silvester dei gratia Sagiensis Episcopus Salutem in domino. Noverit universitas vestra nos ad presentationem . . Abbatisse et Conventus Sanctimonialium Sancte Trinitatis de Cadomo . ad quas ius patronatus Ecclesie Sancti Gervasii de falesia dinoscitur pertinere? eamdem Ecclesiam liberam et vacantem dilecto clerico nostro Willelmo Hacari[no][1] amore dei canonice contulisse. Ut igitur hec nostra donatio Rata permaneat in futurum? presenti scripto et sigilli nostri munimine duximus Roborandam. Actum anno gratie m°cc°. Septimodecimo . Valete.

Endorsement: *Littera de ecclesia de falesia* (13th/14th cent.).
Size: 5.6 × 16 cm.
Seal: missing; parchment tag. Léchaudé d'Anisy, *Extraits*, records the existence of a broken seal.
NOTE
[1] William Acarin, founder of the collegiate church of the Sepulchre at Caen. See Charter 15 and Document 22.

9 *Charter of two brothers, Hugh and John, bakers, to the convent of Holy Trinity, Caen, granting it two-thirds of the tithes of twelve acres of land at Vaux-sur-Seulles.* [1218]

Original charter, Caen, Archives du Calvados, H, Trinité de Caen, carton 26/2, liasse 'Vaux-sur-Seulles'.
Léchaudé d'Anisy, *Extraits*, no. 62.

Notum sit tam presentibus quam futuris quod Ego Hugo furnarius et Ego Johannes furnarius fratres pro salute nostra et antecessorum nostrorum concessimus et dedimus ecclesie et Conventui sancte Trinitatis de Cadomo in perpetuam et puram elemosinam liberam et quietam ab omni servicio et omni redditu et omni exactione seculari duas Garbas decime duodecim acrarum terre in territorio de vaus super seullam . quas duas Garbas nos tenebamus cum predictis duodecim acris de domino Petro Ruaud milite in feodo et hereditate. Quamobrem volumus et concedimus . quod predicta ecclesia et moniales eiusdem loci teneant et possideant predictas duas Garbas decime predictarum duodecim acrarum . libere . pacifice . integre et quiete in pura elemosina. Nos autem et heredes nostri tenemur Guarantizare hoc eis . et si non possemus eis Guarantizare? nos tenemur dare eis decem libras turon[ienses]. Et de hoc faciendo? concessimus in plegium totum tenementum nostrum. Ut autem predicta donacio nostra permaneat semper stabilis et firma? eam presenti carta et sigillis nostris confirmavimus. Actum est anno dominice incarnacionis .m.°cc.° Octavo decimo apud cadomum in assisa coram domino Petro de Teill'.[1]

Endorsement: *Vaux copia est in caterno.* (13th/14th cent.).
Size: 14 × 14.25 cm.
Seals: missing; two parchment tags. Léchaudé d'Anisy, *Extraits*, records the existence of broken seals.
NOTE
[1] Pierre du Thillai, a *bailli* of Normandy, 1205–24(?): Strayer, *Administration*, 111.

10 *Charter of William of Vaux-sur-Seulles granting the abbess and convent of Holy Trinity, Caen, all his meadow at Vaux-sur-Seulles.*
[27 September 1218]

Original charter, Caen, Archives du Calvados, H, Trinité de Caen, carton 26/1, Vaux-sur-Seulles (boxed charter).
Léchaudé d'Anisy, *Extraits*, no. 63.

Notum sit omnibus tam presentibus quam futuris quod Ego Willelmus de vaus pro salute mea et antecessorum meorum concessi et dedi Abbatisse et conventui et ecclesie sancte Trinitatis de Cadom[o] totum pratum meum de vaus possidendum eis in perpetuam et puram elemosinam . et liberam et quietam . ab omni servicio et omni Redditu et omni consuetudine . et omni exactione seculari. Hanc autem elemosinam ego et heredes mei tenemur eis Garantizare.? et si non possemus eis garantizare.? teneremur ad faciendum eis competens excambium in alio feodo meo. Hoc autem totum cum assensu et concessione domini mei Roberti de Cormorlein militis de quo tenebam feodaliter predictum pratum. Factum est hoc . videlicet anno dominice incarnacionis .m.°cc.° decimo octavo in mense septemb[ris] in festo sanctorum Cosme et damiani martirum. Ut autem predicta concessio mea permaneat semper stabilis et firma.? eam mea presenti carta et sigillo meo confirmavi. Et ad maiorem confirmacionem Dominus meus Robertus de Cormorlein miles sigillum meum apponere Curavi.

Endorsement: *Vaux super seullam copia est in cateno* (13th/14th cent.).
Size: 10/10.5 × 19.5 cm.
Seals: two seals pendent from single tags.
(a) Seal of William of Vaux-sur-Seulles: round; 3.5 cm; green wax; emblem: kite-shaped shield; legend: + S' WILLELMI DE VAV[L]IBUS. Léchaudé d'Anisy, *Extraits*, Atlas, plate 15, fig. 23.
(b) Seal of Robert of Cormolain: round; 4.25 cm; green wax; emblem: fleur-de- lys; legend: + [SIGILL]UM ROBERTI D[E] [CORMOR]LAN. Léchaudé d'Anisy, *Extraits*, Atlas, plate 15, fig. 27.

11 *Charter of William of Sallenelles, knight, quitclaiming to Johanna, abbess, and the convent of Holy Trinity a vavassoriate in the island of Jersey that he and his father had held unjustly; in return the abbess paid him ten livres tournois.* [1221]

Original charter, Caen, Archives du Calvados, H, Trinité de Caen, carton 25/1, liasse 'Iles Normandes'.
Printed in *Cartulaire des îles Normandes*, ed. G.F.B. Gruchy, R.R. Marrett and E.T. Nicolle (Société Jersiaise, 1924), no. 320.
Copy by Léchaudé d'Anisy, Paris, Bibl. nat., MS lat., n. acqu. 10077, no.14. Léchaudé d'Anisy, *Extraits*, no. 66.

Universis Christi fidelibus ad quos presens carta pervenerit Willelmus de Salinell'[1] miles salutem in domino. Sciatis universi quod Ego Willelmus de Salinell' miles filius Willelmi de Salinell' militis pro salute mea et salute patris mei et omnium antecessorum meorum cum assensu et concessione [   ][2] filii mei primogeniti concessi reddidi et quietum clamavi ecclesie et .J.[ohanne] Abbatisse et conventui sancte Trinitatis de Cadomo totam vavassoriam et totum tenementum quod quidam homines de insula qui vocantur mali filiastri[3] tenuerant et tenere debent de predictis Abbatissa et conventu in insula de Geresuil . quod tenementum pater meus et ego occupavimus et detinuimus iniuste. Quamobrem volo quod predicti ecclesia et Abbatissa et conventus habeant et teneant amodo totam predictam vavassoriam cum omnibus pertinentiis suis integre . libere et quiete et pacifice salvo iure et feodo predictorum hominum. Pro hac autem quietancia et reddicione predicti tenementi Abbatissa et conventus dederunt mihi et filio meo de caritate domus sue decem libras turon[ienses]. Ut autem totum hoc perpetuam semper habeat firmitatem mea presenti carta et sigillo meo confirmavi. Actum est hoc anno dominice incarnacionis .m.°cc.° vicesimo primo.

Endorsement: *littera de insulis copia est in caterno.* (13th/14th cent.).
Size: 13.5 × 18.2 cm.
Seal: pendent from single tag; round; 3.5 cm; green wax; emblem: kite-shaped shield with horizontal zig-zag design; legend: illegible. Léchaudé d'Anisy, *Extraits*, Atlas, plate 15, fig. 20, depicts legend: + S' WILLERMI DE SALINEL.
NOTES
[1] Sallenelles, cant. Troarn.
[2] Name omitted.
[3] The Malfilâtre family. The fief of seven knights' fees was granted to Robert, earl of Gloucester, by Richard fitz Samson, bishop of Bayeux (1107–33). Cf. *Regesta*, III, no. 58; H. Navel, *L'Enquête de 1133 sur les fiefs de l'évêché de Bayeux* (Société des antiquaires de Normandie, Caen, 1935), 13, 25; 'Recherches sur les institutions féodales en Normandie (région de Caen)', *BSAN*, li (1948–51), 130.

12 *Charter of Johanna, abbess, and the convent of Holy Trinity, Caen, granting William, seneschal of Amblie, a total of 17¼ virgates of land in Bény-sur-Mer (as described in Charter 4) in return for an annual rent of seven sesters of wheat.* [January 1221]

Original charter, Caen, Archives du Calvados, H, Trinité de Caen, carton 26/1, liasse 'Bény'. Léchaudé d'Anisy, *Extraits*, no. 65.

Universis Christi fidelibus ad quos presens scriptum pervenerit. J.[ohanna] humilis Abbatissa et conventus sancte Trinitatis de Cadomo salutem in domino. Noveritis universi nos concessisse et tradidisse Willelmo senescallo de Amblida omnes illas terras quas dominus Johannes de solign[eio] et Hascolius de solign[eio] filius suus dederunt nobis in territorio de Ben[eio] cum margareta filia predicti Hascolii facta moniali in cenobio nostro . videlicet habendas et tenendas de nobis eidem Willelmo senescallo et heredibus suis in feodo et hereditate . Reddendo nobis inde per annum de se et heredibus suis septem sextar[ia] frumenti in mense septembri ad mensuram eiusdem ville. Hec sunt autem terre . videlicet Campum de subtus domum horosie . trium virgatarum terre . Campum in exsarto trium virgatarum et dimidie virgate . Campum retro Gardig' unius virgate et dimidie virgate . Campum ad caput vici unius virgate et dimidie virgate . Campum ad limitem de Dowr' trium virgatarum . et Campum in curceria vie de Cortiseign' quinque virgatarum terre. Quamobrem volumus et precipimus quod dictus Willelmus senescallus et heredes sui teneant de nobis predictas terras . pacifice . libere . integre . plenarie . et quiete ab omni servicio per redditum predictum. Ut autem predicta concessio nostra permaneat stabilis et firma? eam nostra presenti carta et sigillo nostro confirmavimus. Actum est hoc anno gratie .m.°cc.° vicesimo primo . mense Januar[ii].

Endorsement: *copia est in caterno .C.* (13th/14th cent.).
Size: 18 × 15 cm.
Seal: pendent from single tag; oval; 5.5 × 4.5 cm; green wax; in poor condition, but clearly of the abbey of Holy Trinity, similar in design to the well-preserved seal of abbess Juliana de Saint-Sernin attached to a charter of 1252 in Archives du Calvados, H, Trinité de Caen, carton 26/1, liasse 'Vaux-sur-Seulles' and depicted in Léchaudé d'Anisy, *Extraits*, Atlas, plate 12, figs. 1 and 2. Legend: [ABBATI]SSE DE CADOMO.

13 *Charter of Johanna, abbess, and the convent of Holy Trinity, Caen, granting to Mauger of Rosel six plots of land in Rosel (as outlined in Charter 6, but described in more detail here), totalling about six acres, in return for an annual rent of one muid of wheat.*   [January 1221]

Original charter, Caen, Archives du Calvados, H, Trinité de Caen, carton 26/1, liasse 'Rosel'. Léchaudé d'Anisy, *Extraits*, no. 64.

Universis Christi fidelibus ad quos presens scriptum pervenerit. J.[ohanna] humilis Abbatissa et conventus sancte Trinitatis de Cadomo salutem in domino. Noveritis universi nos concessisse et tradidisse maugerio de Rosel omnes terras illas quas domina Philippa de Rosel concessit et assignavit nobis in territorio de Rosel pro frumento quod ipsa nobis reddebat annuatim . videlicet tenendas et habendas de nobis eidem maugerio et heredibus suis in feodo et hereditate . Reddendo nobis inde per annum de se et heredibus suis unum modium frumenti in mense septembri ad mensuram eiusdem ville: Hec sunt autem terre . videlicet campum de viis furcatis unius acre et dimid[ie] quinque pertic[as] minus . Campum de sirecamp' trium virg[atarum] . Campum de villeta unius acre et dimid[ie] et sex perticarum . Campum de virgatis . trium virg[atarum] et quart[e] part[is] virg[ate] . Campum de valle de subtus limitem de lacon' unius acre et dimid[ie] Novemdecim pertic[as] minus . et Campum de Colle . unius virg[ate] . et duarum part[ium] virg[ate]. Quamobrem volumus et precipimus quod dictus maugerius et heredes sui teneant de nobis predictas terras . pacifice . libere . integre . plenarie . et quiete . ab omni servicio per redditum predictum. Ut autem predicta concessio nostra permaneat semper stabilis et firma.? eam nostra presenti carta et nostro [sigillo]¹ confirmavimus. Actum est hoc anno gratie .m.°cc.° vicesimo primo . mense Januar[ii].

Endorsement: *copia est in quaterno* .*C*. (13th/14th cent.).
Size: 14.5/14.75 × 15.2 cm.
Seal: missing; one parchment tag. Léchaudé d'Anisy, *Extraits*, records the existence of a broken seal.
NOTE
¹ Word supplied.

14 *Charter of Guy of Le Manoir (cant. Ryes) to Johanna, abbess, and the convent of Holy Trinity, Caen, of one vavassoriate at Beuville (cant. Douvres), because he is unable to service it.* [1223]

Original charter, Caen, Archives du Calvados, H, Trinité de Caen, carton 26/2, liasse 'Beuville'.
Léchaudé d'Anisy, *Extraits*, no. 67.

Universis Christi fidelibus ad quos presens carta pervenerit dominus Guido de manerio miles salutem in domino. Noveritis universi me reddidisse domine .J.[ohanne] Abbatisse et conventui sancte Trinitatis de Cadomo unam vavassoriam quam tenebam de eis apud Buevillam cum omnibus pertinenciis suis sine aliqua reclamacione de me et de heredibus meis . quam non potui deservire . et quam vavassoriam Willelmus loe tenebat de me racione uxoris sue. Et unde mihi reddebat annuatim quatuor capones et quatuor panes ad Natale et sexaginta Ova ad pascha. Et ut hoc semper firmum habeatur et ratum.? mea presenti carta et sigilli mei munimine roboravi. Actum est hoc . anno incarnationis domini .m.°cc.° vicesimo tercio.

Endorsement: *Buevilla copia est in quaterna* (13th/14th cent.).
Size: 12 × 17 cm.
Seal: pendent from single tag; round; 5 cm; green wax; emblem: kite-shaped shield with inverted 'V'; legend: + S'.GVIDO[NI]S DE MANEREIO. Léchaudé d'Anisy, *Extraits*, Atlas, plate 15, fig. 24.

15 *Charter of the dean and chapter of the Holy Sepulchre, Caen, granting the abbess and convent of Holy Trinity, Caen, land and rent at Villons-les-Buissons for a payment of fifty livres tournois.* [1223]

Original charter, Caen, Archives du Calvados, H, Trinité de Caen, carton 26/1, liasse
'Villons-les-Buissons'.
Léchaudé d'Anisy, *Extraits*, no. 68.

Universis sancte matris Ecclesie filiis ad quos presens scriptum pervenerit
.W.[illelmus] Decanus[1] et capitulum sancti sepulchri de Cadomo Salutem
in domino. Noveritis quod nos concessimus abbatisse et conventui sancti
trinitatis de Cadomo pro quinquaginta[2] lib[ris] tur[oniensis] quas nobis
dederunt . Omnem terram et omnem redditum quem habebamus apud
villon de feodo dicte abbatisse et conventus de dono magistri Willelmi de
villon et ne aliquid in dicta terra vel in dicto redditu de cetero Reclamare
possimus, presentem cartam sigilli nostri munimine roboravimus. Actum
anno gratie .M.°C°C.° vicesimo tercio.

Endorsement: *Villon copia est in quaterno .c.* (13th/14th cent.).
Size: 6 × 17 cm.
Seal: fragment pendent from single tag; green wax; legend: . . . .[SAN]CTI. . . .
NOTES
[1] For the career of William Acarin, a native of Grainville-sur-Odon, an influential clerk of
the *bailli* of Caen and founder of the collegiate church of the Sepulchre at Caen in 1219, see
Strayer, *Administration*, 99; *Antiquus Cartularius Ecclesiae Baiocensis* (*livre noir*), ed. V.
Bourienne (Rouen and Paris, 1902–3), cxvi, and charter no. ccxix. See also Charter 8 (1217)
in which William was presented to the church of St. Gervase at Falaise, and Document 22
(Easter 1217), where he is described as a scribe at the exchequer court held at Falaise. Cf.
R. Jouet, . . .*et la Normandie devint française* (Paris, 1983), 105.
[2] Léchaudé d'Anisy, *Extraits*, gives fifteen *livres tournois*.

16 *Charter of Ivo of Ouistreham and William, his brother, renouncing in
favour of the abbess and convent of Holy Trinity, Caen, their right to the
advowson of the church of Carpiquet and its tithes, saving their fee in
Carpiquet and the tithes they hold in various parts of the same manor.*
[29 September 1224]

Original charter, Caen, Archives du Calvados, H, Trinité de Caen, carton 26/1, liasse
'Carpiquet'.
Léchaudé d'Anisy, *Extraits*, no. 70.

Universis Christi fidelibus ad quos presens carta pervenerit . Yvo
de Oistreha[m] et Willelmus frater suus salutem in domino. Noverit
universitas vestra nos dimisisse in pace in scacario apud Cadomum ad
festum sancti michaelis anno gratie .m.°cc.° vicesimo quarto Abbatisse et
conventui sancte Trinitatis de Cadomo omne ius quod nos dicebamus
habere in presentacione ecclesie de Carpiket et in decimis eiusdem ville.
Habendis sibi et possidendis quiete et pacifice sine aliqua reclamacione

que per nos vel heredes nostros possit fieri de cetero contra ipsas. Salvo nobis feodo nostro de Carpiket . et salvis decimis quas in dicta villa habemus in diversis locis in territorio eiusdem ville . que dignumduximus propriis vocabulis exprimenda. In vavassoria nostra quam nos tenemus de dictis Abbatissa et conventu apud Carpiket percipimus duas Garbas. In vavassoria Brienz.? similiter. In vavassoria Galfridi de Cingeleis.? similiter. In vavassoria Willelmi . Alardi. similiter. In vavassoria . Willelmi Baudri.? similiter.[1] In cultura de vinea[2] in medietate versus Ros.? duas Garbas . et in alia medietate nichil percipimus. In cultura de Puce fondre[3] in medietate versus martelet.? similiter. In cultura de Beu manet .[4] in medietate versus martelet.? similiter. In cultura de hoverlenc[5] versus martelet . similiter. In cultura de saket[6] versus Cadomum . similiter. In cultura de la champainne[7] versus Carpiket.? similiter. In cultura de Dumis . similiter. Exceptis tribus acris versus martelet.? ubi nichil percipimus. In londis vero terciam percipimus Garbam. Et in tribus virgatis terre in via de puce fondre.? duas Garbas. Et in dimidia acra iuxta terram comitis.?[8] similiter. Quod ut ratum et inconcussum in posterum habeatur.? presentem paginam sigillorum nostrorum munimine roboravimus.

Endorsement: *Pro ecclesia et decima de Karpiqueto. copia est in cateno .C.* (13th/14th cent.).
Size: 14.5 × 17.5/18 cm.
Seals: seals missing. Léchaudé d'Anisy, *Extraits*, recorded the existence of a broken seal.
NOTES
[1] Cf. Carpiquet B, **1–4, 54**. Yves and William of Ouistreham appear to be the successors of Ralph fitz Eude, who held the tithe of the fee of the four vavassors, Ralph son of Brienz, Warin de Cinglais, Aelard *nepos*, and Baudric *peregrinus* in Survey B, together with the tithe of half the demesne *culturae*, and the third sheaf from half of the villeins and bordars. See also Document 18 (1185).
[2] Cf. Carpiquet B, *Vinea*.
[3] Cf. Carpiquet B, *De puteo effundre*.
[4] Cf. Carpiquet B, *Cultura de Busmanet*.
[5] Cf. Carpiquet B, *Hovellenc*.
[6] Cf. Carpiquet B, *Cultura de Sachet*.
[7] Cf. Carpiquet B, *De campania*.
[8] Cf. Carpiquet B, *De terra Odonis comitis*.

17 *Charter of W. Thomas, canon of the Bayeux prebend of Merville, recording the settlement of a dispute between himself and the abbess and convent of Holy Trinity, Caen, over the tithes of Escanneville. It was agreed that the tithes of grain, flax and hemp be shared equally between them.*

[August 1224]

Original charter, Caen, Archives du Calvados, H, Trinité de Caen, carton 65 (Escanneville and Beauvoir).

Universis Christi fidelibus presens scriptum Inspecturis.? W. Thomas
Canonicus Baiocensis prebende de matrevilla . In domino salutem. Noverit
universitas vestra quod cum Inter me Ex una parte, et abbatissam et
Conventum Sancte Trinitatis de Cadomo ex altera . super quibusdam
decimis Terre de feodo Eiusdem abbatisse et conventus quam homines de
Eskenevilla tenent ad feodi firmam de predictis abbatisse et Conventu
que est In Cultura earumdem.? Questio verteretur.? post multas alter-
cationes.? lis sopita est Inter Nos . In Hunc modum . videlicet quod Ego
medietatem decimarum omnium Bladi Cuiusconque (*sic*) generis.? similiter
lini et Canabi predicte Terre memoratis Abbatisse et conventui In perpetuum
de assensu venerabilis patris nostri .R.[oberti] dei gratia Episcopi[1] .
W.[illelmi] Decani[2] . et Capituli Baiocensis In pace dimisi . Nulla
Reclamatione a me vel aliquorum canonicorum succedentium In eadem
prebenda.? In posterum facienda vel movenda . Tota altera medietate
dictarum decimarum michi et meis In ea prebenda successoribus In
perpetuum Remanente . Quod ut Ratum In posterum habeatur . venerabilis
pater .R.[obertus] dei gratia Baiocensis Episcopus et Capitulum eiusdem
loci presentem paginam dignum duxerunt sigillorum suorum munimine
Roborandam. Actum est hoc anno gratie .m.°cc.° vicesimo quarto mense
Augusto.

Endorsement: *copia est in caterno* (13th/14th cent.).
Size: 14.5 × 16.75 cm.
Seals: missing; 3 parchment seal tags, 2 with small pouches.
NOTES
[1] Robert des Ablèges, bishop of Bayeux, 1206–31.
[2] William de Semilly, dean of chapter of Bayeux, 1213–26.

18 *Charter of Thomas of Evrecy granting the nuns of Holy Trinity annual
rent of three quarters of wheat in a portion of land at Bougy and alms in
two houses at Caen.* [January 1227]

Original charter, Caen, Archives du Calvados, H, Trinité de Caen, carton 26/1, liasse
'Bougy'.
Léchaudé d'Anisy, *Extraits*, no. 71.

Sciant presentes et futuri quod Ego Thomas de Evrec' miles garanto et
concedo de me et heredibus meis pro salute anime mee et antecessorum
meorum Deo et monialibus sancte trinitatis Cadom[i] quod ipsae percipiant
feodaliter annuali redditu tres quarteria frumenti In septembr[e] ad
mensuram de Bougeio in una petia terre sita apud Bougeium in nigris terris
iuxta meam Culturam . et faciant plenariam Justiciam In dicta petia terre
pro dicto frumento sicuti (*sic*) in sua libera et quieta elemosina. Item

concedo eisdem similiter elemosinam quam habent apud Cadomum de dono Ricardi bordon in duabus domibus sitis extra portam mileti iuxta terram Gaufridi monachi. Ita quod ipsae habeant dictam elemosinam cum predicto frumento et possideant In puram et perpetuam elemosinam sine reclamatione mei et heredum meorum de cetero. Quod ut ratum et stabile teneatur in perpetuum presens scriptum sigilli mei testimonio roboravi. Actum anno gratie .m.CC.xx. septimo mense Januar[ii].

Endorsement: *copia est in quaterno*. (13th/14th cent.).
Size: 8/8.5 × 18.25/18.75 cm.
Seal: missing; one parchment tag. Léchaudé d'Anisy, *Extraits*, records the existence of a broken seal.

19 *Notification of settlement of a dispute between Johanna, abbess, and the convent of Holy Trinity, Caen, and master Lucas of Vaux-sur-Seulles over two-thirds of the tithes of grain in Vaux-sur-Seulles.* [1216 × 1227]

Original charter, Caen, Archives du Calvados, H, Trinité de Caen, carton 26/2, liasse 'Vaux-sur-Seulles'.

Universis Christi fidelibus ad quos presens scriptum pervenerit . . sancte marie magdalene et . . de monte leprosorum Priores et magister herbertus de Andeleio Canonicus Rothom[agensis] salutem in vero salutari. Ad vestram volumus pervenire noticiam . quod cum causa que vertebatur inter .J.[ohannam] Abbatissam et conventum sancte Trinitatis de Cadomo ex una parte: et magistrum Luc[am] de Vallibus clericum ex altera.? nobis a summo pontifice Honorio tercio[1] delegata super duabus partibus decimarum bladi de territorio de Vallibus quas Abbatissa et conventus ad se dicebant quantum ad possessionem et proprietatem de iure pertinere.[2] Datis dilacionibus et induciis quas iuris racio postulabat. Tamdem lis coram nobis fuit sopita in hunc modum . videlicet quod partibus in nostra presencia constitutis.? predictus magister Luc[as] in iure confessus est . omnes decimas supradictas ad iam dictas moniales Abbatissam et conventum quantum ad possessionem et proprietatem de iure pertinere. Easque per quadraginta annos vel amplius dictas decimas vel per se vel per firmarios pacifice possedisse . Exceptis quibusdam decimis quas Abbas et conventus de Cerasio[3] et Abbas et conventus de longis[4] in iam dicto territorio de quibusdam terris percipiunt . bona fide promittens se in iam dictis decimis de cetero nichil omnino reclamaturum. Reservata nobis iurisdictione de eius assensu et voluntate animadvertendi in ipsum . si forte vellet a supradictis aliquo modo resilire. Quod ut firmum et stabile et realiter et personaliter in posterum habeatur, sigillorum nostrorum munimine duximus Roborandum.

Endorsement: *Vaux. copia est in cateno.* (13th/14th cent.).
Size: 19/20 × 20.2 cm.
Seals: missing (3).
NOTES
[1] Pope Honorius III, 1216–27.
[2] Cf. Vaux-sur-Seulles A and B, in which two-thirds of the tithes are claimed to be in the abbey's possession.
[3] Abbey of St. Vigor, Cerisy.
[4] Abbey of St. Mary, Longues-sur-Mer.

20 *Charter of Simon Pevrel granting an annual rent of one mine of wheat from a purpresture of land at Mathieu (cant. Douvres) for the maintenance of a lamp at the altar of St. Lawrence in the abbey of Holy Trinity, Caen.* [August 1229]

Original charter, Caen, Archives du Calvados, H, Trinité de Caen, carton 73 (Mathieu).
Cartulary copy, Caen, Archives du Calvados, H, Cartulaire de l'abbaye Sainte Trinité, pp. 67–9. See Document 25.

Sciant presentes et Futuri quod Ego Simon Pevrel dedi et concessi pro salute anime mee et antecessorum meorum Deo et Luminari Altaris sancti Laurentii martiris[a] In Abbatia monialium[b] sancte Trinitatis Cadom' constituti scilicet unam minam frumenti percipiendam feodaliter[c] annuali redditu per annum In Septembr[e] ad mensuram de matoni' in uno porprisagio sito ibidem iuxta terram que fuit Vmfridi filii marie quod Ricardus pevrel meus avonculus (*sic*) tenet de me feodaliter tenendam et habendam dicto Luminari in puram et perpetuam elemosinam sine reclamatione mei et heredum meorum de cetero. Ita quod dicte moniales poterunt facere feodaliter plenariam Justiciam[d] in dicto porprisagio pro dicto frumento. Et de hoc atornavi eis[e] dictum Ricardum feodifirmarium. Et Ego et heredes mei dictis monialibus[f] successive dictam elemosinam contra omnes homines garantizare Integre tenemur. Quod ut ratum et stabile teneatur In perpetuum[g] presens scriptum sigilli mei testimonio roboravi. Actum anno gratie[h] .M.CC. vicesimo[i] Nono . mense Augusti.

Endorsement: *Math' Una m. frumenti ad mensuram ville* (13th/14th cent.).
Size: 8/8.5 × 24.5/25 cm.
Seal: missing; parchment tag.
[a] *Laurencii martyris*, Cartulaire. [b] *monialium* omitted, Cart.
[c] *feodaliter* after *redditu*, Cart. [d] *iustitiam*, Cart. [e] *eis* omitted, Cart.
[f] *moialibus*, Cart. [g] *Imperpetuum*, Cart. [h] *domini*, Cart. [i] *.M.CC.XX.*, Cart.

21 *Charter of Simon Pevrel granting an annual rent of one quarter of wheat from a purpresture of land at Mathieu for the maintenance of a lamp at the altar of St. Mary in the abbey of Holy Trinity, Caen.* [August 1229]

Original charter, Caen, Archives du Calvados, H, Trinité de Caen, carton 73 (Mathieu).
Cartulary copy, Caen, Archives du Calvados, H, Trinité de Caen, Cartulaire de l'abbaye
Sainte Trinité de Caen, pp. 64–6. See Document 23.

Sciant presentes et Futuri quod Ego Simon Pevrel dedi et concessi pro
salute anime mee et antecessorum meorum Deo et luminari lampadis
altaris sancte marie In abbatia monialium[a] sancte trinitatis Cadom' siti
retro magnum altare[b] scilicet[c] unum quarterium frumenti percipiendum
feodaliter annuali[d] redditu per annum In septembr[e] ad mensuram de
Matoni' In uno porprisagio sito ibidem iuxta terram que fuit Umfridi[e] filii[f]
marie . Tenendum et habendum dicto luminari In puram et perpetuam
elemosinam sine reclamatione mei et heredum meorum de cetero . quod
porprisagium.[g] Ricardus pevrel meus Avonculus tenet de me feodaliter.
Ita quod dicte moniales poterunt facere feodaliter plenariam Justiciam[h] In
dicto porprisagio pro dicto frumento[i] . Et de hoc atornavi eis dictum
Ricardum feodifirmarium.[j] Et Ego et heredes mei dictis monialibus
successive[k] dictam elemosinam[l] contra omnes homines garantizare
Integre[m] tenemur. Quod ut ratum et stabile teneatur[n] In perpetuum[o]
presens scriptum sigilli mei testimonio roboravi. Actum anno gratie[p]
.m.cc.xx Nono . mense augusti.

No endorsement.
Size: 5.6/6 × 28/28.5 cm.
Seal: missing; parchment tag.
[a] *monalium*, Cartulaire.   [b] *alltare*, Cart.   [c] *silicet*, Cart.   [d] *anuali*, Cart.
[e] *Unfridi*, Cart.   [f] *filius*, Cart.   [g] *propisagium*, Cart.   [h] *iusticiam*, Cart.
[i] *frumeto*, Cart.   [j] *feodi firmarium*, Cart.   [k] *sucessive*, Cart.   [l] *ellemosinam*, Cart.
[m] *Integre* omitted, Cart.   [n] *tenatur*, Cart.   [o] *imperpetuum*, Cart.   [p] *domini*, Cart.

Surveys
First Series (A)

Cartulary copy, Bibl. nat., MS lat. 5650.

DATE. c. 1113. The outside dates for the first series of surveys are 1107 and 1131. The reference to the capture of the duke (*sub* St. Aubin d'Arquenay A) is taken to be a reference to the capture of Robert Curthose at the battle of Tinchebray in 1106. The additional reference in the same entry to a transaction made in the following year provides a *terminus a quo* of 1107. If the English surveys in the same cartulary are contemporaneous with the Norman surveys, neither series can be later than 1131, the date by which Holy Trinity acquired the manor of Tilshead in Wiltshire. See Chibnall, *Charters and Custumals*, xxvi–xxxi, who argues that the surveys 'may have been made before 1113', and Tabuteau, *Transfers of Property*, 278–9, n. 52. See Introduction, 14.

Of the following twenty-two estates all but five are to be found in the various charters and confirmations of charters of 1066–1113 published in Musset, *Abbayes caennaises*. The five for which these surveys are the first evidence of possession by Holy Trinity are Saint-Aubin-d'Arquenay, Mâlon, La Fontenelle, Bonnemaison, and Juvigny-sur-Seulles.

Hęc sunt reditiones ho/noris nostrę ęcclesię Sanctę Trinitatis Cadomi

OUISTREHAM A (cant. Douvres)

In Oistrehan habemus xxix^{ta} vilanos plenarios, et dimidium de terra Serli. Unusquisque eorum reddit per annum iiii^{or} solidos et dimidium, et tres quadrantes frumenti et v minas brasii, et ii capones ad Natale Domini, et xx ova ad Pascha, et acram terrę arant per annum, dimidiam partem eius ante Natale et dimidiam post Natale et erciant et seminant de nostro semine, de uno quoque porcorum suorum i d. per annum, et quando ad milia capiunt allecta reddit quodque rete c. Sex homines ibi habemus quos aloers vulgo vocant; quisque eorum tenet ortum suum faciuntque servitia ad propinqua maneria et reddunt per annum xvi d. et quattuor minas avene.[1]

---

[1] Cf. Tabuteau, *Transfers of Property*, 103–4, who argues that allodial tenants were subject to lighter services than other tenants and enjoyed a relative lack of interference, especially in matters of inheritance. In Normandy allodial land did not retain the sense of absolute ownership it continued to have in most of the rest of France. See also J. Yver, review of Carabie, *Propriété foncière* in *RHD* (1943), 104; and L. Musset, 'Réflexions sur *alodium* et sa signification dans les textes normandes,' *RHD*, 47 (1969), 606, who argues that the term disappears from Norman texts by the middle of the twelfth century.

COLLEVILLE-SUR-ORNE A (cant. Douvres)

De Colevilla

In Colevilla habemus xviii acras terrę quę reddunt xviii sextarios.

SAINT-AUBIN-D'ARQUENAY A (cant. Douvres)

In Sancto Albino xii acras et dimidiam. In anno quo comes captus fuit,[1] Helvid' de Sancto Paulo[2] dedit in vadimonio. Vigolent de iiii acros (*sic*) terrę campartum et decem solidos ad festum Sancti Dionisii[3] usque ad viii annos, et in anno sequenti in vadimonio dedit ipsa H[elvid'] Rogerio filio Rainfredi usque ad xx annos v virgas terrę; xxxiiii solidos reddet ad terminum.[4]

CARPIQUET A[5] (cant. Tilly-sur-Seulles)

De Carpiket

f.21r   In Carpichet habemus xii^cim vilanos et dimidium./ Quisque eorum reddit iiii^or minas brasii et i minam avene, tres quadrantes frumenti, xii d. ad ligna, et i berbicem cum agniculo, et ii solidos de pratagio aut facit dimidiam acram prati, et ad Natale iii gallinas et i auquam, xx ova ad Pascha, ii d. de fumagio, de uno quoque porcorum suorum i d., et adhuc vilanum i tredecimum qui dat campartum, et est liber á servitio et debitis eo quod facit brasium, et ix bordarios quorum octo reddunt xi solidos et iii d. Nonus munit aratrum vomere et cultro, et serviunt sicut bordarii, et ii bubulcos; quisque habet i acram terrę, et ita sunt quieti. Habemus adhuc

---

[1] 1106.

[2] Possibly Saint-Paul-du-Vernay, 10 km south-west of Bayeux. Helvida was an abbey official, who was also responsible for releasing the funds involved in the 1083–4 purchases in Doc. 4. Here she is credited with arranging two mortgages: one of four acres for a term of eight years at 10s. per annum and champart, the other of five virgates (1¼ acres) for a term of twenty years for a single payment of 34s. The comparative annual rates per acre are 2s 6d for the shorter term and 1.36s (approx. 1s 4¼d) for the longer term. Cf. Génestal, *Rôle des monastères*, esp. pt. i, 'Le mort gage'.

[3] 9 October.

[4] Cf. Tabuteau, *Transfers of Property*, 278–9, n. 52.

[5] Carpiquet is discussed in great detail in Carabie, *Propriété foncière*, 149–65, mainly, however, in connection with Survey B.

vilanum i qui seminat agros, et erciat, et dat campartum,[1] et est preco,[2] et forestarius et habet i sextarium ordei ante Natale et post Natale aliud, et xii[cim] d. dat per annum.

VAUX-SUR-SEULLES A (cant. Creully)

De Vallibus

In Vallibus terram unius carrucę habemus in dominio et ęcclesiam eiusdem ville et ii garbas decimę et de tercia dat clericus xx solidos per annum et dimidium candelarum de Natale et Purificatione Sancte Marię, et molendinum unum preter hoc quod constitutum est dare participibus nostris, et bercariam unam.[3]

MALON A (cant. Caen-est)

De Marlon

Anschitillus de Cambes[4] habet terram de Marlon in fir/ma pro xxix minas (*sic*) avene et iii sextariis frumenti et dedit abbatisse x solidos eo conventu quod eam debet habere et filii eius nec auferetur ab eis pro altero qui plus offerat. Sed femina putei factoris habet inde iii virgas et reddit inde i minam de his triginta minis.
Teste Ricardo Rufo et Osberto Gisleberto pistore. A parte Anschetilli fuerunt filii eius duo, Fulco de Cambes.[5]

---

[1] The total number of *vilani* is 14½, which corresponds well to the thirteen full villeinages and two half-villeinages of Survey B.

[2] Cf. Carpiquet B, **61**, Adam *precor*, a crier.

[3] Cf. *Abbayes caennaises*, no. 8, 86, 1082 *pancarte*: Roger of Les Moutiers granted Holy Trinity the church with its tithes, one ploughland, and rights in one mill at Vaux.

[4] Cambes-en-Plaine, 1.5 km north of Mâlon.

[5] For a payment of 10s Anschetil of Cambes ensured the 'farm' of Mâlon for the lifetimes of himself and his sons. The witness list seems to have been taken from the original agreement, presumably to add weight to the survey's testimony. See Tabuteau, *Transfers of Property*, 69 and 310, n. 194.

ASNIERES-EN-BESSIN A (cant. Isigny)

De Aneriis

In Aneriis habemus iiii^{or} libras.

GRAYE-SUR-MER A (cant. Ryes)

De Graeio[1]

Decimam[2] de Graeio habemus in vadimonio ab Eudone et ipse tenet eam á nobis,[3] et i vavasorem Fulconem trium acrarum et alium Heldebertum de virga una.

In Graeio habemus terram duarum carrucarum in dominio et duos dimidios vilanos qui dant viii^{to} minas brasii et i quadrantem frumenti et iiii^{or} gallinas et v solidos xl^{ta} ova et i acram de corveę, et ix bordarios qui dant x solidos et campartum et x et viii^{to} gallinas et novies xx ova, et censarios x qui dant xxx^{ta} et iiii^{or} solidos, et novies x[x] ova, et xvii^{tem} gallinas, et furnum qui dat vi^{ta} solidos. Vavasores x de tali honore qualem tenent. Ricardum ętiam de Graeio qui habet duos bordarios et horreum suum et helmos, et hoc totum quod habet Helto dapifer in eadem villa.[4]

f.22r   Willelmus de Sancta Cruce[5] iiii^{or}/ acras, Herfastus i acram, et iiii^{or} bordarios quisque dimidiam acram, et bercarius similiter. Seminator dat xii d. Faber habet virgam terrę et reficit ferra carrucę de ferro nostro, et ita liber est. Herveus acram i.

GRAINVILLE-SUR-ODON A (cant. Tilly-sur-Seulles)

De Grainvilla

In Grainvilla ętiam habet ęcclesia Sanctę Trinitatis vii acras terrę quas tenet clericus ab ea, et facit inde servitium tale, cum abbatissa vadit ad

---

[1] The rubric appears in a space between the following two paragraphs.

[2] Superscript in MS.

[3] Tabuteau, *Transfers of Property*, 322, n. 353, suggests that Odo was the tenant of Holy Trinity, to whom he mortgaged the tithe, which he then continued to hold of the abbey.

[4] Cf. *Abbayes caennaises*, no. 8, 87, no. 22, 131. In charters of 1082 and c. 1080–5 (?) William the Conqueror granted Holy Trinity the services due from Geoffrey Salomon and Helto, the steward, at Graye-sur-Mer.

[5] Sainte-Croix-sur-Mer, 3 km south-west of Graye-sur-Mer. Cf. Graye B, **39**.

curiam, vel cum aliis dominabus cum victu earum ubi necesse fuerit vel in suis legationibus semper cum earum victu. Et terram unius carrucę et duos dimidios villanos, x inter bordarios et censarios et reddunt xx et ii[os] solidos et vi d. et serviunt sicut debent, et ii[os] vavasores: unus commodat palefridum suum ter in anno ille de Longa Aqua,[1] ubi abbatissa voluerit per Normanniam, alius servit sicut vavassor.

LA FONTENELLE A (cant. Villers-Bocage)

De Fontenella

In Puteo et in Fontenella[2] vi acras terrę, et orreum i in dominio, et xiii[cim] censarios qui garbam reddunt et ii[as] gallinas quisque et xx[ti] ova. Sunt et alii xii[cim] qui non tenent nisi ortos suos et reddunt similiter ii[as] gallinas quisque et xx[ti] ova. Hi xx[ti] iiii[or] (*sic*) dant per annum xxx solidos et vi d.

BONNEMAISON A (cant. Villers-Bocage)

Presbiter Sancti Martini de Bona Domo dat iii solidos pro decima quam tenet ab abbatissa. Sunt adhuc vi acre terrę vacuę ibi in duabus mansionibus et xi[cim] vavassores qualescumque. Quidam homo de Bona Domo/ habet acram terrę sicut vavassor.

JUVIGNY-SUR-SEULLES A (cant. Tilly-sur-Seulles)

De Iovinneio

In Iovinneio quartam partem villę per omnia. In hac sunt parte iii villani. Quisque reddit iiii[or] minas brasii et ii[os] solidos et iiii[or] placentas et iiii[or] gallinas et iii gallinas de pulagio et i aucam. De corvedę quisque acram i

---

[1] Possibly Longeau, cant. Trévières, 8 km west of Bayeux.
[2] *Puteus* is mentioned in the 1066 and 1086 *pancartes* of Holy Trinity, but, according to Musset (*Abbayes caennaises*, 170), is not identified. Hippeau, *Dictionnaire*, identifies it as Le Puits in the commune of Sommervieu, 4 km north-east of Bayeux. The same author identifies *Fontenella* as La Fontenelle in the commune of Hamars, canton of Evrecy, some 25 km away. In view of the close textual and geographical relationship between La Fontenelle and Bonnemaison and the fact that a hamlet of Le Puits is situated in the commune of Bonnemaison, it seems unnecessary to accept Hippeau's identification.

arant et seminant de semine abbatissę et secant. Et iii^es vavassores, quorum ii habent xxx^ta acras terrę quisque. Tercius vero v. Et quisque villanorum reddit lx^ta garbas: xx de frumento, xx de ordeo, et xx de avena.

RANVILLE A (cant. Troarn)

[I]¹n Ranvilla in dominio terram unius carruce et iiii^or dimidios vilanos, bordarios ii, censarium i qui dat iiii^or sextaria annone, ii de frumento, ii de ordeo, et alium qui dat sextarium frumenti, et ix vavassores. In molendino vero, vi sextaria annonę.

BAVENT A (cant. Troarn)

De Bavent

In Bavent tres mediatores et x acras terrę in dominio et iiii^or bordarios. Quisque dat xii d. per annum et serviunt sicut debent, et i firmarium qui dat per annum i sextarium frumenti, aliud ordei, ii avene, et i servientem in dominio qui habet acram terrę et censarium qui dat xii d., et vacarium unum. Vavasores ii qui habent xxiiii^or acras terre, et alium adhuc qui habet ii acras, et ii acras in elemosina et vavassorem acrarum xii^cim.

ESCANNEVILLE A (cant. Troarn)

f.23r   *De Eskenevilla/*

In Eskenevilla in dominio xxv acras terrę et inter prata et aliam terram, et iii villanos et dimidium et reddunt vii sextaria braisii et iii solidos et dimidium et iiii quadrantes et dimidium frumenti, et iii berbices in uno anno et iiii in alio, et xi gallinas de pulagio dant inter omnes, et decies xx garbas et x de tribus annonis per annum, et xiii bordarios qui dant xv solidos et serviunt sicut vilani, et i modium salis et ii ambros salis de salinis eiusdem ville, et iii vavassores.

---

¹ Blank space left for rubricated initial.

AMBLIE A (cant. Creully)

De Amblia

De elemosina. In Amblia terram unius carrucę, ix^{vem} modios in molendino, sed x et viiii sextaria tenet inde quidam homo á nobis, et mediatorem sex acrarum terrę. Bordarios iii; quisque dat xii d. et campartum. Vavassores iii.[1]

VILLONS-LES-BUISSONS A (cant. Creully)

De Willon

In Willon terram dimidię carrucę in dominio, iiii^{or} villanos plenos. Quisque reddit iiii minas braisii et i avene, et x solidos de lignis et pratis et arietibus, et ii capones ad Natale Domini, et ova xxx ad Pasca, et i quadrantem frumenti. Quisque arat et seminat i acram de corveę, et iiii^{or} bordarios qui dant xi solidos servientes sicut debent. De duobus vavassoribus ii garbas decimę. Habemus adhuc alios ii: unus/ habet ii acras, et alius iii. Sunt et alii duo: unus habet xl acras et alius xx.

GIBERVILLE A (cant. Troarn)

In Goisbertivilla i modium et a quodam homine iii solidos.

MONTBOUIN A (cant. Bretteville-sur-Laize)

In Monteboen decimam ville in dominio, et xx acras terrę. Aliam terram eiusdem villę tenet Ricardus Herluini filius á nobis.

BOUGY A (cant. Evrecy)

In Bolgeio xv sextaria annonę.

---

[1] Cf. *Abbayes caennaises*, no. 12, 97, *pancarte* of 1066–83, in which the almonry of Holy Trinity was assigned *unum molendinum atque terram unius carruce tresque bordarios cum IIII liberis hominibus.*

ENGLESQUEVILLE-LA-PERCEE A (cant. Isigny)

In Angiscavilla i modium et xv solidos.

GRENTHEVILLE A (cant. Bourguébus)

In Grentivilla ii garbas decimę, terciam partem decime carrucarum Sancti Stephani.

Surveys
Second Series (B)

Cartulary copy, Bibl. nat., MS lat. 5650, ff. 60v–87r.

DATE. c. 1175–80. There are two references in this series of surveys to terms and conditions established in the time of Abbess Dametta (*sub* Vaux-sur-Seulles and Montbouin). In both cases they appear to be subject to reassessment. Since the latest authenticated charter relating to Dametta is dated 1168 × 1178, with a preference towards 1175–6 (*Charters and Custumals*, Charter 2) it seems reasonable to suggest the mid- to late 1170s as the dating of these surveys. Chibnall suggests *c.* 1170 and 'certainly before 1176' for the second series (B) of the English surveys, and 'probably not more than a few months or a year or two' later for the third series (C) (*Charters and Custumals*, xxxii, xxxiv). See Introduction, 14.

CARPIQUET B[1]

v

Jurea de Carpicheto[2]

8	Ricardus Pulcher Avus[3]
4	Baldricus de ibidem
15	Osbertus filius Radulfi
21	Renoldus de Puteo[4]
19?	Ricardus Hurtelov[5]
28	Godoinus palmarius[6]
69	Rogerus de Mota[7]
13	Adam filius Odonis
14	Willelmus peregrinus
1	Radulfus filius Brienz

[1] This entry forms the basis of the lengthy analysis in Carabie, *Propriété foncière*, 149–65. The use of a faulty transcript in war-time led to a few minor errors.

[2] Carpiquet is the only Norman estate for which a list of jurors' names is given. Of the fifteen jurors twelve seem to have come from the vavassors and villeins and, as such, represent ancient tenures. The other three, only one of whom (Roger de La Motte) can be positively identified among the following tenants, were probably representatives of more recent tenures, including burgage tenure. See Carabie, *Propriété foncière*, 153–4.

[3] Also known as *Bel Aiel*. See below, under *De Vilanagiis* and *Campartum de Rusticis de Carpiquet*.

[4] Field-name in Carpiquet; probably shortened version of *puteo effundre* at f. 64r.

[5] Unidentified in the main body of tenants. The only possibility is Richard, the brother of Gilbert *firmarius* among the villeinage tenants.

[6] Probably Godoinus who held on villeinage terms.

[7] La Motte, western quarter of Carpiquet.

16   Johannes brasarius
18   Gislebertus filius Radulfi
27   Willelmus filius Renoldi
63? Wimondus filius Ade[1]
33   Osmundus
         Omnes isti homines dixerunt super iuramentum suum quod quando
36   Adam filius Rogeri recepit maner[i]um de Carpicheto murus erat
f.61r   integer circa grangiam, gran/gia nova, et porte cum seris. Modo non
         est ita.[2]

De vavasoribus[3]

1   Radulfus filius Brienz tenet l acras terrę in vavasoria per servicium
        equi et reddit iiii capones et iiii panes et facit precarias bis in anno
        et invenit vi boves in cariagio vini.
2   Garinus de Cingeleis[4] tenet in vavasoria circa xx acras per servicium
        equi et reddit ii capones et ii panes et invenit ii boves ad cariagium
        vini et facit preces bis in anno.
3   Aelardus xx acras in vavasoria similiter et reddit iii capones et iii
        panes et ii boves ad vinagium et facit precarias.
4   Baldricus tenet in vavasoria viii acras per servicium equi et reddit iiii
        capones et invenit i bovem ad vinagium et precarias.
5   Johannes filius Waudri xl acras in vavasoria per servicium equi et iii
        capones et iii panes et invenit ii boves ad vinagium et precarias.
6   Radulfus de Baiocis[5] lx acras in vavasoria.
7   Wido de Sancto Waler[ico][6] xxx acras in vavasoria et invenit ii boves
        ad vinagium et precarias.

[1] The only other Wimond is *Wimundus Hurtelov* (**63**) who held two demesne portions in Sachet.
[2] Carabie, *Propriété foncière*, 163, argues that it was only the manorial buildings that were leased to Adam fitz Roger, and that the abbey continued to enjoy the direct profits of the manor as a whole. From his position of some prestige Adam accumulated nine plots of land, most of it on the demesne, and became something of a *petit seigneur du village*. It is more likely that Adam received the whole manor as farmer. Cf. Auberville B, tenants **1** and **12**.
[3] The following seven vavassors held a total of 228 acres, composed of 50, 20, 20, 8, 40, 60, and 30 acres.
[4] Cinglais, a forest area 15 km south of Caen.
[5] Bayeux.
[6] Saint-Valéry-en-Caux.

De vilanagiis[1]

8 9 [R]²icardus Bel Aiel et Wido filius Willelmi tenent̄ i[n] vilanagio de xxv acras (*sic*) terrę et faciunt prata et corveas de i acram (*sic*) et dant vi [d.] and[egavensium] vel inveniunt i bovem ad vinagium, et i augam de campartagio et summagio, et iii quarteria frumenti de oblictis, et ii sextaria brasii vel grudi, et i minam avene, et iii gallinas et regarda/ xx ova, et i acram arature et herciature et precarias, et xii[d.] and[egavensium] de leignagio, et ii d. de fumagio et i ovem cum agno ad Pascha, et pasnagium et cariagium ad grangiam de i acra terrę et de camparto tocius terrę suę et campartum,³ et si dederit filiam suam extra vilanagium dabit iii solidos abbatisse et precarias araturę et erciaturę.

10 11 Robertus Braose et Willelmus Hurtelov tenent xxxvii acras in vilanagio per eosdem redditus et servicia.

12 13 Tustinus filius Osmundi et Adam filius Odonis xix acras in vilanagio et per eo[s]dem redditus et servicia.

14 15 Willelmus peregrinus et Osbertus filius Radulfi xxviii acras in vilanagio similiter.

16 17 Johannes brasarius et Willelmus Canutus in vilanagio xxiiii acras similiter.

18 19 Gislebertus firmarius et Ricardus frater eius in vilanagio xxviii acras similiter.

15 20 Osbertus filius Radulfi et Hardoin xxviii acras in vilanagio similiter.

21 22 Reignoldus de Puteo et Ricardus Pais xxv acras in vilanagio similiter.

23 24 Ricardus filius Rualdi et Gaufridus Hueli[n']⁴ in vilanagio xviii acras similiter.

25 26 Renaldus faber et Willelmus filius Pagani xxxiiii acras in vilanagio similiter.

---

¹ The use of the word *vilanagiis* rather than *vilanis* emphasises the importance attached to preserving the services due from the tenements. There are thirteen full villeinages and two half-villeinages totalling 387 acres. The survival of three 28-acre holdings and one half-villeinage of 14 acres suggests that this was the original size of villein holdings. The *summa regardorum*, however, seems to ignore half-villeinages and is computed on the basis of 15 tenancies (see f. 63r). Survey A records 14½ villeins. The overall impression on this estate is one of declining emphasis on cash revenue. As observed by Carabie, the most striking aspect of the tenures in villeinage is the absence of payment of *cens*. In addition to this, it is notable that the option to pay 2s for meadow-work and the 1d pannage payments, recorded in Survey A, are omitted from Survey B. The emphasis seems to have lain with services, especially the *corvées*, and produce rents; in short, the development of Carpiquet as a 'supply' manor. The 1257 Survey §20–24, Carpiquet, records substantially the same obligations.

² Blank space left for rubricated initial.

³ The specific quantities of champart due from villein and bordage tenures form the final section of the survey (f. 64v).

⁴ Cf. Vaux-sur-Seulles B, **12**, *Huelina*.

27 28 Willelmus filius Renaldi et Godoinus xxxvi acras in vilanagio similiter.

29 Willelmus Fawel dimidium vilanagium ix [acras] similiter.

30 Alveredus filius Wimundi dimidium vilanagium similiter per xiiii acras.

31 Falco xxxviii acras in vilanagio similiter.

32 33 Bernardus Petite Boche et Osmundus Normannus in vilanagio xxiiii acras similiter.

f.62r   Omnes isti debent/ operari ad manerium reficiendum.[1]

[Bordage tenure][2]

16 Johannes brasarius tenet iii acras terrę in bordag' pro iii sextar' frumenti et i bovem ad vin[agi]um, iiii capones et xl ova.

31 Falco v virgas in bordag' pro i sextar' frumenti et dimidium bovem ad vinagium et capones ii et xx ova et campartum.[3]

34 35 Robertus larme sa feme[4] et Ascelina de Versu[n][5] in bordag' i acram terrę et i masuram pro i sextar' frumenti, ii capones et xx ova et dimidium bovem ad vinagium et campartum.

36 Adam filius Rogeri ii acras et dimidiam in bordag' pro iii min' frumenti, iii capones, xxx ova et dimidium bovem et dicunt iuratores quod scaeta est abbatisse ex parte Aelevini mortui sine herede. Appreciatur in camparto dimidium modium frumenti.[6]

23 Ricardus filius Ruaudi in bordag' i virgatam terrę pro i min' frumenti, ii capones,[7] xx ova et dimidium bovem ad vinagium.

37 Eudo faber iii virgatas in bordag' pro i sextar' frumenti, ii capones, xx ova.

32 Bernardus Betite (*sic*) Boche xii[d.] and[egavensium] de i domo.

38 Ascelina filia Seyrie iii so[l'] et ii capones de ii acris terrę in bordag' et dimidium bovem et servicium peditis[8] et campartum et xx ova.

39 Gualterus gener ii acras in bordag' pro iii sol', ii capones et xx ova et dimidium bovem et servitium pedditis[9] (*sic*) et campartum.

---

[1] Cf. Villons-les-Buissons B, **6/14**.

[2] There are 12 bordage tenures, 4 of which were held by tenants holding in villeinage at the same time. Two others (**36** and **40**) held no less than ten plots of demesne between them. The total acreage held on bordage terms is small: 15¾ acres, one messuage and one house.

[3] See p. 70, tenant **31**.

[4] 'Tearful for his wife'.

[5] Verson, immediately to the south of Carpiquet.

[6] Cf. tenant **89**, whose regular champart is considerably less than a half muid of wheat.

[7] *gallinas* written above *capones*.

[8] Cf. Villons B, **5–8**.

[9] *ibid.*

40   Robertus de Warda[1] i acram in bordag' pro iii sol', ii capones, xx ova, dimidium bovem ad vinagium et campartum.

41   Albereda uxor Alveredi i acram in bordag' pro i sextar' frumenti et iii sol' and[egavensium], ii capones, xx ova, dimidium bovem et campartum.

42   Uxor Renaldi fil' Rohais i acram in bordag' pro ii sol', ii capones, xx ova/ et dimidium bovem ad vinagium et campartum.

36   [D][2]e dominico de terra elemosine v acras et unam masuram extra monasterium,[3] quam Adam filius Rogeri occupavit cum vii virgatis eiusdem terrę quę valent iii sextaria et i minam frumenti et xvi sol' and[egavensium] et iiii capones et xl ova. Et unam acram et dimidiam de eadem terra quę valent iii sextaria frumenti, et superplus fuit excambiat[um] pro burgo faciendo.[4]

43   Donatio ęcclesię de ibidem est abbatisse. Et habet inde xxx solidos de pensione.

44   Costillu' i minam frumenti.

45   Quidam (*sic*) pars Fornilli Thom' fil' Rogeri est occupatura de dominico.

46 47   Unfr[idus] Rufus et Willelmus Maincoir occupaverunt Keminum.

48   Radulfus Pantouf de porprestura mare xii d. et ii capones.

49   Alveredus filius Guidonis tenet vii[5] acras terrę de vilanagio Odonis comitis qui remansit sine herede, nec habet illas per abbatissam.

50   Decima de feodo Ranulfi de Fresne valet ii modios bladi tercionarii.

51   Decima de medietate culturarum abbatisse valet i modium bladi tercionarii.

52   Masura Johannis filii Normanni reddit iii sextaria frumenti vi gallinas lx ova.

45   Thomas filius Rogeri occupavit masuram illam. Bordagium eiusdem Thome valet iii sextaria frumenti.

53   In novo burgo xlii sextaria iii quarteria frumenti, lxxxvi gallinas/ dccc et xl ova.

       Ibidem virgata terrę locanda est quę valet i minam frumenti.[6]

---

[1] Alias *de la Garde* and *de Garda*.

[2] Blank space left for rubricated initial.

[3] *Monasterium* here probably refers to the church at Carpiquet.

[4] Cf. **53**. The grain value of leased demesne appears to be two sesters of wheat per acre. Carabie adopts this formula to estimate the total extent of leased demesne from the wheat rents at ff. 63v–64r. The same equation applied to burgage tenure here and elsewhere: Carabie, *Propriéte foncière*, 161–2; L. Musset, 'Peuplement en bourgage et bourgs ruraux en Normandie du Xe au XIIIe siècle', *Cahiers de civilisation médiévale*, ix (1966), 197–8.

[5] The two minims are hidden in the gutter; only the *v* is visible on microfilm and photocopy.

[6] See above, n.4: 42¾ sesters of wheat implies 21⅜ acres of land held on burgage terms.

54 1   Radulfus filius Eudonis habet decimam de feodo Radulfi filii Brienz
2 3 4   et Warini de Cingeleis et Aelardi nepotis et Baldrici peregrini. Idem
Radulfus habet decimam de dimidiis culturis de dominico abbatisse
et terciam garbam de medietate rusticorum et de dimidiis bordariis.[1]

[Totals][2]

Summa denariorum de Carpiqueto sine porpresturis lxxiiii sol' et iii d.
Summa brasii grudi et avene sine dominicis decima et camparto xxii
sextar' et i min'.
Summa frumenti sine annicis et decimis et campartis et porpresturis
iiii mod' et vii sextar' et i min'.
Summa porpresturarum i mod' et i min' frumenti et xvi sol'.
Summa decimarum iii mod' vi sextar' bladi tercionarii.
Summa frumenti de campartis viii mod' ii sextar' ii bois'.
Summa ordei de campartis viii mod' et iii quart' et ii bois'.
Summa avene de campartis viii mod' ii boiss'.
Summa frumenti de annico xi mod' et ix sextar' et iii quart'.
Summa regardorum c et quatuor xx^{ti} et iiii tam capones quam
gallinas. Et xii panes. Et m et cccc et quatuor xx^{ti} et x ova. Et xv
augas. Et xv bidentes. Et xv anni.

f.63v
Summa summarum tocius bladii (*sic*) xxvi mod' et ix sextar' et iii
quart' et ii bois' frumenti, et xi mod' et v quart' et ii bo[is']/ ordei,
et ix mod' et ii sextar' et ii bois' avene.

[Wheat rents from demesne][3]

Cultura de Sachet

[1] Cf. Document 18 (1185) and Charter 16 (1224).
[2] Some of the totals (*summae*) are absolutely in accord with an independent tallying of the
figures; others differ by varying, but for the most part small, margins. For example, the
champart totals are entirely accurate (see p. 69, n.2), as are the 'regards' of hens, capons,
loaves, eggs, geese, and sheep. On the other hand, recorded cash payments total 70s (rather
than 74s 3d), and the total wheat from all sources, excluding the demesne, tithes, and
champart, is 63½ sesters (rather than 55½ sesters). The biggest discrepancy occurs in the
case of the malt-grain and oats due from tenures in villeinage. The entry for Richard Bel
Aiel and Wido fitz William (**8** and **9**) records 2 sesters of malt-grain and 1 mine of oats, the
same quantities recorded in Survey A; thus the total for the fifteen tenancies would be 37½
sesters, rather than 22½ sesters as recorded above under *summa brasii grudi et avene*.
[3] The following nine sections represent demesne plots held for wheat rents. The total of
wheat rents due from demesne is a little more than 141 sesters, viz. 11 muids, 9 sesters, 1
mine, and 2 bushels. On the basis of 2 sesters per acre there would be approximately 71
acres, and not 128 as postulated in Carabie, *Propriété foncière*, 161. Carabie's figures are in
error as a result of interpreting *m'* as *modius* (12 sesters) rather than as *mina* (half sester).
The scribe invariably uses *mod'* for *modius* and *m'* or *min'* for *mina*. Normally it is also clear
from the position, i.e. in descending order, whether *modius* or *mina* is meant. Furthermore,
the total calculated on the basis of this formula is very close to that given in the *summae* at
f. 63r, viz. *summa frumenti de annico*: 11 muids, 9 sesters, and 3 quarters (or 141¾ sesters).

55 Anschetillus de Monasterio i sextar' frumenti et ii boisel'.
56 Osb[ertus] Bordon i minam et i b' et dimidium.
57 Daniel vii b' et dimidium.
58 Robertus textor vii b'.
59 Anfridus sutor vii b'.
60 Rogerus Brundos v quat' et ii b'.
61 Adam precor v quart' et terciam partem b'.
60 Roger Brundos vii b'.
62 Aelais Lubias vii b' et dimidium.
63 Wimundus Hurtelov v quart' et ii partes b'.
60 Rogerus Brundos v quart' et ii b' et terciam partem b'.
62 Aelais Lubias v quart' et ii b' et terciam partem b'.
64 Evardus Anglicus iii minas et i b'.
62 Aelais Lubias iii minas et ii b' et terciam partem b'.
60 Rogerus Brundos iii quart' et i b'.
62 Aelais Lubias iii quart'.
36 Adam filius Rogeri iii quart'.
65 Ascelinus filius Odonis ii sextar' et ii b' et terciam partem b'.
63 Wimundus Hurtelov ii sextar' et i b'.

De buissinis Abbatisse

66 Hugo de Mota iii quart'.
67 Regnarius de Ros ii sextar' et i quart' et ii partes b'.
29 Willelmus Fawel v minas.
62 Aelais Lubias i sextar'.
67 Regnarius i sextar' et i b'.
40 Robertus de la Garde vii b'.
68 Willelmus Godelent i sextar' et ii b'.
57 Daniel i minam et duas partes b'.
69 Rogerus de Mota iii sextar' et vii b' et dimidium.
57 Daniel vii b'.
70 Aelardus filius Dere viii b'.
66 Hugo de Mota i sextar' et ii b'.
71 Gaufridus filius Goie i sextar' et ii b'.[1]
12 Tustinus filius Osmundi iiii sextar' et ii b'.
72 Robertus sutor iii minas.
73 Thomas ii sextar' et i quart'.
74 Gauterius Anglicus v quart' et ii b'.
75 Serlo filius Goie i sextar' et duas/ partes b'.

[1] Cf. Graye-sur-Mer B, 21.

68   Willelmus Godelent i minam et duas partes b'.
57   Daniel i minam et duas partes b'.
72   Robertus sutor iii sextar' et ii b' et terciam partem b'.

      Hovellenc

65   Ascelinus filius Odonis xvi sextar' et i quart' frumenti.

      Cultura d[e] Busmanet

36   Adam filius Rogeri ii sextar' et v b'.
75   Serlo filius Goie iii sextar' et i minam.
76   Willelmus Magnus i sextar'.
36   Adam filius Rogeri i sextar' et ii b'.
77   Jon panifex ii sextar' et i b'.
78   Godefridus Parvus xi quart'.

      De puteo effundre[1]

67   Regnarius xi quart' et i b'.
79   Pichot v quart'.
40   Robertus de Garda iiii sextar' et i minam et dimid' quart'.
67   Regnarius xi b' et dimid' b'.
80   Hugo Godelent iii quart'.
81   Ricardus de Mota iii quart'.
69   Rogerus de Mota i sextar'.
66   Hugo filius eius iii sextar' et i b'.

      Vinea[2]

36   Adam filius Rogeri v sextar' et i minam et ii b'.
82   Robertus frater eius vii quar'.
83   Odo filius Giroldi vii sextar' et v b'.

      De terra Odonis comitis[3]

36   Adam filius Rogeri xi quart' et ii b'.

[1] See Introduction, 4, n.2.
[2] An indication that there was or had been viticulture in Carpiquet, albeit on a small scale compared with the Dives valley. Cf. Delisle, *Etudes*, ch. 15, esp. 441–2.
[3] See **49**, where it is stated that the seven acres of villeinage belonging to Count Odo were not held through the abbess.

84 Willelmus Caperu[n] iiii sextar' et vii b'.
83 Odo filius Giroldi ii sextar' et i quart'.

De campania

36 Adam filius Rogeri vi sextar'.
3 Aelardus nepos iii sextar'.
83 Odo filius Giroldi iii sextar'

Cultura borgagii

85 Willelmus de P[er]ceio[1] ix quart'.
40 Robertus de Garda i sextar'.
86 Willelmus textor i minam.
87 Odo faber i minam.
36 Adam filius Rogeri iii sextar'.

Campartum de Rusticis[2] de Carpiquet

v 8 Ricardus Bel Aiel xx^{ti} sextaria bladi tercionarii./
10 11 Robertus Braose et Willelmus Hurtelov i mod[ium] bladi tercionarii.
12 13 Tustinus filius Osmundi et Adam filius Odonis xviiii sextaria.
14 Willelmus peregrinus ix sextaria bladi tercionarii et i minam frumenti
15 Osbertus filius Radulfi i modium tam ordei quam avene et vii sextaria frumenti.
17 16 Willelmus Canu et Johannes brasarius ii mod[ios] bladi tercionarii.
18 19 Gislebertus filius Radulfi et Ricardus frater eius xix sextaria bladi tercionarii.
21 Reinoldus de Puteo xxi sextaria bladi tercionarii.
23 24 Ricardus filius Rualdi et Gaufridus Hueli[n'] xvi sextaria bladi tercionarii.
25 26 Renaldus faber et Willelmus filius Pagani xxv sexter (*sic*) bladi tercionarii.
27 28 Willelmus filius Renaldi et Godoinus xxv sextaria similiter.

---

[1] Possibly Percy, cant. Mézidon.
[2] *Rusticis* is used here to refer to all non-vavassorial tenants (Cf. Escanneville B, **39**). Champart was due from all tenures in villeinage and about half of those in bordage at a rate of approximately one sester of grain per acre. An independent totalling of the champart dues here corresponds exactly with the *summae* of wheat, oats, and barley at f.63r. It also confirms that dry measures for this estate were as follows: 3 bushels = 1 quarter; 2 quarters = 1 mine; 2 mines = 1 sester; 12 sesters = 1 muid. The same formula clearly applies at Escanneville, Gonneville and Beauvoir. Cf. Carabie, *Propriété foncière*, appendix 2, xxiii.

29 Willelmus Fawel ix sextaria bladi tercionarii.

30 Alveredus filius Wimundi x sextaria bladi tercionarii.

31 Falco ii modios bladi tercionarii et i minam frumenti.

33 32 Filius Normand'[1] et Bernardus Petite Boche xviii sextaria bladi tercionarii.

42 Uxor Renaldi fil' Rohais i quarterium ordei de bordagio.

31 Falco de bordagio i sextarium bladi tercionarii.

38 Ascelina Sewrie iii minas bladi tercionarii.

34 Robertus larme sa feme i sextarium bladi tercionarii.

88 Gauterius filius Goie i minam bladi tercionarii.

40 Robertus de Warda i sextarium bladi tercionarii.

45 Thomas filius Rogeri i sextarium similiter.

89 Bordagium Aelevrai v minas bladi tercionarii de ii acros et dimid' terrę.[2]

SAULQUES B[3]

f.65r   *Jurea de Salqua*

[Bordage tenure]

1 Alveredus fullo[4] tenet iii virgas in bordad' (*sic*) pro vi d. et ii panes et ii gallinas, xx ova et summagium et consuetudines.

2 Ricardus filius Godefridi tenet ii acras in bordag' pro xii d. et ii panes et ii gallinas et xx ova et summagium et consuetudines.

3 Radulfus Durand' i acram in bordag' pro vi d. et ii panes et ii gallinas, xx ova et summagium et consuetudines.

4 Ricardus Osmundus filius Ricardi similiter.

5 Godefridus filius Radulfi i virgam pro iii d. et i gallinam, xx ova, summagium et consuetudines.

6 Radulfus Muriel[5] i acram in bordag' pro vi d., ii panes, ii gallinas, xx ova, summagium et consuetudines.

7 Ewaldus v virgas pro ix d., iii panes, iii gallinas, xxx ova, summagium, consuetudines.

---

[1] Although *Filius Normand'* is probably *Osmundus Normannus* on the grounds of his association with Bernard *Petite Boche* among the tenants holding in villeinage, he could also be John, son of Norman, among the demesne tenants (**52**).

[2] Cf. **36**, under the bordage land of Adam fitz Roger.

[3] Situated in the commune of Saint-Georges-d'Aunay, 28 km south-west of Caen.

[4] Probably a fuller, as with tenant **17**, Willemus *folart*. See p. 72, n.5.

[5] Cf. La Rouelle B, **11**.

8 Rogerus de Hamel[1] i masuram (*sic*) in bordag' pro vi d., i panem, i gallinam, x ova, summagium, consuetudines.

9 Herbertus de Hamel i mansuram in bordag' pro ii sol' et ii gallinas et i d. et xx ova.

10 Ricardus de Hamel i virgam pro iii d.

11 Hugo de Vira[2] dimidiam acram in bordag' pro viii d.

12 Radulfus de Pitot[3] i virgam in bordag' pro iii d. et i panem et i gallinam, x ova et summagium.

13 Rogerus de Pitot i acram in bordag' pro vi d., ii panes, ii gallinas, xx ova, summagium, consuetudines.

14 Godefridus de Pitot similiter.

15 Ricardus de Caron[4] i acram in bordag' similiter.

16 Theboldus similiter.

17 Willelmus folart i virgam in bordag' quietam quamdiu serviet.

18 Robertus de Pede Tailhe[5] iii acras in bordag' pro iii sol', ii panes, ii gallinas, xx ova, summagium, consuetudines.

19 Hugo de Broillie[6] similiter.

v 20 Ranulfus/ de Brolio ii acras in bordag' pro xii d., ii panes, ii gallinas, xx ova, summagium, consuetudines et servicia.

21 Geraldus de Salqua ii acras similiter.

22 Geroldus i acram in bordag' pro vi d., ii gallinas, xx ova, summagium et servicia.

[Vavassorial tenure]

23 Willelmus filius Johannis xx acras in vavasoria pro xxii minas avene, iii panes, iii gallinas, xx ova, consuetudines.

18 Robertus de Bedetaille[7] xv acras in vavasoria pro iii panes, iii gallinas, xx ova et servicium equi.

24 Godefridus Lesware xxx [acras] in sua vavasoria [pro] iiii panes, iiii gallinas, xxx ova et servicium equi.

25 Gerardus de Salqua[8] xv acras in vavasoria [pro] iii panes, iii gallinas, xx ova, servicium equi.

---

[1] Le Hamel, hamlet in Saint-Georges-d'Aunay, 2 km north-west of Saulques.

[2] Vire, 24 km south-west of Sauques.

[3] Pitot, hamlet in Saint-Georges-d'Aunay, 1 km north-east of Saulques.

[4] Cairon, cant. Creully, 8 km north-west of Caen.

[5] Pied Taillis, 1 km west of Saulques.

[6] Le Breuil, Saint-Georges-d'Aunay, 0.75 km north-west of Saulques.

[7] Clearly the same as Robert *Pede Tailhe* above. Cf. Bernard *Petite Boche* and *Betite Boche*, Carpiquet B, **32**.

[8] Possibly the same tenant as **21**.

26 Ranulfus filius Hansquitilli x acras in vavasoria pro iii panes, iii gallinas, xx ova et servicium equi. Ipse vero emit absque assensu capituli.

27 Robertus Brito xv acras in vavasoria.[1]

28 In dominico lviii acras et valent lx minas avene.

29 Ricardus Peilleve habet ii garbas de terra abbatisse, et inquirendum est quomodo.

30 Robertus de Ansgerivilla[2] tenet de abbatissa boscum de repentur et terram de foris boscum, sed nescitur quomodo.

31 Willelmus de Binna[3] tenet de abbatissa circa c acras terrę apud Montpiel[4] et i molendinum[5] ibidem.

32 In dominico dimidia feria de Sancto Egidio.[6]

(Eight lines left blank)

LA ROUELLE B[7]

f.66r *Jurea de Rotella*

[Bordage tenure][8]

1 Germanus le Clos tenet ii acras et dimidiam in bordag' pro xii d. et i sextar' avene, ii ii (*sic*) gallinas, xx ova, summagium et servicia.

2 Rogerus le Heir viii acras in bordag' pro ii sol' et ii gallinas et xx ova et campartum.

3 Galterus le Tros x acras in bordag' pro xx d., iiii gallinas, xl ova et campartum.

---

[1] Cf. Charter 2, n. 6; and Carpiquet B, **6**, whose vavasorial services are unspecified.

[2] Angerville, Saint-Georges-d'Aunay, 2 km north of Saulques, and separated from it by Le Bois d'Angerville.

[3] La Bigne, 2 km south-west of Saulques.

[4] Probably Montpied adjoining Pied Taillis.

[5] Presumably a fulling mill. Saulques, Montpied, and Pied Taillis are situated in the foothills of the Collines de Normandie and on streams flowing into the River Odon.

[6] St. Giles f.d. 1 September. Cf. 1257 Survey §81–82, Sauques, Bitot and La Bigne: *la foire de Saint-Georges de Aulnay* and *la moitié de la foire d'Aulnay*.

[7] Situated in the commune of Bonnemaison, canton of Villers-Bocage, 1 km south of Bonnemaison.

[8] Most of the tenants on this estate held on bordage terms, paying cash rents, hens and eggs, and champart from 70½ of the 82⅞ acres they held. Cf. Sallen B, where bordage tenants held 56 acres on champart terms, compared with only 28 acres *in bordagium*.

4 Robertus Cervus vii acras in bordag' pro xviii d., ii gallinas, xx ova
et campartum.
5 Robertus le Clos ii acras in bordag' pro xii d., ii gallinas, xx ova et
servicia.
6 Robertus Wimunt ii acras in bordag' pro iii d., iii gallinas, iii panes
et servicia.

7 Hugo de Bosco ii acras in vavasoria et servicium equi.[1]
8 Robertus Popel dimidiam virgam pro iii d. et i gallinam, xx ova.

[Bordage tenure]

9 Germanus Mori[n] viii acras in bordag' pro xviii d. et ii gallinas, xx
ova et campartum.
9 Idem viii acras in bordag' pro i sextar' avene et ii gallinas, xx ova,
campartum.
10 Rogerus Rex x acras in bordag' pro xviii d., ii gallinas, xx ova et
campartum.
11 Radulfus Muriel[2] iiii acras in bordag' pro ii sol', ii gallinas, xx ova,
campartum de iii acris.
12 Willelmus Fochoi'/ vii acras in bordag' pro xviii d., ii gallinas, xx ova
et campartum excepta i acra.
13 Robertus Berout iii acras in bordag' pro ii d., ii gallinas, xx ova et
campartum de ii acris.
14 Willelmus Cat ii acras in bordag' pro viii d., ii gallinas, xx ova et
campartum.
15 Godefridus filius Aupais virgam et dimidiam in bordag' pro xii d., ii
gallinas, xx ova et dimidiam acram ad campartum.

[Smallholders]

16 Robertus Sochu[n] de suo curtillo iii d., i gallinam, x ova.
17 Amelina i cortillum pro iii d. et gallinam i, x ova.
18 Germanus Florie i clausum et iii virgas terrę pro xii d., ii gallinas, xx ova.

[Bordage tenure]

19 Ranulfus Manchu[n] acram et dimidiam in bordag' pro xii d., ii
gallinas, xx ova.

[1] This sole vavassorial tenant with two acres contrasts with Saulques 10 km away where six
tenants held 105 acres on vavassorial terms.
[2] Cf. Saulques B, 6.

20   Willelmus nepos iii acras in bordag' pro xii d., ii gallinas, xx ova et campartum.
21   Willelmus Harviel dimidiam acram in bordag' pro vi d., ii gallinas, xx ova.
22   Robertus H[er]vei iii acras in bordag' pro viii d., ii gallinas, xx ova et campartum.
23   Herveis i acram in bordag' pro ii sol', ii gallinas, xx ova.

[Tenure unknown][1]

24   Ranulfus de Bosco iiii acras unde nichil sciunt iuratores.
25   Robertus de Cortwandu[n] iii acras similiter.
26   Robertus Harel ii acras similiter.

27   Mansura fabri ii acras pro xii d., ii gallinas, xx ova.

[Demesne]

28   Nemus in dominico quod Robertus Johannis tenebat.
29   In dominico xxi acras que valent xx minas avene.

30   Robertus Blanchart vi acras et relevandum est feod[um].
f.67r   31   Homines de Bellovidere et Sancto Aniano[2] non venerunt qui per/tinent ad predictum manerium.
32   Sanxon de Cortwald' debet iii solidos and[egavensium].

(Six lines left blank)

JUVIGNY-SUR-SEULLES B

Jurea de Iovinneio

[Vavassorial tenure][3]

1   Tustinus tenet xxx acras in vavasoria pro xii d. de vinagio pro ii bobus et servicia.

---

[1] Three instances of uncertainty about landholding terms on a more distant estate. Cf. Tassilly B, **35**.

[2] Saint-Agnan-le-Malherbe, 4.5 km north of La Rouelle. Cf. 1257 Survey §85, La Rouelle and Bonnemaison: *rentes à Saint-Anian*.

[3] Cf. Juvigny A, when there were two vavassors, each with thirty acres, and a third with five acres.

2 Willelmus po[n]ter[1] xxx acras in vavasoria.
Et isti duo debent dare dimidiam partem auxilii quando venerit.

[Villeinage tenure][2]

3 Sello de Monasterio[3] x acras in vilanagio pro iiii sext[ariis] bladi
tercionarii ad mensuram granarii et campart[o] et auga in septembri
et vi[d.] and[egavensium] pro vinag[io], iiii g[allinis], ii pan[is], xx
ov[is] et xii d., summagium et servicia.

4 Rogerus de Monasterio x acras in vilanagio similiter.

5 Gislebertus Pirus x acras similiter.

6 Radulfus Biset x acras similiter.

7 Robertus Ivo x acras similiter.

8 9 5 Ranulfus ad Nummos et Radulfus frater eius et Gislebertus Pirus x
acras similiter.

[Demesne]

10 In dominico v acras et dimidiam in Iovinneio et ii masure vacue et
valent ii sextaria et plenam minam frumenti et ii sextaria ordei et i
minam.

11 Et iii[4]/ campania circa ix acras.

2 Quarta pars presentationis ęcclesię de ibidem est abbatissę.[5] Willelmus
po[n]ter illam tenet qui numquam fuit presentatus.

(Six lines left blank)

VAUX-SUR-SEULLES B

Jurea de Vaus

1 Abbatissa habet in molendino de ibidem et valet xxii modios frumenti
et iii modios et ii sextaria ordei. Eadem habet ii garbas ville preter

---

[1] Possible bridge-keeper or bridge-wright on the River Seulles.

[2] Cf. Juvigny A, when there were three villeins. Here there are six, each with ten acres, which is suggestive of half-villeinages. A few of the obligations appear to be half of what was required in Survey A, but the grain rent of four sesters of mixed grain is twice as much as the four mines required in the earlier survey.

[3] Possibly Les Moutiers-en-Cinglais, cant. Bretteville-sur-Laize, but see Introduction, 21, n.5.

[4] Possible an error for *in*.

[5] This corresponds to the quarter share in all things (*per omnia*) in Juvigny A.

feodum regis et domini cum Ricardo de Wauville[1] et Willelmi de Mainneio,[2] et valent circa v modios bladi.[3] Et molonarius reddit xxxvi solidos et cc anguillas et xxiiii capones et xxiiii panes ad Natale, et cccc ova et xx panes ad Pascha.

2   De dominico: de xliii acris xliii sextaria frumenti de firma. Et de xxiii acris de dominico xx sextaria ordei et avene, et de terra ad campart quę valet iii minas bladi tercionarii.

[Vavassorial tenure]

3   Radulfus Morel xii acras in vavasoria et reddit iii capones et xxx ova et servicia.
4   Willelmus de Molino iii acras in vavasoria et reddit iii capones et xxx ova et servicia.

[Bordage tenure][4]

5   Herbertus de Viana[5] tenet in bordagium et reddit iii gallinas et xxx ova.

6   Odo filius Avice tenet in/ bordag' et reddit iii gallinas et xxx ova.
7   Torgis filius Godefridi in bordag' et reddit ii gallinas et xx ova.
8   Eudo filius Gocelinus in bordag' ii gallinas et xx ova.
9   Radulfus Briquet bord[arius] similiter.
10 Ranoldus Flori bord[arius] i gallinam et vi d. et x ova.
11 Alveredus bord[arius] et debet reddere ii solidos et ii gallinas et xx ova.
12 Huelina bord[arius] et reddit ii solidos and[egavensium] ii gallinas et xx ova.
13 Margareta   bord[arius]   et   reddet   ii   solidos   et   dimidium and[egavensium] et ii gallinas et xx ova.
    Isti omnes debent precaturas.

3   Radulfus Morel tenet clausum quod habuit de abbatissa Dameta pro i quart[erio] frumenti et potest modo inde haberi i sextarium frumenti.[6]

[1] Possible Vauville, cant. Pont l'Evêque.
[2] Magny-en-Bessin, cant. Ryes, 6 km north-west of Vaux-sur-Seulles.
[3] Probably *bladi tercionarii*, i.e. 20 sesters of wheat, 20 sesters of barley and 20 sesters of oats.
[4] The quantities of land held on bordage terms are not given.
[5] Vienne-en-Bessin, 2 km north-east of Vaux-sur-Seulles.
[6] Abbess Dametta occurs in charters of the 1150s and 1160s. See *Charters and Custumals*, 139. The suggestion here and at Montbouin B, **6**, is that these arrangements in Abbess Dametta's time were too favourable towards the tenant. Cf. *Charters and Custumals*, 60, 73: the meadow of Pillsmore in Avening was said to be worth fifty per cent more than its tenant rendered.

14   Donatio ęcclesię de Vaus super Sellam est abbatisse et persona reddit inde xx solidos de pensione, et candelas ad Purificationem.[1]

(Nine lines left blank)

SALLEN B[2]

Jurea de Salam

[Vavassorial tenure]

1   /Willelmus filius Gaufridi tenet vii ving[inti][3] acras terrę in vavasoria sicut ipse dicit et facit servicia.

2   Godardus similiter.

3   Acardus de Lu[4] similiter.[5]

4   Robertus Tirel tenet xv acras terrę in vavasoria et reddit iiii gallinas ad Nativitatem et xl ova et summagium et servicia alia.

5   Honoratus tenet xv acras in vavasoria et reddit iiii panes et iiii gallinas et xl ova et summagium et servicia.[6]

6   Hugo de Verquerol[7] tenet xxx acras in vavasoria et reddit iiii panes et iiii gallinas et xl ova et summagium et servicia.

7   Radulfus Viviani tenet x acras[8] et reddit iii panes et iii gallinas et xxx ova et summagium et servicia.

8   Durandus le Gorge tenet x acras in vavasoria et reddit iiii gallinas et iiii panes et xl ova et summagium et servicia.

9   Robertus sacerdos de ibidem tenet xxx acras et reddit iiii panes et iiii gallinas et xl ova et summagium et servicia.

---

[1] Cf. Vaux-sur-Seulles A, when the priest rendered 20s and half of the candles for Christmas and the Purification.

[2] Situated in the canton of Caumont, 20 km south-west of Bayeux.

[3] It is unlikely that each of these first three tenants held 140 acres; it is far more likely and in keeping with most of the vavasorial tenures that they held twenty-seven acres each.

[4] Probably Luc-sur-Mer. Cf. 1257 Survey §30, Luc: *une vavassorie que tient Jean de Salen, et contient 60 acres de terre, desquelles y a 15 à Salen et 45 à Luc.*

[5] Superscript added in a later hand.

[6] MS adds *et debet relevium suum*, which is then ruled through.

[7] Probably Vercreuil in the commune of Cahagnolles, 8 km north-east of Sallen.

[8] It is reasonable to assume that these ten acres were held *in vavasoria*, as with tenants **1–6**, **8**, **30**. There is a total of 167 acres held on vavassorial terms, and a priest (**9**) with 30 acres.

[Bordage tenure][1]

10 Ranulfus filius Osberti tenet ii acras in bordag' pro xii d. et ii gallinas et xx ova et summagium et servicia.
11 Radulfus Peilevilai[n] tenet in bordag' i acram pro ii sol' et ii gallinas et xx ova et summagium.
11 Idem ix acras ad campartum.
12 Willelmus filius Bence tenet i acram in bordag' pro xviii d. et ii gallinas et xx ova et summagium et vi acras ad campartum.
13 Robertus de Logis[2] i acram similiter et ix acras ad campartum.
14 Willelmus de Cruce ii acras in bordag' pro iii sol' et iiii gallinas et xl
f.69r ova/ et iiii acras ad campartum.
15 Radulfus Tesardus i acram in bordagium pro xviii d. et ii panes et ii gallinas et summagium et servicia et iii acras ad campartum.
16 Samson i acram similiter et ii acras ad campartum.
17 Robertus filius Ase ii acras in bordag' pro iii sol' et iiii gallinas et xl ova et summagium et iiii acras ad campartum.
18 Ricardus Palmaru[m] i acram in bordag' pro xviii d. et ii gallinas et xx ova et summagium et iiii acras ad campartum.
19 Robertus Caruel i acram in bordag' pro xviii d. et ii gallinas et xx ova et summagium et vi acras ad campartum.
20 Gocelinus i acram in bordag' similiter.
21 Radulfus Malpoint iii virgas pro xii d. et ii gallinas et xx ova et summagium.
22 Hubertus de Bosco iiii acras in bordag' pro vi sol' et iii gallinas et xxx ova et summagium.
23 Ranulfus Milet ii acras in bordag' pro iii sol' et ii gallinas et xx ova et i virgatam pro i quart' avene.
24 Regina i acram in bordag' pro xviii d. et ii gallinas et xx ova.
25 Willelmus Bernardi v virgas in bordag' pro ii sol' et ii gallinas et xx ova et summagium.
26 Willelmus Boet i acram in bordag' pro xxii d. et ii gallinas et xx ova et summagium.
27 Wimondus i acram in bordag' pro xviii d. xx ova et ii gallinas et summagium et iiii acras ad campartum.
28 Radulfus Lepus i acram in bordag' pro xviii d. et ii gallinas xx ova
f.69v et summagium./

[1] As at La Rouelle B, the tenants holding in bordage (28 acres) held much more land (56 acres) on champart terms.
[2] Possible Les Loges, 8 km south of Sallen.

29 Ranulfus de Lu i acram[1] pro ii sol' et ii gallinas xx ova et summagium et iiii acras ad campartum.

30 Robertus Achu[m] vi acras in vavasoria pro iii panes et iii gallinas et xxx ova et servicia.

31 Acardus de Lunda[2] i acram in bordag' pro xviii d. et ii gallinas et xx ova et summagium et i acram ad campartum.

[Demesne]

32 Molendinum in dominico et valet xxviii sextaria avene[3] ad mensuram granarii.

33 Donatio ęcclesię de ibidem est abbatissę. Et habet inde de pensione xvi so[l']. Et de dominico suo duas garbas.[4]

(Nine lines originally left blank used for the 1254 settlement. See n.4 below)

GRAINVILLE-SUR-ODON B

Jurea de Grainvilla

1 Robertus filius Rogeri tenet virgam terre et dimidiam in mansura pro v [d.] and[egavensium] de vinagio.

2 Hugo de Voire[5] tenet iii virgas similiter.

---

[1] It is assumed that this acre was held on bordage terms.

[2] Unidentified as a place-name; possible a 'bind' of eels.

[3] Here and at **23** oats are the only grain mentioned.

[4] The survey is followed by the notification of a dispute between the abbess of Caen and Richard of Tilly-sur-Seulles relating to Sallen and settled in 1254, apparently in favour of the abbess, who was empowered to take Richard's pledges and draught animals to Caen:
Item. Recordum assisie Baiocensis pro abbatissa Cadomi coram Roberto de Pontisara ballivo domini Regis, W[illelmo] de Bretevilla, W[illelmo] de Vilers, Enguerram de Vilers, Roberto de Craloeyo, W[illelmo] de Craloeyo, Henrico Talebois, Gaufrido de Bosco, Roberto de Carone, W[illelmo] de Mariscis, Roberto de Sancto Martino, Ansell' de Mortune, Nicholao de Anis', Galtero de Sillie, Henrico de Agneaus, Ricardo de Caigel, Willelmo de Anis' milite, Nicholao de Hablovilla clerico, magistro Petro de Locellis, Johanne Goiel, Roberto [puhel'] presbitero, H' scriptore et pluribus aliis. Actum anno domini m cc l quarto die martis proxima post festum Sancte Lucie contra Richardum de Tele de nammis suis et averiis que quidem domina abbatissa Cadomi potest adducere de Salano apud Cadomum.

[5] Unidentified.

[Vavassorial tenure]

3   Rogerus nepos tenet xv acras in vavasoria et reddit v d. de vinagio
f.70r   et i sextarium frumenti pro ii garbis/ suę decimę, et servicium equi.

4   Helias de Kemino tenet in vavasoria iii acras et dimidiam pro v d. de
vinagio, et ii gallin' et xxx ov' et i sextar' avene pro servicio equi.

5   Wimondus iiii acras in vavasoria pro iiii so[l'] pro servicio et v d. de
vinagio et ii gallin', xxx ov'.[1]

6   Robertus de Vilers[2] tenet xxx acras in vavasoria et debet terciam
partem auxiliorum et serviciorum quę pertinent abbatissę in villa
predicta et servicia omnium suorum hominum residuorum in illa
terra, scilicet vinagium, summagium, precarias. Idem debet adhuc ii
releveia de mortibus patris et fratris sui et servicium equi.

[Mixed tenure][3]

7   Hugo Follus tenet iiii acras in vilanagio pro ii sol' et i auga et ii gallin',
xxx ov' et v d. de vinagio, et campart' ii d. valet,[4] iiii sextar' avene.

8   Melida de Gaveluiz tenet i acram in bordag' pro iii sol' et ii gallin'
et xxx ov', et summag' et campart'.

9 10   Willelmus filius Restoudi et Odo tenent iiii acras in bordag'[5] pro ii
sol' et ii gallin' et xxx ov' et i augam et v d. de vinagio et summagium
et campartum.

11   Radulfus Blondus tenet i masuagium et ii acras terrę [in] feodifirmam
pro ii sol' et ii gallin', xxx ov', v d. de vinagio et i sextar' frumenti et
i quart' ordei et fecit abbatissam heredem sui catalli.

12   Radulfus filius Emme iii virgas in bordag' pro v sol' et ii gallin' et
xxx ov'.

13 14 Radulfus Bober et Rogerus Folqueredi ix acras in vilanagio pro xii
f.70v   d./ et v d. de vinagio et ii gallin', xxx ov' et i auga et i sextar' brasii,
et summag' et campart', quod valet ix sextaria avene.

15 16 Willelmus Arrabi et Willelmus Reigecel ix acras in vilanagio similiter.

---

[1] One of only two vavassorial tenures commuted for cash and possibly for hens and eggs.
The other is at Auberville B, **30**. Tenant **4** (above), however, seems to have commuted his
horse-service for one sester of oats.

[2] Villers, 11 km south-west of Grainville-sur-Odon.

[3] The two nine-acre holdings of **13/14** and **15/16** seem to represent the two half-villeins of
Survey A. If the two vavassors of Survey A are represented by nos **3–6** here, the ten Survey
A tenants described as *inter bordarios et censarios* may be neatly represented by the remaining
ten tenants, viz. **1**, **2**, **7**, **8**, **9/10**, **11**, **12**, **13/17**, **18**, **19**. The mixture of cases used with *pro* for
tenants **7–19** is so confusing that for the most part the suspensions have been retained.

[4] Here and at **19** champart is commuted for a very small cash payment.

[5] *vil'* superscript.

17   Radulfus Bobert et Ranulfus Malart ii acras et dimidiam in bordag'
      pro ii sextar' et i min' avene, iii gallin', xl ov'.
18   Fagelina i acram in firma pro i sextar' frumenti.
19   Radulfus Matefelun i virgam in masura pro vi d. et ii gallin', xxx ov'
      et ii d. pro camparto.

[Purpresture]

20   Enguerannus occupavit dominicam masuram abbatissę cum viii acris
      terrę et reddit inde ut dicit ii sextaria frumenti et iii sextaria et i
      quarterium ordei et iii sextaria avene et ii gallinas, xxx ova et v d.
      pro vinagio et summagium.

[Demesne]

21   Donatio ęcclesię est abbatisse. Martinus de Grainvilla[1] habet illam
      per abbatissam et reddit inde iiii sextaria frumenti et pro ii garbis de
      dominico abbatisse.
22   De dominicis terris quantum habeant et quid valeant inquirendum
      est. Et de terris datis ęcclesię in elemosina similiter. Et de precariis
      quantum valent.

[Grain rents from demesne][2]

23   Coutura quę est iuxta masuram Lesceline iiii acrarum est et valet v
      sextaria frumenti.
24   In Busco Torq'tel v virge et dimidia et valent vii[tem] quateria de avena.
25   Apud Tasnerias due acre et dimidia et valent tres sextaria de avena.
26   Super Magnum Rivum dimidiam acram et valet i minam [de] ordeo.
27   Apud Belveer i virgam et valet i minam de avena.
28   Apud Couvert/ ii[e] virge et dimidia et valet iii quarteria de ordeo.
29   Apud Aguillinis i acram et valet tres quarteria de frumento.
30   Apud Longam Ream tres acras in duobus locis et valent tres
      quarteria frumenti.
31   Apud Sallebec[3] vii virgas et valent septem quarteria de frumento.
32   Apud Pontem Ogeri v virgas et dimidiam et valent i minam de ordeo.

[1] Cf. Document 18 (1185): *magistro Martino de Grainvilla* in the list of witnesses.
[2] The following list of grain rents seems to be the result of the enquiry referred to above in
22 (Cf. Amblie B, **16–21**). Land given in alms and boon works is not included. A total of
32⅞ acres and a portion of meadow was held for a total of 29½ sesters of grain, consisting
of 15¾ sesters of wheat, 9½ sesters of oats, and 4¼ sesters of barley.
[3] Described as a hamlet of Grainville in 1257 Survey §79.

33 Apud Septem Virgas v virgas et valent tres minas de frumento.
34 Apud Cortereie tres virgas et valent tres quarteria frumenti.
35 Apud Petra[m] Mond'r i virgam et valet i quarterium de ordeo.
36 Apud Glaucam Terram tres virgas et valent iii quarteria de ordeo.
37 Iuxta Coutura i acram et valet i sextarium frumenti.
38 Coutura quę est iuxta domum Hengerrandi duarum acrarum et dimidie et valent xiii quarteria de frumento.
39 Apud Holegate i virgam et valet i quarterium de ordeo.
40 Super Vicos i acram et valet i sextarium frumenti.
41 In Campania septem acras per totum et valent xiii quarteria de avena.
42 In via Misseii[1] dimidiam acram et valet i minam de ordeo.
43 Iuxta Keminum Hebreceii i virgam et valet i quarterium de ordeo.
44 Super Londam i acram et valet i sextarium avene.
45 Inter duas culturas quoddam pratum est valens i minam ordei.

Porpresture

46 47 Robertus filius Brete et Willelmus avunculus eius tenent i acram et dimidiam ad malam salsam.[2]
48 Gervasius de Cole/willa tenet i acram apud Colewill[am][3]'in masura.
46 47 Iterum Robertus Brete et Willelmus de Mondrewill[a][4] occupaverunt i acram in duobus locis.

(Six lines left blank)

ESCANNEVILLE B

Jurea de Esquęnevilla

1 De dominico abbatisse xiii acras et dimidiam et valent queque (*sic*) xxvii sextaria frumenti[5] et ii acras prati que valent xx solidos and[egavensium].

---

[1] Missy, 2.5 km south-west of Grainville.
[2] Salt rent.
[3] Coleville, 2 km north-east of Grainville.
[4] Mondrainville, 1 km east of Grainville.
[5] Demesne acres here and below (see **38** and **10**) are valued at 2 sesters of wheat per acre. Cf. Carabie, *Propriété foncière*, 160–2, where the same rate applied at Carpiquet. On the other hand, at Saulques, Grainville-sur-Odon, Vaux-sur-Seulles and Ranville demesne seems to have been valued at about one sester per acre.

[Vavassorial tenure][1]

2 Christianus tenet in vavasoria iiii acras et reddit xii d. de vinagio et servicia et summagium.

3 Durandus filius Bose iiii acras similiter.

4 Rogerus filius Yvel tenet in vavasoria iii acras pro vi d. de vinagio et servicia et summagium.

5 Walterus Lesbaht iiii acras in vavasoria per idem servicium quo Christianus et per eosdem redditus.

6 Radulfus pitore iiii acras in vavasoria similiter.

7 Durandus Wasco[n]i[2] i acram et dimidiam in vavasoria et nichil inde facit.

[Bordage tenure]

8 Garinus Coillart i masuram in bordag' pro xii d. et ii capon' ad Natale.

9 Herbertus filius Roberti Galteri tenet i masuram in bordag' pro vi d. et ii gallin'.

10 Durandus filius Rainbolt occupavit in virguto suo de dominico/ et reddit vi d. et i caponem et i gallinam.

11 Robertus de Gonevilla[3] iiii acras in bordag' pro vi d. et iii d. de vinagio, summagium et campartum.

12 Roche dimidiam acram in masiagio in bordag' similiter.

13 Johannes Grossus dimidiam acram similiter.

14 Robertus le Barbe dimidiam acram similiter.

14 Idem i d. de porprestura.

15 Normannus filius Dionisii dimidiam acram in bordag' pro ix d. et iii d. de vinagio similiter.

16 Willelmus filius Roberti Galteri i masuram in bordag' pro ii sol' similiter.

---

[1] Note the consistently small acreage for vavassorial tenures, viz. 4, 4, 3, 4, 4, and 1½ acres. Cf. 1257 Survey §47, Escanneville, which records four vavassors with five acres each, one with four acres, and a sixth with three acres.

[2] The Gascon. In effect, his only obligation was a salt-rent of 12 bushels (f. 72v). In 1257 a successor still held a vavassoriate, now 4 acres, for the same rent: *Willelmus le Vascoig, i vavassoriam de iiii acris per i pesell salis que valet xii boessellos* (1257 Survey §47); he also held in fee-farm: *Willelmus le Vascoil, i peciam terre, ii sext. et iiii b. fr., ii gall. et xx ova* (1257 Survey §46).

[3] Probably Gonneville-en-Auge, 1 km south of Escanneville. The tenant is the same as Gonneville B, **1**.

[Smallholders]

17 Adelais i masuram pro xii d.
18 Oielor i masuram pro vi d.
3   Durandus filius Bose pro i mas' xii d.
19 Robertus de Sancto Albino[1] i masuram pro vi d. et summagium.
20 Hugo cementarius ii masuras pro iiii sol'.
21 Radulfus Pulcher Filius i masuram pro xii d.
22 Radulfus de Gonnewill[a] pro i masuag' ii so[l'].
23 Radulfus iiii Pedes i masuram pro xii d.
24 Reginaldus filius et Vitalis pro i masuram (*sic*) similiter, xii d. et ii gallinas.
25 Radulfus filius Eudonis i masuram pro i quart' frumenti.
26 Ogerus filius Ingulfi i masuram similiter.
27 Haeis i masuram pro iiii bois' frumenti.

[Villeinage tenure][2]

28 Ernoldus de Fonte iiii acras in vilanagio pro v quarteriis avene et dimidio quarterio frumenti et i auga et dimidia bidente vel xii d et i gallina et dimidia et x ovis ad Pascha et vi d. de vinagio et v d. de censu.
29 Ansquitillus filius Stephani v acras in vilanagio similiter. Un[us] ii so[l'] plus de reliquo.
30 Herbertus circa iiii acras in vilanagio[3] similiter sicut Ernulfus.[4]
31 Rogerus ad Dunas[5] iiii acras similiter in vilanagio.
32 Unfridus filius Gisleberti similiter.
33 Ricardus Piques similiter.
f.72v   34 /Feodum Botart similiter.
35 Omnes isti reddunt campartum et unusquisque illorum septem rusticorum reddit x garbas frumenti, x ordei et x avene et corveas.

36 De terra iuxta granchiam abbatissę ii capones.

31 Rogerus ad Dunas i masuagium pro xviii d.

---

[1] Saint-Aubin-d'Arquenay.
[2] As with the vavassorial tenures, these tenures *in vilanagio* are unusually small, viz. 4, 5, 4, 4, 4, 4 and 4 acres. They may well be the descendants of the bordars who worked *sicut vilani* in Survey A.
[3] *vilag'* in MS.
[4] Ernulfus seems to be a mistake for the exemplar, Ernoldus (**28**).
[5] Les Dunes, on the coast north of Escanneville.

37 Et ii garbas villanag[iorum] et borderiorum et cuiusdam vavasorii,
6 scilicet Radulfi pitore, habet abbatissa ibidem, et ii garbas de feodo
   quod Henricus Lupellus tenet ibidem.

[Demesne]

38 Reginaldus de Marisco[1] tenet i acram de dominico pro ii sextar'
   frumenti et xii d., ii capon', xx ov'.
10 Durandus filius Rainbolt acram et dimidiam de dominico pro iii
   sextar' frumenti.[2]
39 Et ii garbe decime rusticorum et camparta possunt valere et garbe
   vilanagiorum circa i modium ordei et avene et circa iii sextaria
   frumenti et circa iiii sextaria legumen (sic).[3]

[Salt rents]

40 Reginaldus filius Ivel' debet v boissell[os] salis.
29 Hanquitillus filius Sthephani (sic) vi bois'.
33 Ricardus Piquet vii bois'.
41 Gervasius vii bois'.
42 Ricardus de Matrevilla[4] vi b'.
43 Gislebertus de Hommez vi b'.
21 Radulfus Bellus Filius viii b'.
44 Radulfus Gaisclu[n] ii b'.
 3 Durandus filius Bose vi b'.
33 Ricardus Piquet iii b'.
 9 Herbertus Galteri iii b'.
16 Willelmus Galteri iii b'.
45 Durandus filius Ricardi iii b'.
45 Idem vi b'.
46 Odo filius Roce vi b'.
47 Saillehache vi b'.
 5 Galterus Lesbahi vi b'.
48 Durandus filius Garini vi b'.
 7 Durandus Wasco[n]i' xii b'.[5]
49 Acho de Humma ii b'.
50 Galterus filius Quintini ii/ b'.

---

[1] Le Marais, 0.5 km east of Escanneville.
[2] See above, p. 82, n.5.
[3] This seems to be the total value of 35 and 37. The term *rustici* is used to denote villeins
and bordars, as at Carpiquet (*Campartum de Rusticis de Carpiquet*).
[4] Merville, 0.5 km west of Escanneville.
[5] Cf. above, p. 83, n.2.

51   Fulchout vi b'.
13   Johannes Grossus viᵃ b'.
52   Radulfus de Fonte iiii b'.
32   Unfridus filius Gisleberti viii b'.
38   Reginaldus de Marisco iii b'.
53   Uxor Hugonis pauperis i b'.
31   Rogerus ad Dunas i b'.
31   Item idem Rogerus vi b'.
10   Durandus filius Rainbolt iiii b'.
34   Feodum Botart vii b'.
54   Robertus filius Hansquitille vi b'.
15   Normannus vi b'.
17   Adeloia vi b'.
 2   Christianus vii b'.
20   Hugo cementarius vi b'.
45   Durandus filius Ricardi iiii b'.
11   Robertus de Gunnevilla iiii b'.
55   Albereda filia Hosmel' ii b'.
29   Item Hansquitillus filius Stephani ii b'.
17   Item Adeloia ii b'.

56   Summa: cc et iiii boissellos qui faciunt xxxiiii summas.[1] De decima
     comitis apud Waravilla[2] xix summas salis. Hoc sal prefatum totum
     debet reddi ad festum Sancti Michelis.
     Summa denariorum lxiiii sol' et vii d.
     Summa frumenti ii modios iiii sextaria iii quarteria.
     Summa ordei vi sextaria et iiii sextaria leguminis et xiiii sextaria et
     iii quarteria avene et xxiii tam capones quam gallinas et v augas et
     iiiiᵒʳ xxᵗⁱ ova et x.[3]

---

[1] The total of the individual salt rents is 202 bushels. It seems that one (cart)load of salt
comprised 6 bushels, which also seems to have been the standard obligation, with 16 of the
41 rents being 6 bushels.
[2] Varaville, 3 km south-east of Escannevile. See Boussard, *Henri II*, 90, on the extent of the
possessions of the count of Evreux.
[3] The totals are correct for barley, legumes, oats, hens and capons, and eggs, but they differ
from the sum of the individual items for cash (62s 11d), wheat (approximately 3 muids), and
geese (7). The number of geese is corrected in the grand totals for the group of estates
(Escanneville, Gonneville and Beauvoir) at f. 74r. The wide discrepancy for wheat may be
accounted for if there were 16 sesters to the muid rather than the more usual 12 (see Note
on Currency, Land Measures and Dry Measures). An independent tallying of wheat rents
results in 36 sesters 2½ quarters and 1 bushel.

GONNEVILLE B[1]

De Gonnovilla

[Fee-farm tenure]

1   Apud Gonnovillam Robertus de ibidem[2] tenet in feodifirmam circa
    ix acras et reddit iii sextaria frumenti et iii sextaria ordei et vii
    sextaria avene et ii capones, xxx ova, iii d. de vinagio et reddit ad
    co[n]tharium[3] et portat.
2 3 Herbertus Galteri et Willelmus frater eius[4] circa iiii acras et dimidiam
    ad feodifirmam ibidem pro iii min' frumenti et iii min' ordei et iii
    sextar' avene et i min' et portat ad granarium.
4   Ricardus Rainoardi circa iiii acras et dimidiam similiter et ii capones/
    et xxx ova et iii d. de vinagio.

[Bordage tenure]

5   Albereda filia Oismel'[5] i masuagium in bordag' pro xii d., iii capon',
    ii pan' et xxx ov'.

6   Summa denariorum ii so[l'] vi d. et vi sextaria ordei et xiiii sextaria
    avene et ix tam capones quam gallinas et ii panes et c et x ova.[6]

BEAUVOIR B[7]

Jurea de Bello Videre

[Bordage tenure][8]

1   Oricus tenet iii acras in bordag' pro iii sol', ii capon', xxx ov'.

---

[1] Cant. Dozulé.
[2] See Escanneville B, **11**.
[3] Probably has the sense of an aid or gift, from *congiarium* or *contiamium*.
[4] See Escanneville B, **9** and **16**.
[5] See Escanneville B, **55**.
[6] The totals are correct for barley, oats, and loaves, but differ from the sum of the individual items for cash (1s 6d), hens and capons (7), and eggs (90). Two hens and twenty eggs may have been omitted from the entry for 2/3. Wheat renders, totalling 6 sesters, have been omitted altogether.
[7] Beauvoir was a hamlet situated in the parish of Gonneville. Cf. Archives du Calvados, H. Trinité de Caen, carton 65, 'Escanneville et Beauvoir'. Hippeau, *Dictionnaire*, 21, erroneously identifies it as part of Esson, cant. Thury-Harcourt.
[8] Only **1, 2, 8** and **9** are defined as bordage tenure. **3-7** were held on virtually the same terms, and may be assumed to fall into the same category.

2 Sello ii acras in bordag' pro xviii d. et i sextar' avene, ii capon', xxx ov'.

3 Stephanus Oain i acram pro xii d., ii capon', xxx ov'.

4 Radulfus Tope circa iiii acras pro v sextar' avene, ii capon', xxx ov'.

5 Anfrida filia Ade ii acras pro ii sextar' avene, ii gallin', xx ov'.

6 Albereda Gallica i acram pro i sextar' avene, xx ov', ii capon'.

7 Albereda uxor Durandi et sui participes ii acras pro ii sextar' et i min' avene, iiii capon', xxx ov'.

8 Costentinus iii acras in bordag' pro iii sextar' avene et i min' et ii capon', xxx ov'.

9 Hugo de Bolu[n] i acram in bordag' pro i min' frumenti et i min' avene ii capon', xxx ov'.

[Demesne]

10 De i virgata de dominico v bois' avene.

[Vavassorial tenure]

11 Gislebertus Go[de]fredi tenet in vavasoria x acras pro vi d. de vinagio ii capon', xxx ov' et debet servicium equi.

12 Isti omnes portant bladum ad granarium.

13 Summa denariorum viii sol' et i minam frumenti et xv sextaria et iii quarteria et ii boissellos avene et xxvi tam capones quam gallinas et ccc et x ova.[1]

[The grand totals for Escanneville, Gonneville and Beauvoir][2]

f.74r **14** Summa denariorum de Eskenevilla et Gonnovilla et Bellovidere lx et xv sol' et i d. and[egavensium].
Summa frumenti ii modios xi sextaria et i quarterium.
Summa ordei i modium et iiii sextaria leguminis.

---

[1] The totals are correct for wheat and oats, but incorrect for cash (6s 2d), hens and capons (22), and eggs (280). The *summa* and the total of the individual quantities of oats, 15 sesters, 3 quarters, 2 bushels, and 14 sesters, 3 mines, 5 bushels respectively, confirm the equation 3 bushels = 1 quarter, 2 quarters = 1 mine, and 2 mines = 1 sester. Cf. Carpiquet B, *Campartum de Rusticis.*

[2] These grand totals represent the result of adding the document's given totals for each estate and, for the most part, are quite accurate. In general, they do not allow for discrepancies between the given totals and the sum of the individual items. The exceptions are the seven geese due from the seven villeinage tenures at Escanneville (only five are recorded in the *summa*), and the six sesters of wheat due from the three tenures in fee-farm at Gonneville, which were omitted from the Gonneville *summa* but seem to have been included in the grand totals here.

Summa avene iii modios viii sextaria i minam et ii buissellos.

Summa regardorum lvii[1] tam capones quam gallinas et vii augas et ii panes et d ova et x.

Summa salis liii summas.

BOUGY B

De Bogeio

1   Apud Bogeium xxiiii acras terrę in dominico quę valent xxiiii sextaria bladi tercionarii.

2 3   Willelmus sacerdos et Radulfus frater de i masuagio iiii sol' et iiii capones, xl ova.

4   Abbatissa habet ii garbas de predictis xxiiii acris[2] et de feodo filiorum Ursi quod fuit Agnetis de Ria[3], quod Herbertus de Arreio[4] tenet, et Robertus Corbi' et Rogerus bucularius, que valent iiii sextaria frumenti et xvi sextaria ordei et ii sextaria et i minam [   ][5] et i sextarium vech' et i sextarium siliginis et iii minas avene.

AUBERVILLE B[6]

r

Jurea de Osbertivilla super mare

[Demesne]

1   Herbertus de Bollevilla[7] tenet xiii acras in dominico pro xviii sol', et ii panes et ii capones.

2   Guarinus de Osbertivilla tenet xl acras in vavasoria per servicium equi. De regardo inquirendum est.[8]

2   Idem tenet de dominico xii acras pro xii sol', iiii panes, iiii capones et ii augas, xl ova.

---

[1] The separate *summae* total 58, viz. Escanneville (23), Gonneville (9), and Beauvoir (26).

[2] Cf. 1257 Survey §38, Maizet: . . .*Est contenu, avec le chappitre de Bougy, que l'abbaye avoit à Maiset une dixme sur un certain fief, et que l'abbaye percevoit 2 gerbes de dixme sur 24 acres de terre.*

[3] Ryes, 7 km north-east of Bayeux.

[4] Arry, 1 km west of Bougy.

[5] Blank space, probably for *avene*.

[6] Cant. Dozulé.

[7] Bourgeauville, 7 km south-east of Auberville.

[8] The entry might have made more sense if it had been included with the vavassors (below), but it seems to have been included here because the tenant also held demesne.

f.74v **3** Hugo filius Garini tenet xii acras de dominico pro x sol'/ et iiii capones, xl ova.

4 Boso Brito xi acras [in dominico] pro ix sol', iiii capones.

5 Johannes de Hais vi acras in dominico pro iiii sol' vi d., ii capones, ii panes.

6 Jordanus textor in dominico iii acras pro v sol', ii panes, ii capones, ii panes, xxx ova et servicium diei.[1]

7 Bosso de Fossa iiii acras in dominico pro iii sol' et ix d., i gallinam.

8 Robertus de Fossa iiii acras in dominico pro vii sol', ii panes, ii capones, ii panes, xxx ova, i auga (*sic*).

8 Idem v virgas de dominico pro xv d.

9 Gaufridus filius Wimarc i acram in dominico pro xii d.

10 Hugo filius Wimarc circa i virgam de dominico pro xii d. vel iii augas.

11 Boso filius Wimarc ii acras in dominico pro xxi d., i caponem.

12 Willelmus Moltu[n] iiii acras et iii virgas in dominico pro iiii sol' et vii d., ii capones, ii panes, xx ova.

13 Henricus filius sacerdotis vii acras in dominico pro x sol' viii d., ii capones.

14 Willelmus de Pirou iiii acras in dominico pro viii sol', ii panes, ii capones, ii panes, xx ova.

15 Boso de Monasterio[2] circa iiii acras in dominico pro vi so[l'], ii capones.

16 Herbertus de Fossa iii virgas de dominico pro ii sol', i caponem.

17 Symon textor iii acras in dominico pro ii sol' ix d., iii panes, iiii capones, et iii panes et xxx ova.

18 Robertus Cardonnel i acram in dominico pro ii so[l'] et iiii d.[3]

7 Boso de Fossa occupavit i acram de dominico.

f.75r **11** Boso filius Wimarc de/ dominico occupavit circa i acram.

19 Andreas occupavit tantum de dominico unde debebat reddere ii capones.

17 Simon similiter.

12 Willelmus Montu[n] occupavit i virgam de dominico.

20 Gocelinus de Monasterio occupavit pratum.

21 22 Willelmus Rex et Rogerus occupaverunt pratum.

23 Flori occupavit pratum similiter.

---

[1] Loaves are recorded twice in many instances, presumably because the one quota of loaves represented part of the rent proper, and the other part of the *regarda*. See also tenants **7** (3rd entry), **8**, **10** (2nd entry), **14**, **15** (2nd entry), **17**, **24**, **30** and **31**. Alternatively they may represent renders made at different times of the year, for example at Easter and Christmas.

[2] Possibly Les Moutiers-en-Cinglais. Cf. Juvigny B, **3** and **4**.

[3] Probably the value of one goose. See **10**.

De campartis

8 Robertus de Fossa de suo masuagio xii d., ii capones, ii panes, ii gallinas, xxx ova et ii augas et ii panes.

24 Willelmus Fortis i masuagium pro vi d., ii capones, ii gallinas, ii panes, xxx ova et ii augas, ii panes.

20 Gocelinus de suo masuagio similiter.

21 22 Reges similiter.

25 Hugo Monacus similiter et xii d. plus.

26 Willelmus similiter.

18 Robertus Cardonnel xii d. de suo masuagio et regarda similiter.

27 Willelmus filius H[er]menent vi d. de suo masuagio et regarda similiter.

23 Flori xii d. de suo masuagio et ii capones et i augam, xxx ova.

15 Boso de Monasterio de suo masuagio vi d., ii capones, ii gallinas, ii panes et xxx ova, ii panes, ii augas.

20 Gocelinus de Monasterio similiter.

28 Robertus Rollant de suo masuagio vi d., ii panes, ii capones, xxx ova, ii augas, ii augas (*sic*), ii panes.

29 Isti xii tenent in vilanagia (*sic*) et reddunt campartum et quisque eorum occupavit in suo porpriso.

De vavasoribus[1]

30 Thomas de Osbertivilla tenet in vavasoria iiii acras pro vii sol', ii panes, ii capones, xxx ova, ii panes, i augam.[2]

7 Boso/ de Fossa tenet circa xx acras in vavasoria pro iii panes et iii capones, xl ova, ii panes, iii augas et servicium equi.

10 Hugo filius Wimarc ix acras in vavasoria pro iii panes, iii capones, xxx ova, iii panes et servicium equi.

31 Radulfus Pigache[3] vi acras ad feodifirmam pro vi so[l'], iiii pan', iiii capones, xl ova, iiii panes et servicium equi.[4]

[1] The rubric appears between entries **28** and **29**.
[2] One of only two vavassors to have the principal vavassorial obligation of *servicium equi* commuted for cash. The other is at Grainville-sur-Odon, Grainville B, **5**.
[3] Pick-axe, or possibly a reference to pointed shoes, a style deplored by Orderic Vitalis, and many other later commentators. Cf. *Ord. Vit.* (ed. Chibnall), iv, 186.
[4] There appears to be virtually no distinction here between the obligations *in vavasoria* and *ad feodi firmam*, apart from the cash rent paid by the latter.

[Demesne]

32 In dominico vi acras et dimidiam de terra lucrabili quę valent xiii so[l'] et ii acras et i virga (*sic*) prati in dominico quę valent xviii so[l'] et ii garbe vilanagiorum sunt abbatissę de decima quę valent circa xx sextaria bladi cum camparto. Omnes isti faciunt precarias bis in anno de aratura et herchatura et vadunt ad fena.[1]

33 Item de Osbertivilla. Donatio ęcclesię de Osbertivilla est abbatissę et Willelmus sacerdos de Bolevilla tenet de abbatissa sicut homines iuraverunt et dicunt. Omnes bruerię de ibidem in dominico sunt. De reperta de mari medietas est abbatissę, reliqua repertorum, salvo regis iure.[2] Et portant predicti homines de Osbertiwilla bladum usque ad navem ubicumque continget illam honorari.

12 Willelmus Montu[n] recepit in stauramento iiii boves et xl bidentes, vi postes, ii panernas, iiii trabes et ii modios bladi et i caream et i carigatam fęni per manum Garini sacerdotis.[3]

12 1 Idem Willelmus et Herbertus de Bolewilla receperunt de stauramento per manum abbatisse iiii boves qui fue/runt appreciati lx so[l'] et vi sextaria bladi tercionarii.

f.76r

35 Techa mortuus est sine herede. Terra ipsius in manu abbatissę.

(Six lines left blank)

BAVENT B

Jurea de Bavent

[Fee-farm tenure]

1 Saffredus tenet iii virgas terre in feodo firmam et reddit inde xii d. and [egavensium], i quarterium ordei et i caponem, i gallinam, xxiiii ova.

2 Radulfus mercennarius tenet i acram terre in feodo firmam et reddit iii quarteria frumenti, ii capones, i gallinam, xl ova.

3 Ranulfus de Bavent tenet campum de Mara et reddit inde i sextarium frumenti, ii capones, xxiiii ova.

---

[1] These boon works seem to apply to the twelve tenants holding in villeinage. See **29**.

[2] Cf. *TAC*, cap. lxvii, *De verisco*, and Document 3.

[3] From this and the following entry it seems that William Montu' and Herbert de Bolewilla had received the manor of Auberville as farmers on the abbey's behalf.

4 Avicia tenet acram et dimidiam terrę et facit inde pratum falcari, quod est unius acre et dimidię, et reddit iii gallinas, xxx ova, vi d. de vinagio.

5 Herbertus filius Odonis tenet dimidiam virgatam terrę in feodo firmam et reddit inde xii d., xi gallinas,[1] xx ova.

3 Ranulfus de Bavent tenet iii acras terrę de feodo Martelli nepotis avi Ranulfi. Inde solebat reddere Mar/tellus iii sextaria inter ordeum et avenam, iii capones, xxx ova.

6 Ansgerus tenet dimidiam acram terrę et reddit inde iii quarteria frumenti, iii capones, i gallinam, xl ova.

3 Item Ranulfus de Bavent tenet dimidiam acram terrę, in qua est masuagium suum, et dimidiam acram terrę propinquam masuagio quam habet Ranulfus ex caduco et solebat inde reddere iii minas frumenti, vi capones, lx ova.

7 Billeheut[2] tenet dimidiam acram terrę et reddit inde xii d., ii capones, xx ova.

8 Hugo de Grocet[3] tenet i vavasoriam x acras terrę et reddit inde ii capones, xxx ova, vi d. de vinagio.

9 Jordanus de Bavent tenet ii acras terrę de feodo Sancte Trinitatis quam tenuit antecessor eius Robertus presbiter, qui solebat interesse placitis domine abbatisse apud Bavent et Cadomum et debet replegiare homines abbatisse apud Waravillam vel alibi si necesse fuisset.

3 Totale tenementum Ranulfi de Bavent est xx acrarum terre quas tenet in feodo firmam et reddit inde xiiii sextaria iii quarteria bladi,[4] scilicet v sextaria ordei, viii sextaria avene i partem minus,[5] iii minas frumenti. Qui Ranulfus pro totali tenamento de Bavent, quod ipse ętiam prenominati tenent, reddit xviii sextaria bladi. Qua' abbatissa debent (*sic*) habere pasturam suam per omnia nemora comitis Ebroicensis apud Bavent[6] et per omnia pascua.

10 Summa denariorum exceptis nummis de prato falcando iiii so[l'].
Summa frumenti vi sextaria et i minam.
Summa ordei vii/ sextaria et iii quarteria.
Summa avene ix sextaria et i quarterium.

---

[1] The figure is more likely to have been one or two hens, although it would need to have been four hens in order to make the total 31 as indicated in the *summa*.

[2] Cf. Ranville B, **25**.

[3] Possibly Gruchy, commune of Rosel, 7 km north-west of Caen.

[4] The actual total of the following rents is 14 sesters and 1 quarter

[5] i.e. 7¾ sesters of oats.

[6] Probably the extensive woodland to the south of Bavent. For the restoration of Bavent and other property to the count of Evreux, see *Ord. Vit.* (ed. Chibnall), iv, 183–7. The association of the counts of Evreux with Bavent goes back to at least Robert Curthose's time. See Document 15; David, *Robert Curthose*, 71, 75.

Summa caponum et gallinarum xxxi.
Summa ovorum ccc et xlii.[1]

MONTBOUIN B

Jurea de Monteboani

1 2　Hugo le Bret[2] et Rogerus Tolem'[3] tenent circa xii acras terrę ad feodifirmam. Unde reddunt vi sextaria bladi tercionarii ad mensuram de Monteboaini et ii gallinas et xx ova et summagium firme deferende apud Cadomum.

3　Walterus le Bret tenet i bordag' de i acra et dimidia pro xviii d. and[egavensium] ad feriam prati[4] et ii gallinas et xx ova et summagium et campardum vel i minam frumenti in voluntate abbatisse.

4　Ricardus de Ruello tenet ii vavasorias terrę de lxx acris et nesciunt servicium eius preter summagium suorum hominum.

5　Willelmus Leflac tenet xii acras terrę pro vi sextar' bladi tercionarii unde Gislebertus le M[er]le[5] reddit i minam frumenti et summagium.

6　Gislebertus le M[er]le tenet circa xxx acras terrę pro x sextar' bladi tercionarii et summag'.

6　Idem tenet i clausulum ante suam domum, unde reddit xii [d.] and[egavensium] et ii gallinas et xx ova.

6　Idem tenet circa iii acras terre de dominico quas habuit sicut dicunt de Dameta abbatissa pro[6] i min' avene et ii gallin' et xx ov'. Et valent vi sextaria bladi tercionarii.[7]

7　Safr[edus] le Chevalier tenet xxiiii acras terrę in vavasoria pro servicio equi et summag'.

---

[1] The totals for cash and oats are correct. Those for wheat, barley, poultry, and eggs are out by small amounts. In the case of wheat and barley they are one sester too high, capons and hens are seven too few, and eggs are 24 too many.

[2] The Breton.

[3] Possibly a family name.

[4] A longstanding fair, which, according to Sauvage, predates the first reference to the town of Caen. It was a ten-day event, commencing three days before the feast of St. Denis (9 October) and lasting until the vigil of St. Gabriel (16 October). See R.N. Sauvage, 'Le *cri* de la foire du pré à Caen', *Bulletin de la société de l'histoire de Normandie*, xii (1913–18), 351–4.

[5] In modern French *le merle* means blackbird, and with adjectives has a figurative meaning, e.g. *vilain merle*, nasty customer.

[6] Abbess Dametta occurs in charters of the third quarter of the twelfth century. See *Charters and Custumals*, 139.

[7] This appears to be a reassessment of the three demesne acres at a rate of two sesters per acre.

v 7 8   Idem tenet cum Hugo Normant xxiiii acras terrę et reddunt inde ii
           sextaria frumenti et iii sextaria ordei et iii sextaria avene et summagium.

   8   Idem Hugo Normant tenet domum suam de dominico.

   8   Idem tenet bordagium de escaeta pro xii [d.] and[egavensium] et ii
           gallin' et xx ov'.

8 3   Idem tenet cum Waltero le Bret feodum Fulconis de xxx acris de
           dominico ad firmam pro ii sextar' frumenti et iiii sextar' ordei et iiii
           sextar' avene. Et valet ii sextaria frumenti et xvi sextaria ordei et avene.[1]

   9   Gislebertus de Gorloai'[2] tenet dimidiam acram et dimidiam virgam
           in bordag' pro xii [d.] and[egavensium] et ii gallin' et xx ov', et
           summagium et campartum circa i quarterium ordei.

10 11   Thomas de Cingeleis[3] et Stephanus Rosceli' tenent xl acras in
           vavasoria et non faciunt servicium preter summagium.

   12   Gislebertus de Saceio[4] tenet xii acras in vavasoria et non facit
           servicium preter summagium.

   13   Willelmus Canu et fratres eius tenent ii acras in bordag' pro iiii sol'
           and[egavensium] et ii anseribus et ii gallinis et xx ovis et campardum
           quod valet i minam ordei et summagium.

   14   Willelmus le M[er]le dimidiam acram et masagium in bordag' pro
           xviii d. and[egavensium] et ii gallin' et xx ov' et campart' quod valet
           i quarterium ordei et summagium.

   15   Fulco de Monteboani tenet dimidiam acram et masagium in bordag'
r   pro vi [d.] and[egavensium] et ii gallin' et xx ov' et campart' quod/
           valet i quarterium ordei et summagium.

   16   Gaufridus Leflac tenet dimidiam acram et masagium in bordag' pro
           ii sol' and[egavensium] et ii gallin' et xx ov' et campart' quod valet i
           quarterium ordei et summagium.

   17   Gislebertus de Cingeleis tenet xl acras terrę in vavasoria et facit
           servitium.

   18   Hugo le M[er]le tenet i acram et masagium in bordag' pro xii [d.]
           and[egavensium] et ii anseribus, et ii gallin' et xx ova,[5] et campardum
           et summagium et ii gallin' pro porprestura.

   19   Robertus de Aceio[6] tenet i acram terrę et debet ire ad placita
           abbatisse in patriam.

---

[1] A reassessment involving a doubling of barley and oats.
[2] Possibly 'Gornaio' (Gournay) in the commune of Saint-Aignan-de-Cramesnil, 14 km south
of Caen.
[3] Cinglais, forest area 15 km south of Caen.
[4] Sassy, 4 km east of Montbouin.
[5] The confusion of cases with *pro* in this entry makes the intended extensions more
questionable than usual.
[6] Assy adjoins Montbouin.

20   Omnes predicti feodi faciunt precarias bis in anno.

21   Summa denariorum xiii sol' vi d. and[egavensium].[1]
Summa frumenti xiii sextaria iii quarteria i boissellum.
Summa ordei et avene iii mod' vi sextaria ii. . .[2]
Summa gallin' xxiiii et iiii anseres ccxx [ova].

De elemosinaria[3]

Redditus qui pertinent ad elemosinariam
22   Gauchier le Bort tenet xxiiii acras ad feodifirmam pro vi sextar' ordei
ad mensuram de elemosinaria. Et ii garbas decime de Monteboain
que reddunt circa xx sextaria bladi. Et valent vi sextaria frumenti/ et
xix sextaria ordei et xix sextaria avene.[4]

f.78v

23   Summa frumenti vi sextaria.
Summa ordei et avene iii mod' viii sextaria.[5]

TASSILLY B[6]

Jurea de Tasilleio

1   Willelmus Coillart tenet i masuram quę reddit viii [d.] and[egavensium].
2   Radulfus Canu[7] reddit i minam frumenti de dimidia acra in masagio
et ii capones.
3   Gislebertus Caperu[n] reddit i minam frumenti de dimidia acra in
masagio et ii capones.
4   Adam Anglicus reddit i minam frumenti de dimidia acra in masagio
et ii capones.
5   Herbertus Anglicus i minam frumenti de dimidia acra in masagio et
ii capones.
6   Robertus Coisnebeli' similiter.

[1] Five lines were orginally left blank; the *summae* are entered in a later hand. they are correct for cash, hens, geese, and eggs.
[2] The manuscript is torn. Either quarters or bushels would have followed.
[3] William the Conqueror and Matilda specified one villein (*unum rusticum*) and two parts (i.e. two-thirds) of the tithes of Montbouin for the use of the almonry: *Abbayes caennaises*, no. 12, 97.
[4] A reassessment involving almost a doubling of the original rents.
[5] The *summae* are entered in the same later hand as entry **21** and take into account the revised quantities indicated in **22**.
[6] Cant. Falaise.
[7] Possibly one of the brothers of William Canu mentioned in Montbouin B, **13**.

[Bordage tenure][1]

7   Albereda la Rossel ii so[l'] and[egavensium] et ii gallinas et xx ova
     de i virga terrę.

8   Willelmus Gui[d]o ii so[l'] and[egavensium] et ii gallinas et xx ova et
     campardum de i virga terrę.

8   Idem tenet dimidiam acram ad campardum.

9   Emma uxor Rogeri xviii [d.] and[egavensium] et ii gallinas et xx ova
     et campardum de dimidia acra et masagio.

10   Uxor Hugonis molendinarii iii anseres.

11   Willelmus de Aisi[2] xii d. et ii gallinas et xx ova et campardum de acra
     et dimidia.

12   Robertus Gervasius xviii d. et ii gallinas et xx ova et campardum de
     i acra et masagio.

13   Walterus Ausent similiter.

14   Albereda Croclę xii d. et ii gallinas et xx ova de masagio.

15   Vitalis Caisnel xii d. de masagio.

16   Willelmus de Gardigno xviii d./ et ii gallinas et xx ova et campardum
     de iii virgis et servic'.

17   Diera la Cuierdasne[3] xii d. et ii gallinas et xx ova de masagio.

18   Robertus de Uxeio[4] xii d. et ii gallinas et xx ova de masuagio.

19   Robertus Loste ii sol' et ii gallinas de masuagio.

20   Maria de Lo[n]del[5] ii sol' et ii gallinas et xx ova de masagio.

21   Robertus Loherenc ii sol' et ii gallinas et xx ova et campardum de ii
     acris et iii virgis.

22   Rogerus Loherenc xii d. et ii gallinas et xx ova de masagio.

[Vavassorial tenure]

23   Helyas de Rocha[6] tenet iii acras et dimidiam in vavasoria pro ii
     gallinis et servicio.

24   Willelmus le Chevalier xl acras in vavasoria.

25   Radulfus le Gros lxxii acras.[7]

26   Ricardus de Uxeio xvi acras in vavasoria et reddit ii gallinas.

---

[1] Tenants **8, 9, 11–13, 16** and **21**, in possession of a total of 8¼ acres on champart terms,
are specifically referred to as bordars in the demesne section. See below, **36**.

[2] Aisy, 4 km north-east of Tassilly.

[3] Probably a conflation of *cuir d'asne*, ass-hide. Cf. tenant **30**.

[4] Ussy, cant. Falaise (nord), 4 km west of Tassilly.

[5] Le Londel, Barbery, 11 km north-west of Tassilly.

[6] La Roche, hamlet in the commune of Falaise.

[7] Presumably *in vavasoria*.

27 Willelmus le Prior xii acras in vavasoria et reddit ii gallinas.
28 Ricardus Marchie xxxvi acras in vavasoria et facit servicium sicut alii vavasores.
29 Reinerus de Ebrocis[1] vii acras in vavasoria et reddit ii gallinas.
30 Ricardus Cuirdasne[2] xviii acras in vavasoria et reddit ii gallinas.
19 Robertus Loste ii acras in vavasoria et reddit ii gallinas.

31 Omnes isti summagium et precarias faciunt.

32 Willelmus Pantol de Almanesch'[3] habet ii garbas decime de feodo
29 abbatisse preter sexta[m] garbarum quam Reinerus de Ebroicis
f.79v   habet. Et Willelmus dedit suam partem/ in maritagio cum filia sua
         Radulfo filio Vitalis Caisnel.[4]

34 Donatio ecclesię eiusdem ville est ipsius abbatisse.[5]
35 Radulfus de Crevecorio[6] tenet x acras in vavasoria sed nesciunt servic'.

De dominico

36 Dominicum abbatisse de Cadomo apud Tasilleium, scilicet:
    x acras terrę quę valent x sextaria ordei.
    Item alię acre x quę valent viii sextaria ordei.
    Item alię x acre quę valent x sextaria ordei.
    Item alię x acre quę valent ix sextaria ordei.
    Item alię x acre quę valent vii sextaria ordei et i minam.
    Item x acre quę valent ix sextaria ordei.
    Item viii acras quę valent vii sextaria ordei.

    Item x acre que valent viii sextaria avene.
    Item x acre vii sextaria avene.
    Item x acre ix sextaria avene.
    Item x acre viii sextaria avene.

---

[1] Evreux, dép. Eure.
[2] Cf. tenant **17**.
[3] Almenèches, 40 km south-east of Tassilly. Given the proximity of Amenèches and Evroul this William Pantulf could well be a descendant of the William Pantulf, benefactor of St. Evroul: *Ord. Vit.* (ed. Chibnall), iv, 73.
[4] The son of tenant **15**.
[5] Cf. Charter 2 and 1257 Survey §71, Tassilly: *Presentatio ecclesie de Tassilleio pertinet domine abbatisse.*
[6] Crèvecoeur-en-Auge, 25 km north-east of Tassilly.

Item x acre v sextaria avene.

Item viii acras et dimidiam v sextaria et i minam avene.

Item xiii acre quę sunt ad campardum quę valent circa iiii sextaria avene.

Item viii acre et i virga quas bordarii tenent ad campardum valent circa iiii sextaria ordei.[1]

Acra et dimidia de prato falcabili est in dominico et ii acre et dimidia prati quas iiii boves pascunt qui sunt abbatisse et valent iii minas ordei et ii sextaria et i minam avene.

28 Ricardus Marchie occupavit circa iiii acras de dominico et adhuc tenet sed nesciunt quo/modo nec finem inde audierunt.

24 Willelmus le Chevalier habet sicut dicunt circa iiii acras de dominico et adhuc tenet sicut ipse nobis dixit, sed habuit saisinam suam et garbas suas eodem anno per iudicium curię regis.

37 26 Robertus le Chevalier dicit quod Ricardus de Uxeio tenet feodum suum de dominico, sed alii dicunt quod terra illa fuit in manu abbatisse pro defectu heredis.

38 Item terra quę est subtus fossatum valet circa iiii sextaria avene, sed nesciunt quantum terrę ibi habetur quam (*sic*) est cum terra Willelmi Crassi[2] communis.

(Six lines left blank)

RANVILLE B

Jurea de Ranvill[a]

[Vavassorial tenure]

1 Rogerus vavasorius[3] tenet in vavasoria xl acras terrę et servicium debet equi, iii capones, xxx ova et invenit ii boves ad vinagium et facit precarias.

2 Willelmus filius Johannis tenet totidem acras similiter.

[1] See above, tenants **8, 9, 11–13, 16, 21**.
[2] Cf. Round, *CDF*, no. 456, witness to charter of 1171.
[3] This is the only use of the word *vavasorius* in Survey B. Cf. Introduction, 23.

f.80v

3 Willelmus de Abovevilla[1] tenet in vavasoria xviii acras per servicium equi et invenit ii boves ad vinagium, ii capones et xxiiii/ ova et facit precarias.

4 Robertus Rex tenet xii acras in vavasoria per servicium equi et invenit i bovem ad vinagium, ii capones, ii capones (*sic*), xxiiii ova et facit precarias.

5 Thomas firmarius tenet xii acras in vavasoria per servicium equi et invenit i bovem ad vinagium, i gallinam et i caponem, xxiiii ova et facit precarias.

6 Ricardus filius Ernaldi tenet xl acras in vavasoria per servicium equi et invenit iiii boves ad vinagium et facit precarias.

[Fee-farm tenure]

7 Ricardus de Longa Valle[2] tenet ad feodifirmam vii acras et reddit iii sextaria frumenti et iii sextaria ordei et ii gallinas et xxiiii ova et reddit viii [d.] and[egavensium] ad fena falcanda et facit precarias.

8 Johannes filius Radulfi tenet ad feodifirmam v acras et reddit ii sextaria et iii quarteria frumenti, ii gallinas, xx ova et facit precarias.

9 Galterus de Ranville tenet ad feodifirmam i . . . .[3] et reddit i sextarium frumenti, ii gallinas, xxiiii ova et affert bladum suum ad granarium et facit precarias.

10 Hugo prepositus tenet ad feodifirmam ii acras et dimidiam et reddit ii sextaria frumenti ad granarium, ii gallinas, xxiiii ova, viii [d.] and[egavensium] ad fena falcanda et xii [d.] and[egavensium] ad Quadragesimam Capientem[4] et facit precarias.

11 Parent dimidiam acram et dimidiam virgam in feodifirma et reddit i quarterium frumenti ad granarium et xii [d.] and[egavensium] ad feriam prati,[5] ii gallinas, xxiiii ova et facit precarias et corveas.

12 Willelmus de Longa Valla dimidiam acram in feodifirmam et reddit i minam frumenti ad granarium et xii[6]/ [d.] and[egavensium] ad feriam prati ii gallinas, xxiiii ova et facit precarias.

f.81r

13 Acelina filia Acardi i masuagium et reddit vi [d.] and[egavensium] ad feriam prati, ii gallinas, xxiiii ova.

14 Goislenus tenet i acram ad feodifirmam et reddit iii minas ordei, ii gallinas, xxiiii ova et facit precarias.

[1] Cf. Round, *CDF*, no. 456: charter of William Abovilla to St. Stephen's, Caen (1171).
[2] Longueval, 2.5 km south-west of Ranville, on the River Orne.
[3] Blank in MS.
[4] Ash Wednesday. A variation of *caput quadragesima*.
[5] See Montbouin B, **3**.
[6] Only *x* is visible on microfilm or photocopy. The two minims are concealed in the gutter of the MS.

15   Erenborga filia Johannis acram et dimidiam ad feodifirmam et reddit iii minas frumenti ad granarium, ii capones, ii gallinas, lx ova et facit precarias.

16   Reignoldus filius Sup'licie tenet viii acras in feodifirmam et reddit ii sextaria frumenti, ii sextaria avene, i sextarium ordei ad granarium, ii capones, xxiiii ova et facit precarias.

17   Johannes Salemon tenet i masuagium et i acram terre in feodifirmam et reddit iii minas frumenti ad granarium, ii capones, xxiiii ova et xii [d.] and[egavensium] ad feriam prati et facit precarias.

18   Johannes Geroldi tenet ad feodifirmam iii virgas et reddit v quarteria frumenti ad granarium, ii gallinas, xxiiii ova et facit precarias.

19   Johannes de Monte[1] tenet iii virgas in feodifirmam et reddit ii capones, xxiiii ova.

20   Osulfus Heriz tenet in feodifirmam i masuagium et reddit ii gallinas xx ovii (sic) et ii solidos and[egavensium].

20   Idem tenet i virgam terre et reddit ii gallinas, xx ova et vi [d.] and[egavensium] et facit precarias.

21   Willelmus Flandrensis v virgas terrę in feodifirmam et reddit i sextarium ordei, ii gallinas, xx ova et facit precarias.

[Villeinage tenure]

22   Radulfus Godefridi tenet in vilanagio viii acras et reddit i sextarium frumenti et v quarteria ordei et ix quarteria avene et ii capones et iii gallinas biennio[2] xxx ova per annum et facit i virgam prati quietam ad granchiam et vi [d.] and[egavensium] reddit ad corveam et/ ii virgatas arature, i ante Natalem et aliam post, et portat dominicum ad granarium.

10   Hugo prepositus totidem per idem servicium.

23   Hugo Ansgoti similiter.

24   Willelmus le Meschin[3] tenet in feodifirmam iii virgas terrę pro i min' frumenti ad granarium, ii gallin', xxiiii ov' et facit adducere avera quę capta sunt usque Cadomum quando illi capta traduntur et facit precarias.

---

[1] Possibly Le Haut de Ranville.

[2] This seems to mean 2 capons and 3 hens in alternating years. The *summa* of 57 capons and hens at the close of the survey allows for a year in which three hens are due.

[3] *Meschin* comes from the Arabic *meskin*, poor, wretched. As a noun, young man, young nobleman; as an adjective, young.

De dominico de ibidem[1]

25   Billeheut[2] tenet iii virgas pro iii quart' avene.

26   Osanna i acram et dimidiam pro i sextar' frumenti.

27   Herbertus P[er]chardus xiii acras et dimidiam pro xvi sextar' frumenti.

27   Herbertus P[er]chardus iii virgas pro iii quart' ordei.

10   Hugo prepositus ii acras pro vii quart' frumenti et i sextar' ordei.

28   Willelmus Salemon iii acras et dimidiam pro iii sextar' et i min' ordei et i min' frumenti et ii sextar' avene.

29   Rogerus Restoldi v virgas et dimidiam pro iii min' frumenti et i quart' ordei.

30   Radulfus Otto iii virgas pro iii quart' frumenti.

31   Radulfus Docher iii virgas pro[3] iii min' ordei.

32   Alveredus de Scarda i acram pro v quart' frumenti.

33   Gudemanus i acram pro v quart' frumenti et i quart' ordei.

34   Osmondus de Longa Villa[4] i acram pro iii min' frumenti.

35   Symon frater eius i acram similiter.

36   Hugo de Longa Villa i acram pro i sextar' frumenti.

37   Johannes Fortis i acram pro vii quart' ordei.

38   Willelmus Hefovache iii virgas pro i quart' frumenti et i min' ordei.

22   Radulfus Godefridi iiii acras et dimidiam pro ii sextar' et iii quart' frumenti et ix/ quart' ordei et v quart' avene.

f.82r

24   Willelmus le Meschin viii acras pro ix sextar' frumenti.

24   Idem iii acras in Camoret pro iii min' avene.

24   Idem de ix virgis prati appreciatis circa xxiiii solidos.

39   Abbatissa habet ibidem et in omnibus pertinentiis ville de Ranvill[a] in terris pratis et pascuis et in omnibus aliis septem partes et abbas de Sancto Severo v.[5] Et Willelmus de Hummet[6] iiii partes. Pręcarie valent circa xx sol'. Similiter debet habere abbatissa vii boisellos in molendino[7] sicut habet vii partes eiusdem Willelmi sicut homines dicunt super suum iusiurandum.

---

[1] A total of 49⅜ acres of demesne was leased for 40 sesters of wheat, 5½ sesters of oats, 11¾ sesters of barley, and 24s for the nine virgates of meadow.

[2] Cf. Bavent B, **7**.

[3] *pro* appears before *iii virgas* in MS.

[4] Longuevalle, 1 km north of Ranville.

[5] Saint-Sever, Benedictine abbey 12 km west of Vire.

[6] Cf. Round, *CDF*, no. 456 (1171). William du Hommet was a witness to the charter of William Abovevilla (Ranville B, **3**). He may also have been related to Richard du Hommet, constable of Normandy from before 1154 to *c.* 1179–80, and became constable himself in 1179: Delisle/Berger, Introduction, 'notes bibliographiques', 429–31, 485–6. See also Boussard, *Henri II*, 363–4; W.L. Warren, *Henry II* (London, 1973), 308, n.2; Round, *CDF*, nos. 460 and 484; *Regesta*, III, xxxvii.

[7] Cf. 1257 Survey §139, Ranville: *un moullin à vent*.

[Totals][1]

40   Summa denariorum lix sol' et x d. cum[2] pratis et precariis.
Summa frumenti iiii modios ix sextaria et i quarterium.
Summa ordei xx sextaria et i minam.
Summa avene ix sextaria et iii quarteria.
Summa caponum et gallinarum lvii.
Summa ovorum dlx.

VILLONS-LES-BUISSONS B

Jurea de Willon

Hoc est dominicum abbatisse[3]

1   Dominicum manerium et virgutum.[4] Et v virge terrę iuxta virgutum.
In Cultura Iuxta[5] iiii acre et i virgata.
Ibidem ii acras versus Cambas.[6]
Apud Fossam ii acras.
Apud Longum Boel i acram.
In Muchelov v virgas.
In Planis ii acras.
Ultra Miricent iii acras et dimidiam.
Iuxta/Willelmum filium Abb'ti dimidiam acram.
Apud Macerias dimidiam acram.
Desuper Miricent dimidiam acram.
In via Monasterii[7] v virgas.
Post Willelmum filium Hunfridi i acram.
Versus vicum de Carun[8] i acram.

---

[1] The total grain rents do not seem to take into account tenants **10** and **23** who held on the same terms as tenant **22**. It is also possible that the egg rents of all three villeins have been omitted, which accounts for the *summa* shortfall of 90. The total for hens and capons is accurate (see p. 101, n.2).

[2] MS reads *com*.

[3] The following 32 demesne plots total 49¾ acres, and were worth, according to the final entry (**35**), five muids of wheat and twelve mines of oats *de herbagio*. Cf. Survey A's half-ploughland in demesne. Ten of the field-names can be identified in the land of Ralph, the bailiff (Document 5).

[4] Probably for *virgultum*, copse or woodland.

[5] Cf. Document 5, *iuxta Culturam*.

[6] Cambes-en-Plaine, 1.5 km south-east of Villons-les-Buissons.

[7] 'Church Road'; the church of Villons lay to the south-west of the village.

[8] Cairon, 3 km west of Villons-les-Buissons.

In via Monasterii iiii acras.
Apud fossam Grimete i acram.
Ibidem i virgam.
Apud Mesler iii virgas.
Ibidem iii virgas.
Ad Fosete iii virgas.
Ibidem dimidiam acram.
Apud Longum Estrac i acram.
Ibidem i acram et dimidiam.
Ibidem v virgas.
Apud fossam Levodel iii virgas.
Apud Wendic' v virgas.
Apud Marete iii virgas.
Apud Nigras Terras dimidiam acram.
Ibidem i acram et dimidiam.
Apud Sevet dimidiam acram.
Apud Picois iii virgas.
In cultura in Genesteit[1] x acras.

[Vavassorial and quasi-vavassorial tenure][2]

2 Feodum Willelmi filii Unfridi l acras in vavasoria et debet servicium equi et iiii panes et iiii capones de regard' ad Natale.

3 Sello filius Huberti tenet v acras et debet servicium equi et viii candelas ad Natale.

4 Willelmus filius Ivonis vi acras et debet servicium equi et ii capones et xx ova.

5 Vitalis filius Nigelli ii acras et dimidiam et debet servitium peditis et ii capones et xx ova.

6 7 Mainardus et Hamel[inus] i acram et dimidiam et faciunt servicium
f.83r peditis, et ii eidem dimidiam acram unde/ nullum faciunt servicium.

8 Godefridus de Leone iii virgas et debet servicium peditum et ii gallinas.

8 Idem dimidiam acram unde debet idem servicium et i caponem.

9 Robertus Mainardi dimidiam acram et reddit i minam frumenti ad mensuram Cadomi.

---

[1] Les Genetets, fields in south Villons.
[2] Tenants 2–8, with a total of 66¾ acres, owed escort service by horse (3 tenants with 61 acres) and on foot (4 tenants with 5¾ acres), and appear, in part at least, to be the successors of the vavassors of Survey A with 65 acres. Cf. Carpiquet B, **38**, **39**.

10 Sello filius Unfredi i acram in masuagio pro ii sextar' frumenti et vi [d.] and[egavensium], parvo (*sic*) terrę et ii capon' et xxx ov'.

11 Ricardus de Cambis iii virgas pro iii min' frumenti et ii capon' et xx ov', et ii dietas cooperture.

8 Godefridus de Leone iii acras et dimidiam pro viii min' avene.

12 Adam de Quareus[1] dimidiam acram pro xviii [d.] and[egavensium] et ii gallin' et xx ov'.

13 Matheus filius Muriell' circa i acram pro i min' frumenti et i min' avene et ii gallin' et xx ov'.
Omnes supradicti veniunt ad precarias.

[Villeinage tenure][2]

6 14 Mainardus filius Vitalis et Willelmus filius Auberti xx acras in vilanagio et reddunt xx garbas frumenti et xx ordei et xx avene de garbagio, et ii panes et ii anseres et xii [d.] and[egavensium] ad feriam prati, et i quarterium frumenti et ii sextaria brasii ad mensuram elemosine, et ii capones ad Purificationem, et i minam avene et xii [d.] and[egavensium] ad Pascha, et xxx ova et vi [d.] and[egavensium] ad festum Sancti Johannis pro fenagio, et de uno quoque porco i [d.] and[egavensium] in autumpno de porcagio, et campartum tocius terrę. Et debent summagium/ apud Monteboein et Anglica Villa et Anbliam et Sanctum Stephanum et Bougeium et Grentevillam, Petripontem et Willun.[3] Et unaquaque e[b]domada ii sextaria farine portant ad elemosinariam apud Cadomum et reficiunt masuagia manerii et fosseta et ea quę ad manerium pertinent. Et portant linum[4] ad aquam et carwam et referunt et reddunt presto et linosium.[5] Et aportant campartum suum ad granchiam et faciunt corveam de i acra et seminant de semine abbatisse et secant et afferunt ad granchiam et taxant ibidem.

6 7 Idem Mainardus et Hamel[inus] Corteis tenent xx acras in vilanagio similiter sicut precedens.

---

[1] A quarry.

[2] The following four twenty-acre holdings in villeinage correspond with the four full villeins of Survey A.

[3] Carting services to Montbouin, Englesqueville-la-Percée, St. Stephen's at Caen, Bougy, Grentheville, and Pierrepont (near Amblie), and Villons-les-Buissons. Cf. 1257 Survey §25, Villons-les-Buissons: *Sujection d'apporter le bled de l'abbaye, scavoir de Bougy et Montbouin et de plusieurs autres lieux et parroisses.*

[4] The original word was *lignum*.

[5] Cf. Birdsall, *La Trinité*, 239: 'They carry flax and hemp to the water and they carry back the retted flax and hemp'. The nearest river is the Mue.

15 16 Radulfus filius Hunfridi et Radulfus Ruffus, Herveus clericus,
17 18 Ascelina filia Cobla tenent xx acras in vilanagio similiter sicut
precedens.
19 20 21 David Picot et Hamel[inus] Godefridi et Rogerus filius Reinoldi
tenent xx acras in vilanagio similiter sicut precedens, preter
medietatem vilanagii q[uod] non reddit garbagium nec frument' nec
aven'. Et de denariis v [d.] and[egavensium] minus quam unum de
aliis vilanagiis.

[Bordage tenure]

6 Idem Mainardus filius Vitalis tenet acram et dimidiam in bordag' pro
iiii sol' et iiii d. ad feriam prati et i capon' ad Purificationem et x ov'
ad Pascha, et summagium et campartum et alia servicia.

f.84r **22** Hamel[inus] faber i masuagium in bordag' pro ii sol' et vi/ d. et ii
gallin' et xx ov', et servic'.
23 Gisleta ii acras et masuagium et bordag' pro iii sol' ad Pascha et i
auga et i pan' et i capon' et x ov', et canpartum (*sic*) et servic'.
24 Gondoinus Brunus i virgam in masuagio in bordag' pro ii sol' ad
feriam prati et i capon' et x ov', et campartum et servic'.
17 Herveus clericus i acram et dimidiam pro iii sol' ad Pentecosten et i
capon', x ov', et campartum et cętera.
25 Hamel[inus] filius Ricardi ii acras et i masuagium in bordag' pro
iiii sol' ad feriam prati et ii gallin' et xxx ov', et campartum et
cętera.
26 Ricof filius Ricardi in bordag' v acras pro i min' brasii et i anser' et
i pan' et i capon' et x ov', et campartum et cętera.
27 Renoldus faber iiii acras in bordag' pro iii sol' ad feriam prati et i
pan' et i anser' et i capon' et x ov', et campartum et cetera, et i quart'
avene.
28 Ricardus clericus iiii acras in bordag' pro iii sol' ad feriam prati et
pan' et anser' et ii capon' et x ov', et campartum et cetera.
29 Rogerus de Cambis de masuagio vi [d.] and[egavensium] ad feriam
prati.
Omnes debent ire ad moltam ad molendinum abbatisse apud
Anbliam.[1]

30 31 Herveus Picot et David et Wimondus vendiderunt i masuram cum
32 toto porpriso Hamel' pro xxx sol'.

[1] Amblie, 7 km north-west of Villons.

33 Decimam abbatisse de foris quę est de feodo Ranulfi Britonis et Willelmi de Carun valet viii sextaria bladi tercionarii. Abbatissa habet ii garbas de toto feodo de/ Willun quicumque illud teneat de
4 ea, exceptis xviii acris de feodo Willelmi filii Ivonis quas tenet de ea.

34 De feodo Rogeri t[ut]rici fug[itivorum] pro latrocinio inquirendum est ibidem.[1]

35 Dominicum de Willun valet v modios frumenti ad mensuram eiusdem ville et xii minas avene de herbagio.

(Four lines left blank)[2]

AMBLIE B

Jurea de Amblia

[Vavassorial tenure]

1 Reginaldus de Amblia tenet ii acros (*sic*) in vavasoria et reddit xii d. et servicia.[3]
2 Rogerus Malesperu[n] xxiiii acras in vavasoria[4] et reddit iiii panes et iiii capones et servicium equi. Molas molendini de villa adducit.
3 Rogerus Auber xxiiii acras in vavasoria, similiter.[4]
4 Tustinus Toroudi tenet iii acras in vavasoria et reddit ii capones et i gallinam et xxx ova et servicia.
5 Ricardus Flandrensis tenet i masuagium et dimidiam acram terrę in vavasoria et facit servicia.
6 Ivo iii virgas terrę in vavasoria pro ii capon' et i gallin' et xxx ov' et facit servicia.
7 Geroudus de Planch'[5] tenet ad feodifirmam i acram et dimidiam

---

[1] Cf. 1257 Survey §25, Villons-les-Buissons; *Sujets de amener les larrons à Caen, auxquels ceux de Villons estoyent sujects ayder.*

[2] Entry added in a very small later hand: *In Insula de Guernereio xliiii s' ad firmam reddit Ricardus Johannes qui manet ad Campion Hamel.*

[3] Unlike the cases of the two vavassors at Auberville-sur-Mer B (**30**) and Grainville B (**5**), this cash rent does not seem to be the result of commutation of vavassorial services.

[4] **2** and **3** probably represent two of the three vavassors of Survey A. The holding of the third vavassor seems to have become extremely fragmented, with portions as small as an half-acre. The 1257 Survey §9, Amblie, records two vavassors, each with 24 acres for four capons and four loaves. It also gives part of the Latin text: *Isti vavassores predicti debent adducere mollas molendini sine precio, cum propriis expensis suis, et propter hoc mollunt sine multura.*

[5] Les Planches, 2 km west of Amblie.

f.85r   virgam pro i/ min' frumenti et i bois' et ii capon' et xxx ov' et servicia.

8   Radulfus Norreis tenet iii virgas terrę in bordag' pro iii quart' frumenti.

8   Item idem pro i acra terrę i sextarium ordei.

9   Robertus Torquetil i masuagium scilicet abbatissę et reddit v sol' et vi d. et ii capones et xxx ova.

10   Odo filius Radulfi tenet masuagium abbatisse pro vi sol', iii capon', xxx ov' et servicia.

9   Item Robertus Torquętil i acram in masuagio in vavasoria pro ii capon' et servic'.

11   Hamel[inus] de Aurivalle[1] tenet i acram in bordag' pro iii sol', ii gallin', xx ova et servic' et campartum.

12   Robertus filius Ricardi tenet iii virgas in bordag' pro iii sol', ii capon', xxx ov', servicia et campartum.

13   Radulfus filius Roberti dimidiam acram in bordag' pro i min' ordei, ii gallin', xx ov'.

14   Abbatissa habet ii garbas de vavasoribus terrę Eudonis de Morevilla quę valent vi sextaria frumenti et xx sextaria ordei. Et camparta valent i minam ordei. Omnes isti faciunt precarias.

15   Abbatissa habet ibidem molendinum quod valet x sextaria et iiii boissella frumenti et iiii modios et iii minas ii boissellos ordei,[2] et i porc[arius] d[at] v solidos et xv panes facticios, c ova.

16   De dominicis Amblie et de feodo Reginaldi de Petriponte[3] quantum habetur et quantum valent inquirendum est.[4]

f.85v   **17**   Osmundus Sapiens tenet apud Petripontem v/ acras in feodifirma pro dimidium modium bladi tercionarii, et iii capones et i gallinam et xl ova reddit.[5]

18   Dominicum abbatisse apud Ampliam (*sic*) xviii sextaria frumenti ad mensuram eiusdem ville et ii modios et iiii sextaria ordei.

19   Decima iiii sextaria frumenti, xx sextaria ordei.

20   Numerus terrę de dominico l acre.

21   In redditu domorum tam de borderiorum quam vavasorum (*sic*) xviii sol'.

(Five lines left blank)

---

[1] Orival, 3.5 km south-west of Amblie.

[2] Clearly this was an important and valuable mill, to which those holding on bordage terms at Villons-les-Buissons had to travel (Villons B, **29**).

[3] Pierrepont, 2 km south of Amblie.

[4] **17–21** appear to be the result of this enquiry. Cf. Grainville B, **22–45**.

[5] Cf. 1257 Survey §14, Pierrepont: *L'abbaye avoit la dixme de 5 acres à Pierrepont, plus du domaine fieffé par faisant des rentes en orge at fourment, chappons, poulles et oeufs.*

GRAYE-SUR-MER B

Jurea de Graeio

1 Anfrida de Valeta[1] tenet in bordag' i virgam terrę pro xii d., ii gallin', xx ov', et campartum.

2 Ranulfus de Valeta i acram in vilanagio pro v sol' and[egavensium], ii gallin', xx ov', et summagium.

3 Betranus de Valeta i virgam et dimidiam in bordag' pro xii d., ii gallin', xx ov', et servicia et campartum.

4 Alexander de Valeta iii virgas in bordag' pro xii d., ii gallin', xx ov', et servicia et campartum.

5 Radulfus de Quetehou[2] i virgatam in bordag' pro ii sol', ii gallin', xx ov', et servicia et campartum.

6 Robertus filius Restoudus virgam et dimidiam in bordag' pro xii d., ii gallin', xx ov', et servicia/ et campartum.

7 Unfridus filius Ansgeri ii acras in feodifirmam pro xii d. et iiii sextar' frumenti, ii gallin', xx ov', servicia et campartum.

8 Willelmus Julina i masuagium et dimidiam acram et dimidiam virgam in bordag' pro iii sol', ii gallin', xx ov', et servicium et campartum.

9 Willelmus Graver[en]c tenet i cotagium in bordag' pro xii d.

10 Willelmus de Mara[3] x acras in vilanagio pro iii sol' et iiii min' avene, ii gallin', xx ov', servicia et campartum.

11 Ricardus Bonus Homo i masuagium et i virgam in vilanagio pro xviii d., ii gallin', xx ov', et campartum.

12 Radulfus de Cumbeas[4] vii acras in vilanagio pro iii sol', iiii min' avene, ii gallin', xx ov', et campartum.

13 Fulco coquus dimidiam acram et i masuram in vilanagio pro iii so[l'], ii gallin', xx ov', et campartum.

14 Osb[ertus] Anglicus i masuagium in vilanagio pro xii d., ii gallin', xx ov'.

15 Ranulfus Iger i masuagium et i virgam in vilanagio pro xii d., ii gallin', xx ov'.

16 Radulfus Sapiens i masuagium et dimidiam acram in vilanagio pro iii sol', ii gallin', xx ov', et campartum.

17 Robertus Nigra Capa i masuagium pro xii d., ii gallin', xx ov'.

---

[1] La Valette, north-western fields of Graye-sur-Mer. Cf. *TAC*, 63, notes 5 and 8, where it is argued that the word comes from *valseta*, a whale fishery.
[2] Quettehou on the east coast of the Cotentin.
[3] Probably a reference to the marshland to the east of Graye-sur-Mer on the River Seulles.
[4] Cambes-en-Plaine.

18 Godardus Ferlart i acram in vilanagio pro ii so[l'], ii gallin', xx ov', et campartum.

19 Gaufridus Mosteil i masuagium et dimidiam acram in villanagio pro xii d., xx ov', ii gallin', et campartum.

20 Robertus Anglicus i acram et suum masuagium pro iii so[l'], ii gallin', xx ov', et campartum.

f.86v 21 Gaufridus Goiz[1] i masuagium et virgam et dimidiam in villanagio/ pro iii sol', ii gallin', xx ov', et campartum.

22 Rogerus Anglicus v virgas et i masuagium pro iii sol', ii gallin', xx ov', et campartum.

23 Gaufridus Faciens Nichil i masuagium et i acram pro xii d., ii gallin', xx ov', et campartum.

24 Gaufridus Torgis dimidiam acram similiter.

25 Rogerus Herb[erti] i masuagium de acra et dimidia in bordag' pro iii sol', ii gallin', xx ov', et campartum.

26 Julianus filius Basili virgam et dimidiam in masuagio pro i min' et ii boissell' frumenti.

Omnes isti faciunt summagium et servicia.

Abbatissa habet ibi furnum qui reddit xx solidos.

[Vavassorial tenure]

27 Rainaldus de Roqua tenet in vavasoria i acram pro ii gallin', xx ov', et servic'.

28 Henricus Gravere[n]c v acras in vavasoria pro ii gallin', xx ov', et servic' equi.

29 Attardus Acelinus x acras in vavasoria pro ii gallin', xx ov', et servic' equi.

30 Julianus Wagel ii acras et dimidiam in vavasoria pro ii gallin', xx ov', et summag'.

15 Ranulfus Wiger ii acras et dimidiam similiter.

31 Radulfus filius Sellonis i acram in vavasoria similiter.

32 Robertus filius Sellonis v virgas similiter.

21 Gaufridus Goi[2] i virgam et i masuagium in serganteria.

33 Radulfus Herb[erti] i acram in vavasoria pro ii gallin', xx ov' et summag'.

34 Heuta filia Morini i acram similiter.

34 Idem iii acras ad feodifirmam pro iiii sextar' frumenti.

35 Robertus Maug[er] i acram sicut Heuta.

[1] Cf. Carpiquet B, **71**.
[2] Cf. Carpiquet B, **71**.

36 Willelmus Rainoard[i] iii/ acras in vavasoria pro ii gallin', xx ov', et servic'.

37 Ricardus Pagani filius iii virgas in feodo.

38 Regina de Vallibus[1] i acram in vavasoria et facit servicia.

39 Henricus de Sancta Cruce[2] iiii acras in vavasoria.[3]

40 Ricardus de Rouechestria[4] tenet in vavasoria apud Graeium suum feodum de abbatissa.

41 Ricardus de Graeio tenet in vavasoria ibidem de abbatissa circa xviii acras.

Omnes isti faciunt precarias et servicia.

---

[1] Probably Vaux 1.5 km west of Graye-sur-Mer, rather than Vaux-sur-Seulles.

[2] Cf. Graye-sur-Mer A: *Willelmus de Sancta Cruce iiii^{or} acras*.

[3] See Carpiquet B, **6**, Sauques B, **27**, and Escanneville B, **7** for unspecified or no services from vavassors. Nor are they specified for tenants **40** and **41** below.

[4] Rochester, Kent.

Cartulary Documents

The following documents from Paris, Bibl. nat., MS lat. 5650, are printed in cartulary order.

1 *Final concord between Abbess Johanna and Robert fitz Richard of 'Scrotonia'. Robert quitclaimed the rights and property of his uncle in Villons-les-Buissons in return for ten livres angevins and the right to have one of his daughters received into the convent.* [20 January 1183]

Round, *CDF*, no. 432.
Printed in Delisle/Berger, II, no. 638.
Valin, *Le duc de Normandie*, no. 21.

f.13v *De pace facta inter abbatissam et Robertum filium Ricardi de Scro/tonia de*
f.14r *hoc quod predictus Robertus clamabat in Willon*

Notum sit tam presentibus quam futuris quod talis fuit finis inter Johannam abbatissam Cad[omi] et Robertum filium Ricardi de Scrotoria in curia domini Regis Henrici filii Matildis imperatrix (*sic*) apud Cadomum in plenaria assissa (*sic*) coram Willelmo filio Radulfi tunc temporis Senescallo Normannie et Roberto comite Mellensi et Henrico episcopo Baiocensi et H[enrico] abbate Fiscannensi et Petro abbate Cadom[i] et Godefrido abbate Sancti Severi, Rogero de Arreio, Henrico de Novo Burgo, comite Augi, Johanne de Solinneio,[1] Waquelino de Ferrariis, Hugone de Gorn[aio], Ricardo de Belfou, Enger[ano] Patric, Willelmo camerario Tancarvill[e], Bertrano de Verdun, Radulfo Taixun, Henrico de Tilleio, Willelmo Pingui, Walterius de Brionia, Willelmo de Merula, Roberto de Briecuria, Hamone pincerna, Ricardo Bevrel, Gaufrido Fiquet, Jordane de Landa, Roberto de Curleio, Roberto de Liveto, Ricardo Gifardi, Albino de Vira, Regin[aldo] de Doit, Gaufrido Duredent, Herberto filio Bernardi, Paride clerico, Radulfo de Warlanomonte, Radulfo vicecomite, Ranulfo de Pratariis, Doone Bardulfo,[2] Willelmo de Manerio, Roberto de Manerio, Ranulfo de Grandi Valle, Radulfo de Clinchamp, Willelmo Silvani, Radulfo de Breseio, Thoma de Botemonte, Roberto de Lunviler, Hugone Buschardi, Ricardo de Argentiis, Roberto de Capella, Hugone de
f.14v Liveto, Alano de Putot, Philippo/ de Croleio, Philippo Suhardi, Ricardo

---

[1] Cf. Charter 4.
[2] Brother of Thomas Bardulf (Charter 3). Cf. Delisle/Berger, *Introduction*, 'notes bibliographiques', 463.

de Graeio, Radulfo de Carun, Dina[n] de Carun, Thoma portitore, Henrico Lupello,[1] Willelmo Escorcheville, Gaufrido de Boesvilla, Roberto de Lu, Roberto Belet, Willelmo Belet, Willelmo de Caluiz, Radulfo abbate, Maugero Feru[n], Benedicto de Loches, Johanne Briton[e], Arturo et Willelmo fratre eius sacerdot[ibus], Johanne de Grantia, Osberto, sacerdotibus, Radulfo de hospicio, Michaele filio Garini, Ranulfo nepote Nigelli, Gisleberto de foro, et multis aliis, quod prefata abbatissa dedit predicto Roberto x libras andeg[avensium] et concessit ei quod faceret monialem unam de filiabus prelocuti Roberti ita quod ipse inveniret illi filię suę pannos et caritatem daret monialibus quando reciperetur in sanctimoniale[m] in abbatia Sanctę Trinitatis de Cad[omo].[2] Et prefatus Robertus dedit et concessit predicte abbatisse illud iuris et hereditatis quod habebat et clamabat apud Willun ex parte Ranulfi de Willun avunculi sui, et obtulit super altare Sanctę Trinitatis huiusmodi donum per textum eiusdem ęcclesię. Et iuravit super sacrosancta ęcclesię in eius capitulo coram abbatissa et conventu et clericis et laicis qui aderant quod prefatam teneret conventionem nec admodo reclamaret quidquam ibidem nec quisquam per eum. Et hoc factum fuit ad octavas Sancti Hylarii/ apud Cadomum, anno ab incarnatione domini M°CLXXXII[3] quo tenuit rex curiam suam ibidem ad Natale cum duce Saxon[ie]. Et ibi adfuerunt Ricardus filius Henrici, Rogerus filius Landrici, Martinus de Hosa, Johannes filius Luce.

2 *Rental for Ouistreham. This list of rents follows immediately the entry for Grentheville in the first series of surveys. As in that survey Saint-Aubin-d'Arquenay and Colleville are closely associated with Ouistreham.* [n.d.][4]

De Hoistrehan

Ricardus buisu[n]	v sol'
Gerelmus	iiii sol'
Petrus	iiii
Hugo	iii
Johannes	ii
Willelmus	v
Willelmus	iiii
Robertus	v

[1] Cf. Escanneville B, **37**.
[2] MS: *ead'*.
[3] The correct date is 1183. For the great assembly at Caen, Christmas 1182, see Haskins, *Institutions*, 183. Cf. Document 16.
[4] Probably early twelfth century. See Introduction, 27.

Goiffridus	ii
Hugo	vi
Robertus	iiii
Odo	iiii
Osanna	iiii
Grente	iiii
Audulfus	iii
Divenses	iiii
Fulco	v
Huismelinus	iiii
Rogerius	iii
Ricardus	iii
Osbertus	ii
Uxor Engelier	ii
Hulricus	iiii
Osmundus	ii
Martinus	iii
Sthephanus (*sic*)	iii

Septem bordarii, unusquisque reddit xii d. atque servitium quod pertinet.
Molendinum iiii modios tertiam partem frumenti et xv solidos.
Molendinum minor unum modium et v solidos.
In duobus annis, tria milia anguillarum.
Portus Oistrehan[1] x solidos.
Unfridus v solidos.
Et quidam bordarius de Porto xii d.

In Sancto Albino[2] v censarios: Robertus reddit iii solidos,[3] Rogerius ii,[4] Godefridus ii, Gunduinus iiii ad feriam Sancti Dionisii.[5] Rogerius v solidos ad festum Sancti Martini.[6]

f.24r   In Colevile[7] v censarios et iii bordarios/ qui reddunt xii d. Guarinus censor ii solidos, Robertus iii, filius Balduini ii solidos, Hamelinus iii, reddentes ad feriam prati.[8] Etardus iii solidos Nocte Natalis Domini.

---

[1] Le Port de Sainte-Marie. Cf. 1257 Survey §5, Ouistreham: *Plus on percevoit des rentes au port de Sainte-Marie, après nommé le Port, qui estoyent pour droict de bourgage. Mesme à Saint-Aubin, mesme à Colleville.*

[2] Saint-Aubin-d'Arquenay.

[3] Note in margin: *nota bene*, with a pointing finger.

[4] *ii* superscript.

[5] 9 October.

[6] 10 November.

[7] Colleville-sur-Orne.

[8] Festival centering on feast day of St. Denis. See Montbouin B, **3**.

3 *The abbey's fish-market and shipwreck rights at Ouistreham. A late addition in the left margin and across the foot of the page.*[1]   [1230]

Omnes isti iuraverunt insimul una domine . .[2] abbatisse Cadom[i] apud Hoistrehan anno gratie m°cc°xxx°, in festo Sancti Martini, scilicet Sello de Hoistrehan, Willelmus de Grania, W[illelmus] le t[er]rier, Robertus medicus, Johannes filius Willelmi, Torgis Boenpain, Willelmus Sansonis, [H]ugo le Breton, [D]urandus Lenerio, [D]urandus benedicti, [C]onstentinus de Insula, Willelmus filius Willelmi, Ro' Michael, Martinus Fouchier, Ricardus [Jo]hannis, Rogerus Costan'e, Ricardus le vavasor, Willelmus canonicus.[3]

Domina . . abbatissa vel famuli eius [d]ebent habere pisces [a]d meliorem mercatum quam nullus homo et nullus homo habeat et nullus homo non debet tinere.. illos pisces, [n]isi famuli domine .. abbatisse ab illo loco recesserint. Debet habere salmones et turgones et [a]losas et lampreas et porpedes et omnes francos pisces et omne verece quod acciderit apud Oist[rehan] aurum vel vairum vel mantellum sine atachia nisi habeat aliquem sequentem de homine venienti[4] et debet et potest[5] [ ]i emere suum sal et suum vinum et suam buscam et omnia alia sibi et monasterio necessaria.

4 *List of purchases of vineyards in Argences, urban property in Calix, and tithes at Vaux-sur-Seulles by Abbess Matilda.*   [1083 × 1084]

De vineis Argentiarum

---

[1] The first letter of several words is missing as a result of the trimming of the MS.
[2] There were probably two abbesses in 1230. Isabella de Crèvecoeur was elected on 17 July. Her predecessor was Johanna. See *Charters and Custumals*, 139–40.
[3] Four of the family names are recognisable in the 1257 Survey §3, Ouistreham: viz. *de Insula, Fouquier, Torgis* and *Leterier*.
[4] Cf. *TAC*, cap. lxvii:
De verisco dixerunt quod naufragium, de quo nullus evadit qui sciat cujus hominis fuerit, illud est veriscum, et de eo Dux debet habere aurum et argentum, ebur et rohallum, varium, grisum sine fibulis, sabelinas et pannos sericos, trossellum ligatum, dextrarios, francos canes et aves, accipitres, nisos, et falcones.
Also Cf. 1257 Survey §7, Ouistreham:
. . . tout le varec apartenoit à l'abbaye excepte l'or et escarlette et le manteau sans attache et destrier, plus avoit le saulmon et lamproye . . . Plus s'il venoit une baleine, elle apartenoit à l'abbaye . . . L'abbesse avoit et prenoit des harencs aux bateaux qui en peschoyent.
[5] *potest* appears at the end of the entry after *necessaria*, but the drawing of a hand pointing at *emere* suggests that *potest* should be linked with *emere*.

Eo anno quo regina Matildis migravit á seculo,[1] emit Matildis abbatissa in Argentiis[2] apud fraxinum de Gisleberto bonum dimidium arpennum vineę [pro] vi lib[ris] et x sol[idis] quos Bernardus posuit in manu uxoris illius de cuius hereditate fuerat, quod frater eiusdem mulieris concessit, et sui tres infantes. Huius emptionis sunt testes Tustinus sacerdos, predictus f.24v Bernardus, Fulcoudus/ Willelmus et filius eius Tustinus.

Eodem tempore vendidit Osbernus de Billeio[3] predictę abbatissę unum arpennum et dimidium vineę in territorio Argentiarum concessu fratris sui Hugonis atque Turoldi nepotis sui pro xv lib[ris]. Test' Bernardi, Widelini, et aliorum hominum ipsius abbatissę.

Radulfus Bos vendidit eodem termino iam dicte abbatissę i acrum terrę ad Caluiz[4] pro xxxiii sol[idis]. Cuius rei sunt testes Ra[dulfus] fatuus infans, Odo de Sellis,[5] Godefridus et Wimundus.

Ricilda filia Restoldi vendidit domine abbatisse unam virgam terrę ad Caluiz pro xii sol[idis]. Cuius rei testes sunt Godefridus, Wimundus, Godefridus de Herovivilla, Ricardus gener Grentonis.

Godefridus filius Alberiadis vendidit eidem abbatissę dimidium acrum terrę in suo virgulto ad Caluiz pro xx sol[idis] et Matildis eius soror vendidit unum acrum terrę ad Caluiz pro xxx sol[idis] et alterum dono dedit Sanctę Trinitati et abbatissę pro beneficio orationum concessu Godefridi sui fratris, huius rei sunt testes Radulfus fatuus infans, Wimundus.

Ranulfus et Tustinus filii Godefridi de atrio Sancti Petri vendiderunt prenominate ęcclesię unum acrum et dimidium terrę ad Caluiz pro iiii[or] lib[ris]. Cuius rei testes sunt Radulfus fatuus infans, Godefridus, Wimundus, Bernardus, Gislebertus de Calido Furno,[6] et Hugo filius eius.

f.25r Geroldus de Castello[7] et Inge' uxor eius filia Godefridi iu/venis cuius allodium fuerat vendiderunt predicte abbatissę dimidium acrum terrę in suo burgo pro xx sol[idis]. Cuius rei testes sunt Radulfus fatuus infans, Godefridus et Wimundus.

---

[1] Matilda died on 2 November 1083.
[2] Argences, cant. Troarn.
[3] Billy, cant. Bourguébus, 5 km south-west of Argences.
[4] Calix, Caen.
[5] Cf. Document 9.
[6] Chauffour, commune Exmes, dép. Orne. Cf. below, Hugo de Calfur.
[7] Probably Caen castle, which enjoyed burghal status.

Amisus filius Ilberti de Oximis[1] vendidit supradicte abbatisse unum arpennum vineę apud Oximas pro vi lib[ris]. Huius rei sunt testes Tustinus haste vilani, Hugo de Calfur. Ex parte illius Robert[us] sacerdos de villa Barge[2] et Ulricus.

Heroldus regis portarius concessit Sanctę Trinitati et Mathili (*sic*) abbatissę suam dominicam decimam et decimam suorum hominum qui habebant in villa quę dicitur Vallis[3] pro qua concessione ipsa abbatissa dedit ei iii lib[ras]. T' Godefridi, Wimundi, Bernardi, Rogerii, Hugonis, et cuiusdam sui hominis.

Gislebertus filius Hunfridi vendidit unum acrum prati abbatisse ad Caluiz pro 1 sol[idis]. T' Godefridi, Reinaldi capellani, Godefridi, Wimundi, Corsardi.

Hęc omnia superscripta empta sunt de nummis operis. T' Adelise abbatissę Witonie[4] et Helvidis de Sancto Paulo[5] et Roze[6] quę hanc peccuniam (*sic*) liberaverunt.

5 *Memorandum concerning the land of Ralph, the bailiff of Villons-les-Buissons, totalling 27 plots of land (frustae) and two dwellings (mansiones).*[7]
[n.d.]

De Wilon (rubric)

De terra Radulfi pretoris Wiloni, est hoc commemoratio.
Duas frustas terrę sunt ad Fornas, una est ex una parte vię, altera de alia. i frustra (*sic*)/ ad Runcerium, i f[rusta] ad Seviet, i f[rusta] ad Quadratos, i f[rusta] ad Picos, i f[rusta] ad Vetus Busonem, ii f[rustae] ad fossam

---

[1] Probably Exmes, dép. Orne. Cf. *Abbayes caennaises*, no. 12, 97: *Uismes*.

[2] Barges, cant. Exmes, dép. Orne.

[3] Vaux-sur-Seulles.

[4] There is no abbess of this name at Winchester (Nunminster), but it may be Alice, or Athelits, who was appointed in 1084. D. Knowles, C.N.L. Brooke and V. London, *The Heads of Religious Houses England and Wales 940–1216* (Cambridge, 1972), 223.

[5] Cf. Saint-Aubin-d'Arquenay A: *Helvida de Sancto Paulo*.

[6] Cf. *Abbayes caennaises*, no. 25, 135: Roza, a witness on the abbey's behalf in a deed of 1079–1101.

[7] At least nine of the field-names can be identified among the abbey's demesne acres in Villons (Villons B, 1), *viz.* Seviet, Picos, Grimet, Longum Estrac, via de Cairon, Genestarium, Macerias, Longum Boel, and Planos. Cf. the list of assarts of Simon of Felsted in *Charters and Custumals*, 44–5, Felsted B.

Grimet, ii f[rustae] de monte in Vallo, i f[rusta] ad Longum Estrac, i f[rusta] in via de Caron,[1] duas [frustas] ad Marches, mansio Radulfi, mansio Ranulfi de Caron, i f[rusta] in via de Barberes,[2] i f[rusta] ultra Genestarium,[3] i f[rusta] ad Macerias, i f[rusta] ad Muta Gerof, i f[rusta] ad Furnas, i f[rusta] iuxta Culturam, i f[rusta] ante Crucem, i f[rusta] ad Longum Boel, i f[rusta] ad Muce Lupu[m], i f[rusta] in Hortolatione, i f[rusta] ad caput eius, i f[rusta] ad Planos.

6 *Record of the sale of an unspecified piece of land from Roger of Sallen to Ralph fitz Ansered and his heir, on condition that the latter continued to help Roger in his pleas. Ralph, in turn, made the abbey of Holy Trinity his heir to the property, as a result of which the abbess took over the responsibility for the above aid to Roger. On Ralph's death the abbess was to receive both the land and the tithe.*   [late eleventh/early twelfth century]

f.31r   *Carta* (rubric)

Rogerius de Salam et Hosmundus frater eius vendiderunt unam terram Radulfo filio Anseredi et heredi suo, eo conventu quod, si in plaga qua ipse moraret, adiuvaret eum in placitis suis si ab illo requireretur, et ubicumque eum residentem inveniret, illud idem auxilium ab eo haberet si requireret. Adiuncto ętiam quod quando de sua terra dominica auxilium daret, aut Radulfus quantum rectitudo foret de terra tali scilicet vastata
f.31v   dare, daret aut quietum eum dimittere faceret. Nunc autem/ ipse Radulfus de hac terra hereditat Sanctam Trinitatem et abbatissam facturam illud idem auxilium Rogero post obitum Radulfi quod ipse faciebat illi, concesso eidem Radulfo quicquid habebat abbatissa in eadem terra, ipse vero e[t] decimam illius terre. Post obitum autem suum et terram et decimam. Hoc donum posuit super altare Sanctę Trinitatis teste Petro filio Nigellii et Ranulfo Ulgeri filio et Radulfo filio Ivonis á sua parte. A parte autem abbatissę Rainnolfus de Balge,[4] Ricardus fatuus infans, Ricardus de Lu,[5] et Hunfridus Farsit et Rainaldus et Odo de Herofivilla[6] et Rogerus de Carpiket, et Vitalis prefectus abbatisse, et Willelmus pelliparius et Vitalis

---

[1] Cairon, 2.5 km south-west of Villons.
[2] Barbières, 3 km north-west of Villons. There is a *Delle Barbière* in the north-west corner of Villons.
[3] Probably Les Genetets to the south-east of Villons.
[4] See Document 7, Ranulfus de Baugeio. Baugy, commune of Planquery, canton of Balleroy, a possession of the Templars from 1148.
[5] Possibly the Richard of Luc-sur-Mer in *Abbayes caennaises*, no. 8, 86.
[6] Hérouville-St.-Clair.

filius carpentarii et Radulfus filius Wantarii, Arturus filius Hermenfredi,[1] et Wimundus de Caluiz,[2] Herbertus nepos Godefridi.

7   *Grant by Turold Papillon of the tithes of his vavassors at Amblie on his daughter, Hawisa, becoming a nun at Holy Trinity.*   [Before 1109 × 1113][3]

Papilio dedit filiam suam Haevisam cum decima suorum vavassorum Hamblo esse monacam in monasterio Sanctę Trinitatis, concedente matre et fratribus et sororibus. Huius rei testes sunt ex [parte] Turoldi filius eius, Ricardus et Mauricius et Hugo eius capellanus et Robertus de Fontaneis, Reignaldus de Petrapont[4] et Radulfus de/ Amblia et Pinel de Briusie.[5] Et ex parte domine Cecilie Rogerius monacus prior de Bec et Gaufridus capellanus et Hugo capellanus, Turstinus Malet, Ricardus de Graeio,[6] Herbertus filius Dodemani, Ranulfus de Baugeio,[7] Fulco camerarius, Willelmus parmentarius.[8]

8   *Grant by Hawisa, the widow of Robert Marmion, of land in Saint-Georges-d'Aunay and Jurques on her becoming a nun at Holy Trinity.*
[1106][9]

Round, *CDF*, no. 425.

Anno quo rex Anglorum Henricus Normanniam sibi subiugavit,[10] Hadeguisa coniux Roberti Marmionis in ęcclesia Sanctę Trinitatis Cadomi monialis facta, dedit eidem ęcclesię et sororibus terram quam habebat in Sancto

---

[1] Cf. Document 13 (before 1106).
[2] Cf. Document 4: Wimund was a prominent witness in matters relating to Calix in 1083.
[3] Cf. *Abbayes caennaises*, no. 27. The *pancarte* of 1109–1113: *Toroudus [Papeillun deciman hominum suorum] de Amblia [dedit] monasterio Sanctę Trinitatis pro Hatuissa filia sua ibi monacha facta, concedente conjuge et filiis et filiabus suis.*
[4] Pierrepont, 2 km south of Amblie.
[5] Possibly Brieux, cant. Evrecy.
[6] Witness to Document 8.
[7] Witness to Document 6.
[8] Witness ot Document 8.
[9] Cf. *Abbayes caennaises*, no. 27 (*pancarte* of 1109–1113): *[Hadvisa conjux Roberti Marmionis] in ęcclesia Sanctę Trinitatis facta monialis, dedit eidem ęcclesię et sororibus terram quam habebat in Sancto Georgio et in Jurcas et molendinum de la Boiste et le Parket totam sic[ut] habuit eam Robertus Marmion d[ie] qua f[uit] vivus et mortuus, concedente HENRICO rege et filiis Hadvisę Rogerio, [Heltone et Manasse qui donum s]up[er altare] posuerunt, ea conventione quod mitteret ipsa unam de parentibus suis in ęcclesia ut monialis Deo serviret.*
[10] 1106.

Georgio[1] et in Jurcas,[2] et molendinum de la Hoiste[3] et le Parket[4] totam, sicut habuerat eam Robertus Marmion, eo die quo vivus et mortuus fuit, concessu filiorum suorum, Rogeri Marmionis scilicet et Heltonis et Manasses, qui etiam cum matre sua donum super altare posuerunt. Fuerunt autem testes huius doni á parte sua Willelmus Marmion, Herluinus de Fonteneio, Rogerus de Moeio, Godefridus filius Roberti, Willelmus de Ulfieres, Robertus Aculeus, Hamon filius Roberti del Maisnil Ursin, Robertus filius Roberti filii Ernesii et Gersenda mater eius. A parte vero Sanctę Trinitatis testes sunt Gislebertus de Aquila, Willelmus de Aspres, Ricardus de Graeio,[5] Ricardus rufus, Ri/cardus de aula, Gaufridus brasciator, Rainaldus Durel, Arturus portarius, Willelmus parmentarius,[6] Vitalis prepositus.

f.32v

9 *Grant by Wiger of Sainte-Mère-Eglise[7] to the abbey of Holy Trinity, Caen, of land at Mortefemme.[8]* [Before 1082]

f.32v *De dono Guigerii Sanctę Marie ęcclesię*

Guigerius de Sanctę Marię ęcclesię dedit Sanctę Trinitati terram quam habebat in villa quę dicitur Mortua Femina et in ea manent vi liberi homines. Denique hoc donum fecit coram regina gratia adipiscendi misericordiam eius ut ipsa sibi auxiliatatur (*sic*) adversus omnes opprimentium calumpnias, at per hoc donum annuerunt Guigerius et Albericus nepotes eius coram quibus et factum est. Cuius rei testes sunt ex parte reginę Giraldus marescallus et Odo de Selles[9] et Osmundus de Versun et de hominibus abbatisse Bernardus et Gislebertus atque

---

[1] Saint-Georges-d'Aunay.
[2] Jurques, cant. Aunay-sur-Odon.
[3] La Bouette or La Boite, cant. Aunay-sur-Odon.
[4] Le Parquet, cant. Aunay-sur-Odon.
[5] Witness to Document 7.
[6] Witness to Document 7.
[7] Dép. Manche.
[8] Mortefemme, cant. La Haye-du-Puits, dép. Manche. Cf. *Abbayes caennaises*, nos 8, 27.

    Text of no. 8: *Wigerius quoque de Sanctę Marię ęcclesia dedit eidem ęcclesię terram quam habebat in villa quę dicitur Mortua Femina pro salute animę suę, suis nepotibus Wigerio et Alberico assensu[m] prebentibus.*

    Text of no. 27: *Wigerius quoque de Sancte MARIę ęcclesia dedit [eidem ęcclesię] de terra quam habebat in villa [quę dicitur Mortua] Femina pro salute animę [suę suis nepotibus] Wigerio et Alberico a[ss]ensum prebentibus; in ipsa terra manent quattuor liberi homines et XII^cim hospites.*

[9] Cf. Document 4, witness to sale by Ralph Bos.

Godefridus Calucenses[1] et Boso de Hoistrehan atque Turstenus. Ex parte vero eius idem nepotes ipsius et quidam homo suus Radulfus nomine, et Maugerius qui[dam] et Rabellus et Serlo.

10 *The farm of the abbey's property in Jersey by Abbess Matilda to Osmund of Canville for 26 livres per annum.*[2]   [1066–1113][3]

De firma de insulis

Donna abbatissa M[atildis] Sanctę Trinitatis dedit ad firmam Osmundo de Canvilla[4] quicquid habebat in insulis de Gersoi sicut tenuerant clerici id ante eum propter xxvi li[bras] denariorum, et hoc usque ad x annos, eo pacto ut transacto termino si congregationi visum fuerit ipsi eam relinquent quamdiu illis placuerit, sin autem alii dabunt. Infra ipsum quoque terminum/ si viderint eum supra modum gravari in ipsis erit si aliquam misericordiam remissionis cuiusque illi facere voluerint. Denique in ipsis similiter erit facultas firme alii dandę vel ei relinquende non in ipso. Pecunię vero reddende tres termini sunt he: ad [   ][5] redditurus est centum solidos et ad Pentecosten centum atque ad festivitatem Sanctorum Petri et Pauli[6] alios. Si vero moneta mutanda fuerit, ad Nativitatem reddet quod ad festum sanctorum apostolicorum redditurus fuerat fortis monete. Huius rei testes sunt Bernardus, Anffredus.

11 *Memorandum of a grant by Cecilia of six acres in fee at Colleville to Boso.*[7]   [Early twelfth century][8]

---

[1] Of Calix in Caen.
[2] All the early *pancartes* refer to the abbey's possession of property in Jersey, but none agree as to its exact composition. Cf. *Abbayes caennaises*, 55, 84, 94, 97; J. Walmsley, 'Note sur les possessions de l'abbaye de la Trinité de Caen aux îles Normandes', *AN*, 37 (1987), 228, Table 1.
[3] Tabuteau, *Transfers of Property*, 265, doc. 772, adds 'probably 1084'. L. Musset, 'Sur les mutations de la monnaie normande au xiᵉ siècle: deux documents inédits', *Revue numismatique*, 6th ser., 11 (1969), 291–3, is inclined towards a slightly later date, *temp.* Robert Curthose.
[4] Canville-la-Rocque, near Portbail in the Cotentin.
[5] Blank in MS. Christmas and Easter are possibilities, although Christmas is the more likely, given that adjustments were made then.
[6] 29 June.
[7] Cf. Delisle/Berger, II, 201.
[8] The transaction probably took place before Cecilia became abbess in 1113, when she was acting for the abbess in the later years of Matilda's abbacy, since she is not specifically referred to as the abbess who gave the land to Boso.

f.33r   [I]sti[1] sunt testes et auditores qui audierunt et viderunt quod donna
abbatissa dedit Bosoni[2] vi acros terre in feodo et iiii agros et domum quam
fecerat in Colavilla reddidit filio eius propter decimam quandam quam
ei dederat in Colavilla presente donna Cęcilia. Nigellus de Oistrehan,
Rogerius filius Erphasti, Durandus Boisardus,[3] Fubertus de Siccavilla,[4]
Radulfus prepositus, Wimundus, Vitalis Stephanus.

12   *Memorandum that Robert of Calix made the abbey of Holy Trinity heir
to his estate in Calix for 500 livres and a palfrey worth ten livres (for the
benefit of his wife) on condition that Robert and his wife, Adeliza, could
hold the property for Robert's lifetime and that Adeliza could become a nun
at Holy Trinity if she wished. [c. 1152 – c. 1178]*

Copy in Archives du Calvados, H, Trinité de Caen, Recueil de mémoires et d'extraits, f. 26r.
Léchaudé d'Anisy, *Extraits*, no. 47.[5]

f.33r   *Carta'*

Dameta dei gratia Sanctę Trinitatis de Cadomo abbatissa et omnis conventus
eiusdem ęcclesię tam presentibus quam futuris, salutem. Sciendum est
f.33v   quod Robertus de Caluiz hereditavit monasterium. Sanctę Tri/nitatis de
Cadomo de tota sua terra, videlicet de domo propria et de omnibus his
quę ad eum pertinent tam in hominibus quam in campis et in pratis et in
uno furno et in censis et in reguarz (*sic*) et in omnibus eschaementis quę
ad donum pertinent et maxime totam illam terram quam habebat invadiatam,
et reddidit eam super altare, et se ipsum cum uxore sua ea conventione
quod Dameta abbatissa et presens conventus cenobii concesserunt quod
predictus Robertus teneret et domum et terram quantum temporis vitę suę
vellet. Pręterea concesserunt quod si ipsa Adeliz vellet fieri monialis eam
reciperent. Et pro hoc pacto tenendo dedit abbatissa Roberto ccccc
lib[ras][6] sicut fuit aspectum inter eos, et insuper dedit abbatissa unum
palefridum uxori suę appreciatum x lib[ras] andeg[avensium]. Et hoc
affidiavit tenendum ex parte abbatisse Radulfus Ulfier et Robertus de
Corsout. Et iterum affidiavit hoc tenendum Robertus de Caluiz et Adeliz
uxor sua et Rogerius Alis sororius eius et Serlo Torel et Henricus filius

---

[1] Rubric and initial letter omitted.
[2] Probably Boso of Ouistreham, a witness on the abbess's behalf in Document 9.
[3] Cf. Document 13: *Odo frater Durandi Bosart.*
[4] Secqueville-en-Bessin or Secqueville-la-Campagne.
[5] Léchaudé d'Anisy, *Extraits*, refers to an original charter with a broken seal, but this has
not been located.
[6] This is a very unlikely sum; perhaps 500s is meant.

Willelmi et Odo brunus. Affidiaverunt ętiam quod si aliquis in predictam terram calumpniam faceret iuxta possibilitatem suam eam cenobio defenderent. His inter/fuerunt cum abbatissa et cum conventu: Radulfus capellanus, Benedictus capellanus, Johannes capellanus, Bernadus clericus, Radulfus Ulfier, Robertus de Corsout, Guigenus et Guare, Willelmus de Vals,[1] Gaufridus filius Reinaldi, Otoerus de Grantia. Ex parte Roberti Rogerius Alis, Matheus de Scherie, Hugo Bordel.

13 *Grant by Duke Robert of houses, rents, and fishing rights in Caen, from the castle wall to the River Orne, and of a market and tolls at Ouistreham.* [1087–94]

Transcript in T. Stapleton, *Archaeological Journal*, 3 (1846), 26.
Round, *CDF*, no. 423.
Regesta, I, no. 324 [1087–1091].

Carta consulis Roberti

Ego Robertus Willelmi Anglorum Regis filius Normannorum atque Cenomannorum princeps pro salute animę meę meique patris et matris atque antecessorum meorum do concessu Henrici mei fratris ęcclesię Sancte Trinitatis de Cadomo et Cecilię meę sorori[2] sanctisque monialibus ibidem Deo servientibus id totum quod erat mei iuris extra murum Cadomi usque ad predictam ęcclesiam ita solutum et quietum ut in meo tenebam dominio, Vallem Guę[3] totam videlicet atque domos cunctas usque ad murum et usque ad aquam Olnule cum omnibus redditibus, piscationem quoque aquę Olnule totam sicut Rex habebat in suo dominio.[4] Ad hoc autem mercatum in villa que dicitur Oistrehan et teloneum et tantum quantum tenet territorium eiusdem ville. Huius rei fuerunt testes et liberatores Simon de Camilleio[5], Savericus filius Cane, Radulfus capel/lanus de Airi, Rogerius Poignant, Rogerius Mala Corona dispensator, Toraldus hostiarius. Ex parte Henrici filii regis affuerunt Rannulfus filius Ulgerii, Odo camerarius eiusdem Henrici. Ex parte Sanctę Trinitatis fuerunt receptores et testes:[6] Godefredus de Caluiz, Gislebertus de Caluiz, Johannes filius Godefridi coci, Rainaldus filius Anschitilli de Herovilla[7] et

---

[1] Vaux-sur-Seulles.
[2] Cecilia appears to have been acting as abbess long before 1113.
[3] Vaugueux in Caen.
[4] William the Conqueror. Cf. *Abbayes caennaises*, no. 17, 116; charter of 18 July 1083.
[5] Camilly, commune of Bénouville.
[6] The witnesses on behalf of Holy Trinity are omitted from *Regesta*, I, no. 324.
[7] Hérouville-Saint-Clair.

Odo eius frater, Godefredus filius Herberti, Radulfus de Folebec[1], Odo frater Durandi Bosart,[2] Arturus filius Ermenfredi.[3]

Sig+num Roberti comitis
Signum + Henrici Regis Willelmi filii
Signum Radulfi capellani
+ Signum Rogerii de Curcella
Signum + Gaufridi de Calmunt
Signum + Willelmi camerarii
Signum + Roberti de Montfort
Signum + Gualterii de Meduana
Signum + Hugonis Brittonis
Signum + Rogerii dispensatoris
Signum + Roberti Balduini filii
Signum + Ricardi Painel
Signum + Symonis de Chimilleio
Signum + Saverici filii Canę

14 *Ouistreham Survey. This survey appears without introduction or rubric. It is enigmatic in the extreme and impossible to associate firmly with the main surveys, A and B, or with other documents in the cartulary. There is no survey for Ouistreham in the second series of Surveys.* [n.d.]

f.38r Unfredus tenet xii acros et dimidium terre ad Ostrehan.
Petrus v acros.
Unfredus xvi acros.
Nigellus filius Gaufridi lx [acros] et in istis manent ii liberi homines de v acros et iii dimidios rusticos de xviii acris et i bordarius [de dimi][4] dio acro.
Savaricus liber de dimidio acro.
Petrus lx acros et in istis manent iiii[or] liberi homines de xx acris et dimidius rusticus de vi acris et i borderius.
Robertus Brotin lx acros et v et in istis manent iii liberi homines de xi acris et i rusticus de xii acris et vii bordarii.
Goislenus camerarius cvii acros et i molendinum de iii modiis et in ista manent vii liberi homines de xlvii acris et iii bordarii, ii liberi homines de iiii acris.

[1] Foulbec.
[2] Cf. Document 11.
[3] Cf. Document 6.
[4] Space left blank in MS.

Filius Raineri Insani xxx acros et in istis manent v liberi homines de iii acris et dimidio et dimidium rusticum de vi acris et ii borderii.

Ricardus xii acros et in is manet i borderius.

Malored xi acros.

Grip ii acros.

Sanson lxi acros et in is manent ii liberi homines de vi acris et i rusticus et i borderius.

Osmundus v acros.

Goscelinus xxxv acros et in is manent iii rustici.

Godefredus xxxiii acros et de his tenet mater sua v acros.

Rogerius xl/ acros l[1] in is manent v liberi homines de xi acris liiii bordarii.

Albericus filius Mot est lxii acros et in is manet (sic) i rusticus et iiii borderii.

Fromundus sacerdos lx acros et in is manent v liberi homines de xiii acris.

Rogerius xx acros et in is manet i borderius.

Odo xxiiii acros de is tenet i rusticus xiiii [acros] et i borderius.

[E]t in dominico tenet episcopus[2] xiii bordarios, et iii tenent iiii acros, et vi rusticos plenarios et iiii rusticos dimidios de ci acris, et v liberos homines de xxiii acris.

Et in dominico Adelaide[3] xviii liberos homines de viii[to] et xx[ti] acris et ii rusticos plenarios et ii dimidios et xxii bordarios de iiii acris et ii mansuras devastatas de xx acris.

15 *Account of the despoliation of the estates of Holy Trinity under the rule of Robert Curthose. All but two of the affected estates appear in Holy Trinity's most comprehensive pancarte, that of 1082 (Abbayes caennaises, no. 8). Only seven of the following estates are included in Survey A, and only eight in Survey B.* [late eleventh/early twelfth century]

Printed in Haskins, *Institutions*, 63–4.
Round, *CDF*, no. 424.

[1] Possibly a mistake for *et*.

[2] There is no other reference to the possessions of a bishop at Ouistreham.

[3] This could be a reference to Adelaide, a daughter of Thurstan Haldup, *vicomte* of the Cotentin and a major benefactor of Holy Trinity (see *Abbayes caennaises*, 48). But there is no direct reference to her. A *pancarte* of 1066–83, however, does mention an Adelaide:

Dedimus . . . villam ętiam quę dicitur Ostrehan cum cunctis appendiciis, hoc excepto quod Godefridus ibi tenuit, concedentibus Gisl[eberto] Crispino Ricardoque Balduini filio, per pecuniam scilicet quam regina eis dedit atque Adeladis concessit. (*Abbayes caennaises*, no. 11, 94).

f.39v   Willelmus comes Ebroicensis ex quo rex Willelmus finivit aufer[t] Sanctę Trinitati et abbatissę et dominabus vii agripennos[1] vinę et duos equos et xx solidos rotomagensium nummorum et salinas de Escrenevilla[2] et uno quoque anno xx libras de Gauceio[3] et de Bavent.[4]

Ricardus filius Herluini duas villas, Tassillei et Montboen.[5]

Willelmus camerarius filius Rogeri de Candos[6] decimam de Hainovilla.[7]

Willelmus Baviel xx boves quos sumpsit apud Osbernivillam.[8]

Robertus de Bonesboz eandem villam depredavit.

Robertus de Uz terram de iiii puteis[9] et de Cierneio.[10]

Willelmus Bertrannus duos vavasores et eorum decimam et v solidos quoque anno apud Columbellas.[11]

Ricardus de Corceio[12] iiii[or] libras et xx oves.

Nigellus de Oillei ii boves.

Rogerus de Avesnes[13] in equis et in denariis et in aliis rebus viiii libras.

Robertus Pantolf in denariis et in aliis rebus vi libras.

Willelmus Judas xx solidos.

Rogerus dispensator[14] et Rogerus de Scutella xi boves et ii[os] equos et predam de Folebec[15] et homines vulneraverunt et verberaverunt in pace.

Robertus de Molbrai lxviii libras quoque anno post mortem regis. Eudo vicecomes xx boves.[16]

Adelofdus camerarius episcopi Baiocensis terram de Anglicivilla.[17]

---

[1] Cf. *abbayes caennaises*, no. 8, 84; the *pancarte* of 1082 records the donation of 7 arpents of vineyards at Argences and another 7 arpents at Aubevoye.

[2] Escanneville.

[3] Gacé, commune Laize-la-Ville, dép. Orne.

[4] Bavent, south of Escanneville.

[5] Tassilly and Montbouin, *post obitum* donations of Richard fitz Herluin to Holy Trinity 1066–1083: *Abbayes caennaises*, no. 8, 83, no. 11, 94.

[6] Cf. *Regesta*, II, no. 1439: possibly Roger, the brother of Robert de Candos, *vicomte* of Rouen.

[7] Hénouville, cant. Duclair, dép. Seine-Maritime.

[8] Auberville-sur-Mer.

[9] Quatrepuits. Cf. *Abbayes caennaises*, no. 8, 87.

[10] Cesny-aux-Vignes.

[11] Colombelles, cant. Troarn. Cf. *Abbayes caennaises*, no. 8, 88: the donation by Robert Bertran of two freeman and their tithes to Holy Trinity. Robert and William appear as witnesses to charters of William I and II: *Regesta*, I, nos. 4, 150, 168, 170, 308, 310.

[12] Courcy.

[13] Possibly Avernes-Saint-Gourgon, dép. Orne.

[14] Cf. text and witness list of Document 13, *Carta consulis Roberti*. In the text he is described as *Mala Corona*.

[15] Foulbec, cant. Beuzeville, dép. Eure: *Abbayes caennaises*, no. 8, 86.

[16] Probably Eude, son of Turstin, *vicomte* of the Cotentin, whose sister, Adelaide was one of the early nuns at Holy Trinity: *Abbayes caennaises*, 159–60.

[17] Englesqueville-la-Percée.

Ranulfus vicecomes,[1] Ricardus de Corceio xv libras de terra de Grandicampo,[2] et Ranulfus idem et iii boves et ii equos de Duxeio[3] et de Aneriis[4]
et v acros annone in Aneriis/ et decimam de Boivilla.[5]

Ingelrannus prata de Grai.[6]

Comes Henricus pedagium accepit de Chetehulmo[7] et de omni Constan-
tino,[8] et super hoc facit operari homines Sanctę Trinitatis de eadem villa
et patria ad castella suorum hominum.

Alveredus de Ludreio aufert Sanctę Trinitati tres boves apud Teuvillam[9]
et terram de eadem villa devastat.Et Willelmus de Veteri Ponto[10] prata de
predicta villa.

Et Hulmum[11] aufertur Sanctę Trinitati iniuste.

Adeloldus[12] predictus camerarius episcopi aufert annonam de Grandicampo
et quamplures alias.

Hugo de Redeveris[13] aufert v modios vini et vineam quoque anno ad
Vernun.[14]

Fulco de Aneriis i equum et viii solidos et iii minas de favis, et omnem
terram devastat, ita quod nullus ibi lucrare potest.

Willelmus Bertrannus accepit de Osbertivilla[15] duos boves et postea viros
misit in carcerem.

Willelmus de Rupieres[16] accepit boves et porcos domne abbatissę et
homines super terram eius interfecit.

---

[1] Probably Ranulf Meschin, *vicomte* of Bayeux, who became earl of Chester in 1121:
Abbayes caennaises, 171; *Regesta*, II. xviii.

[2] Grandcamp-les-Bains. Cf. *Abbayes caennaises*, no. 8, 86, no. 12, 97, no. 22, 131.

[3] Ducy-Sainte-Marguerite, cant. Tilly-sur-Seulles.

[4] Asnières-en-Bessin. Cf. *Abbayes caennaises*, no. 8, 87, no. 22, 131: in the *pancarte* of 1082
the donation to Holy Trinity consists of 36 acres, in that of *c.* 1080–5 it consists of 30 acres.

[5] Beuville, cant. Douvres. There is no evidence that the tithes of Beuville belonged to Holy
Trinity. The church, allod, and tithes of Beuville had been granted by the same Ranulf
vicomte of Bayeux to the abbey of St. Etienne: *Abbayes caennaises*, no. 18, 121–2.

[6] Graye-sur-Mer.

[7] Quettehou, dép. Manche.

[8] The Cotentin.

[9] Thiéville, commune of Douville, near St.-Pierre-sur-Dives.

[10] Vieux-Pont, 5 km east of Thiéville.

[11] Le Homme, now l'Isle-Marie, cant. Sainte-Mère-Eglise, dép. Manche. Part of the early
endowment of Holy Trinity included the *burgum* of Le Homme with all its rents: *Abbayes
caennaises*, no. 8, 84.

[12] Above, *Adelofdus*.

[13] Reviers, cant. Creully.

[14] Vernon, dép. Eure. Cf. *Abbayes caennaises*, no. 8, 84–5: donations of 3 arpents of
vineyard by a Godelef and his sister, and an unspecified quantity of land by Billeheut, who
had received it from her father as a dowry (*pro conjugio*).

[15] Auberville-sur-Mer, cant. Dozulé.

[16] Rupierre, cant. Troarn.

Idem Willelmus pecuniam metatoris abbatisse de Ruvvres[1] accepit et annonam fecit inde ferri, et apud Ranvillam[2] duos viro[s] interfecit et complures vulneravit.

Et item Robertus de Guz aufert ei unum equum apud Monboen.[3]

Hugo paganus aufert abbatissę silvam de Salan[4] et sacerdotem verberavit in pace.

Et Willelmus Gernu[n] silwam (sic) incidit et evellit quantum potest.

f.40v Ranulfus frater Igeri sai/siavit terram abbatissę super hoc quod ipsa sibi terminum respondendi dederat, et inquirendi si deberet ei inde rectum facere. Brenagium[5] autem interrogant et Rainaldus Landu[n] et alii ministri abbatisse et monent eam placitare.

Inde Robertus de Genz aufert ei terram de Donmaisnil[6] et annonam inde tulit et oves et boves et alia multa et vi adhuc detinet.

Et Radulfus de Cortlandu[n] ponit terram abbatissę in gravatoria et vi vult ibi eam tenere quod nunquam fuit amplius.

Documents 16–22 follow Survey B and are written in a variety of thirteenth-century hands.

16 *Deraignment by Abbess Johanna, whereby she proved her right to a house, probably in Caen.* [January (?), 1183][7]

Printed in Delisle-Berger, I, 349, no. 5.
Round, *CDF*, no. 437.
Valin, *Le duc de Normandie*, no. 22.

f.87r Sciendum est quod Johanna Abbatissa Sancte Trinitatis Cadom[i], anno ab incarnatione domini MCLXXXIII disraisnavit domum que fuerat Wiguenni Britonis adversus Evainnum et Benedictum qui faciebant se de parentela illius. In curia domini Regis in plenaria assisa coram Willelmo filio Radulfi tunc temporis senescallo domini Regis in Normannia et Willelmo de Sancto Johanne, Radulfo Tesson,[8] Henrico de Tilleio,[9]

[1] Rouvres, cant. Bretteville-sur-Laize. Cf. *Abbayes caennaises*, no. 8, 87, no. 22, 131.
[2] Ranville.
[3] Montbouin.
[4] Sallen.
[5] For *bernagium*, an ancient contribution to the maintenance of the duke's hunting dogs: Haskins, *Institutions*, 39–40, 82.
[6] Doumesnil, cant. Bretteville-sur-Laize. Cf. *Abbayes caennaises*, no. 8, 88.
[7] Probably at the same assise as Document 1. Fourteen of the eighteen witnesses here appear in Document 1.
[8] Ralph Tesson appears in a fragment of an exchequer memorandum roll of *c.* 1200: H. Legras, 'Un fragment de rôle normand inédit de Jean Sans Terre', *BSAN*, 29 (1913), 25.
[9] Legras, 'Un fragment', 23, 26.

Willelmo de Mara,[1] Hamone pincerna, Ranulfo de Pra[t]eriis,[2] Radulfo vicecomite, Henrico Lovet, Gaufrido Duredent, Jordano de Landa, Roberto de Livet, Roberto de Culleio,[3] Ricardo filio H[enrici], Roberto de Manerio, Willelmo de Caluz, Roberto Belet, Rogero de Arreio,[4] Thoma de Botemont, et pluribus aliis tunc presentibus.

17 *Donation of a house by William of Calix, a leper, in return for the prayers of Holy Trinity and being received into a lazar-house.*

[Late twelfth century]

Sciendum quod Willelmus de Caluz[5] leprosus dedit abbatie Sancte Trinitatis et misit super altare per i cultellum assensu sue coniugis domum quandam apud Caluz valentem v sol[idos] annuatim et regard[a] ut esset particeps orationum abbatie et reciperetur ad maladeriam beati Thome.[6] Testibus Arturo, Willelmo fratre Arturi, Willelmo episcopo, Roberto blondo, presbyteris, Radulfo de Wallani monte,[7] Johanne Britone, Radulfo de hospitio, Roberto filio Raginaldi.

18 *Record of an assize held at Caen at which 'recognizance' (a local inquest) was denied Ralph fitz Eude on the grounds that the charter evidence alone was sufficient to support the abbey's claim to the advowson of the church of Carpiquet.*

[1185]

Printed in Delisle-Berger, II, no. 647
Round, *CDF*, no. 438.
Boussard, *Henri II*, 292, n. 1.
Trans. in C. Petit-Dutaillis, *La monarchie féodale en France et en Angleterre* (Paris, 1933), 182–3.

Anno ab incarnatione Domini $m^oclxxx^{mo}v^{to}$ [8]

[1] *Vicomte* of Saint-Mère-Eglise. Cf. Valin, *Le duc de Normandie*, no. 18.
[2] Presles, cant. Vassy.
[3] Cully, cant. Creully.
[4] Arry, 1 km west of Bougy, Possibly Roger *bucularius* of Bougy B.
[5] It is tempting to identify him as William of Calix, a prominent money-lender of Caen, and a constant witness in charters of the 1180s and 1190s. Cf. Haskins, *Institutions*, 180–1. See also Charter 3 and Documents 1 and 16.
[6] Cf. 1257 Survey §125, 'Rentes diverses versées par l'abbaye': *Saint-Thomas, qui estoit une leproserie, avoit distribucions sur l'abbaye*. The hospital of St. Thomas Becket was founded towards the end of the twelfth century. See *Histoire de Caen*, ed. G. Désert (Toulouse, 1981), 39.
[7] Cf. Charter 3 (1178 × 1183) and Document 18 (1185).
[8] Date added later in a different and clumsier hand.

Radulfus filius Eudonis[1] attulit breve domini Regis ad assisam apud Cadomum ad Willelmum filium Radulfi tunc temporis senescallum Norm-[annie][2] et ad alias iusticias que tunc tenebant assisas, per quod breve dominus Rex precipiebat eis quod facerent recognosci per legales homines quis presentavit ultimam personam que mortua erat in ecclesia de Karpik[et], unde contencio erat inter abbatissam de Cadomo et Radulfum filium Eudonis. Abbatissa dixit quod ecclesia Sancte Trinitatis habuerat eam a fundamento ecclesie sue de dono Regis Willelmi et Mathildis Regine et confirmata[3] erat abbatie per carta[s] Regis Willelmi et per cartam Regis Henrici filii Mathildis imperatricis. Quibus auditis, Barones Scacarii et Willelmus filius Radulfi et alie iusticie domini Regis consideraverunt super Scacar[io] quod illa recognitio non debebat fieri, nec abbatissa placitare debebat super ecclesia illa que confirmata est abbatie per cartas dominorum Norm[annie]. Et ita remansit inde quieta abbatissa versus Radulfum filium Eudonis de calumpnia quam faciebat in ecclesia illa per iudicium Baronum Scacarii super Scacar[io], coram Willelmo filio Radulfi, Willelmo de Mara,[4] Hamone pincerna,[5] Roberto de Harecort, Johanne Archidiacono de Arenis,[6] Roberto Archidiacono de Noting[ham], Ricardo Bevrel, Willelmo de Caluz,[7] Jordano de Landa,[8] Rogero de Arreio,[9] Ansquitillo, Osberto capellano, Radulfo de Lexov[io], Roberto de Bernaio, Sehero de Quinceio,[10] Radulfo Tesson,[11] Gilleberto de Tileriis,[12] Radulfo de Wall[ano]mont,[13] Petro de Argentomo,[14] Nicholao pigace,[15] Johanne

---

[1] See Carpiquet B, **54**, **43**. The fact that the jurors at the time of Survey B acknowledged Ralph's possession of a wide range of tithes, including the third sheaf from half of the non-vavassorial population suggests that there was some basis for his claim to the advowson of the church (cf. Charter 16), even if it was on an alternating basis with the abbey. This challenge seems to place a date not later than 1185 for Survey B. Ralph may also have been a tenant at Escanneville (Escanneville B, **25**).

[2] William fitz Ralph, seneschal of Normandy from *c.* 1177–1200. See Boussard, *Henri II*, 527; J. Le Patourel, 'Guillaume Fils-Raoul, sénéchal de Normandie', 321-2.

[3] MS has *conformata* with a superscript *i* after the *f*.

[4] Cf. Document 16.

[5] *ibid.*

[6] John d'Eraines, archdeacon of Sées (Haskins, *Institutions*, 184).

[7] Cf. Document 16.

[8] *ibid.*

[9] *ibid.* and Bougy B, **4**.

[10] Seher de Quincy, constable of Nonancourt (Haskins, *Institutions*, 327, 334–5), and a witness to charters of 1176–8 and 1184.

[11] Cf. Document 15.

[12] Appears in exchequer fragment roll of *c.* 1200: Legras, 'Un fragment', 25–6.

[13] Cf. Document 16.

[14] Argentan, dép. Orne.

[15] Cf. Auberville B, **31**.

pigace, Rohard[o], Arturo,[1] servientibus, Gaufrido de Rapendona,[2] Roberto Lacaille, et pluribus aliis, et Radulfo scriba de Cadomo, magistro Martino de Grainvilla,[3] magistro Gaufrido de Haia.

19 *Godfrey of Tourlaville (dép. Manche) inherited his grandfather's messuage in Froide Rue in Caen and had the obligations changed from bleeding the abbey's oxen to payment of a pepper rent.* [late twelfth century]

Godefridus de Torlaville recognovit coram Johanna abbatissa et monialibus Sancte Trinitatis Cadomi quod ipse debebat tenere hereditatem suam de abbatia Sancte Trinitatis Cadomi, scilicet quandam masuram in Frigido Vico quam tenuit de eadem abbatia Osbertus faber avus prefati Godefridi, qui Osbertus solebat saignare[4] boves abbatie predicte, et ea die qua saignabat boves habebat liberationem suam de abbatia, scilicet panem et cervisiam. Iste Godefridus, cum nesciret facere servitium quod fecerat avus suus, fideliter promisit et iuramento confirmavit se redditurum prefate abbatie quandam libram piperis annuatim ad feriam prati. Hii afferunt cum prefato Godefrido coram domina abbatissa: Willelmus de Maletot, Salomon sellarius, Radulfus filius Bentie, Odo Brun de Frigido Vico, Alexander de Frigido Vico. Idem Alexander dixit quod comederat sepe de liberatione quam habuerat prefatus Osbertus de abbatia.

20 *Charter of Abbess Cecilia granting permission to Erengot to move the abbey's mill from Froide Rue to Gémare.* [1113–27]

Ed. T. Stapleton, *Archaeological Journal*, 3 (1846), 26.
Round, *CDF*, no. 426.

Cecilia filia regis dei gratia abbatissa sancte Trinitatis Cadomi presentibus et futuris ad quos littere iste pervenerint salutem. Sciatis quod ego concessi Erengot molendinario ducere et facere molendinum nostrum quod erat in Frigido Vico super terram suam in Gamara.[5] Et Erengot crevit nobis redditum molendini de uno modio frumenti et de uno modio ordei. Et

---

[1] Cf. Document 17.
[2] Cf. Legras, 'Un fragment', 29, 23; Haskins, *Institutions*, 335, no. 15 (charter of 1186) where Geoffrey of Repton is described as *baillivus regis*.
[3] Cf. Grainville-sur-Odon B, **21**.
[4] Probably a Latinized French word (*saigner*, to bleed). For the similar practice of bleeding horses, which went back to Roman times, see E. Miller, *The Abbey and Bishopric of Ely* (Cambridge, 1951), 283, n. 1. I am indebted to Professor Miller for providing this reference.
[5] Gémare in Caen.

sciendum quod molendinus non reddebat ante nisi duos modios nostre abbatie. Et sic concessimus ei molendinum tenendum in feodo hereditarie sibi et heredibus suis. Ego feci molendinum de meis lignis et refacere debeo quando deterioraverit. Bladium (*sic*) de abbatia nostra debet moliri ad molendinum. Et Erengot et heredes eius habebunt de nostro bladio tredecimum sextarium de moutura et ei computabitur in suo redditu cum dica. Hoc totum factum est concessu Ivonis Taillebosc salvo suo redditu.[1]

21 *Grant by Abbess Alicia to William fitz Stephen of a field in fee for wood to repair the mill. Previously the abbess had provided the wood for repairs, but now only in the event of destruction by fire.* [*c.* 1135]

f.88r   Aelicia abbatissa Sancte Trinitatis dedit Willelmo filio Stephani in feodo et hereditate totius conventus concessu unum campum qui desuper vallem est, habens quandam foveam in uno capite, tali convencione quod ipse Willelmus debet invenire ligna ad refaciendum molendinum suum que ipsa abbatissa solebat ante invenire. Set si per infortunium evenerit quod ardeat, ipsa debet ei invenire omnia ligna ad reficiendum illud. Teste Beatrice de Pomeria,[2] Aubereda de Maiseht[3] cum pluribus aliis.

22 *Record of a judgement made at the Exchequer at Falaise that the abbess of Holy Trinity, Caen, was not obliged to adhere to the terms of an agreement with Ralph of Trois-Monts, knight, concerning eleven sesters of grain from the mill of Gémare in Caen.* [Easter 1217]

f.88v   In scacario de termino Pasche anno gratie m°cc° septimo decimo apud Falesiam iudicatum fuit quod abbatissa Sancte Trinitatis Cadom[i] non faciet excambium Radulfo de Tribus Montibus militi de undecim sex[tariis] bladi quos idem Radulfus habebat in molendino de Gaimare per cartam dicte abbatisse quam idem Radulfus inde habebat factam finem assensu capituli sui, cum ipsa nichil possit dare alicui vel excambire ita quod sit ad detrimentum domus sue. Iudicatum eciam fuit quod carta illa non valebat, et quod debebat dilacerari, et ibidem per iudicium dilacerata fuit. Coram

---

[1] Ivo Taillebois, *dapifer* of William II and the first husband of Countess Lucy, was dead by 1098: *Regesta*, I, xxiv.
[2] Possibly La Pommeraye, cant. Thury-Harcourt.
[3] Maizet, cant. Evrecy.

domino Gar[ino] Silvan[ectensis] episcopo,[1] domino Galt[ero] domini Regis camerario,[2] comite Roberto de Alenc'[3] qui cartam illam diceravit (*sic*), Roberto episcopo Baiocensis,[4] H[ugone] episcopo Constanc[iensis],[5] Jordano episcopo Lexov[iensis],[6] W[illelmo] episcopo Albric[iensis],[7] S[ilvestro] episcopo Sagien[sis],[8] W[illelmo] de Mortuo Mari,[9] Amaurico de Croo', Fulc[one] Paenel, Ricardo de Vernon', W[illelmo] constabulario Norm[annie],[10] Fulc[one] de Aunou, Henrico de Sancto Dionisio, Milone de Leveiis,[11] Petro de Teill',[12] Ren[aldo] de Villa Terrici,[13] Bartholomeo Droc, Ricardo de Fonten', Roberto de Meisnill', Roberto de Petrafiste,[14] Garino de Nuill[eio], Rogero pescheneiro', Fulcone de Cantelou, Hugone de Bougneio, Roberto de Freschen', Roberto filio Herneis, Roberto de [ ]villa,[15] Roberto de Cruis, Galfrido Rossel, W[illelmo] de Mara,[16] Ricardo Carbonel, W[illelmo] Carbonel, magistro Galfrido de Cortun', Roberto de Vaus, Geraldo de Arreio,[17] Ricardo de Floreio, W[illelmo] Acarin[o] clerico qui tunc in scacario scribebat,[18] Ricardo pigace tunc serviens baill[iv]e.

Documents **23–27** are copies of charters in the *Cartulaire de l'Abbaye Sainte Trinité de Caen*, Caen, Archives du Calvados, H, Trinité de Caen, probably a sacristan's cartulary.[19]

23 *Charter of Simon Pevrel granting an annual rent of one quarter of wheat from a purpresture of land at Mathieu for the maintenance of a lamp at the altar of St. Mary in the abbey of Holy Trinity, Caen.*   [August 1229]

[1] Warin, bishop of Senlis, 1214–17.
[2] Walter the young, one of the constables of Philip Augustus.
[3] Count Robert of Alençon was one of the principal defectors to Philip Augustus in 1202–4.
[4] Robert, bishop of Bayeux, 1206–31.
[5] Hugh, bishop of Coutances, 1208–38.
[6] Jordan, bishop of Lisieux, 1202–18.
[7] William, bishop of Avranches, *c*. 1212–18.
[8] Silvester, bishop of Sées, 1202–20.
[9] William of Mortemer, bailiff of La Lande and of Caux.
[10] William du Hommet. Cf. Ranville B, **39**.
[11] Milo of Lévis, *bailli* (Strayer, *Administration*, 95).
[12] Peter of Thillai, *bailli*.
[13] Renaud of Ville-Thierry, *bailli*.
[14] Robert of Pierrefitte, castellan of Pommeraye.
[15] The MS is too damaged to make out the whole word, even under ultra-violet treatment.
[16] Cf. Documents 16, 18.
[17] Arry, 3 km south-west of Bougy.
[18] According to Strayer, *Administration*, 99, this is the first appearance of William Acarin, the founder of the collegiate church of the Sepulchre at Caen. Cf. Charters 8, 15.
[19] *Charters and Custumals*, xxiv.

Caen, Archives du Calvados, H, Trinité de Caen, *Cartulaire de l'Abbaye Sainte Trinité de Caen*, 64–6, no. 11. [124, no. 54, summary].
Original, Charter 21.

Sciant presentes et futuri quod ego Simon Pevrel dedi et concessi pro salute anime mee et antecessorum meorum Deo et luminari lampadis altaris Sancte Marie in abbatia monalium (*sic*) Sancte Trinitatis Cadomum siti retro magnum alltare (*sic*), silicet (*sic*) unum quarterium frumenti percipiendum feodaliter anuali (*sic*) redditu per annum in Septembris [a]d mensuram de Matoni[o], in uno porprisagio sito ibidem iuxta terram qua fuit Unfridi filius (*sic*) Marie tenendum et habendum dicto luminari in puram et perpetuam elemosinam sine reclamatione mei et heredum meorum de cetero quod propisagium (*sic*), Ricardus Pevrel meus avonculus tenet de me feodaliter. Ita quod dicte moniales poterunt facere plenariam iusticiam in dicto porprisagio pro dicto frumeto (*sic*). Et de hoc atornavi eis dictum Ricardum feodi firmarium. Et ego et heredes mei dictis monialibus sucessive (*sic*) dictam ellemosinam (*sic*) contra omnes homines garantizare tenemur. Quod ut ratum et stabile tenatur (*sic*) imperpetuum presens scriptum sigilli mei testimonio roboravi. Actum anno domini M°CC°XX° nono mense Augusti.

24 *Charter of Simon Pevrel granting an annual rent of one quarter of wheat from a purpresture of land at Mathieu for the maintenance of a lamp at the altar of St. Lawrence in the abbey of Holy Trinity, Caen.*

[August 1229]

Caen, Archives du Calvados, H, Trinité de Caen, *Cartulaire de l'Abbaye Sainte Trinité de Caen*, 66–7, no. 12. [125, no. 56, summary].

Sciant omnes presentes et futuri quod ego Simon Pevrel dedi et concessi pro salute mee et antecessorum meorum Deo et luminari Sancti Laurencii martyris in ecclesia monialium Sancte Trinitatis Cadomum constituti, scilicet unum quarterium frumenti percipiendum feodaliter annual (*sic*) redditu per annum in Septembris ad mensuram de Matonio in uno porprisagio sito ibidem iuxta terram qua fuit Umfridi filii Marie quod Ricardus Pevrel meus avunculus tenet de me feodaliter tenendum et habendum dicto luminari in puram et perpetuam elemosinam sine reclamatione mei et heredum meorum de cetero. Ita quod dicte moniales poterunt facere feodaliter plenariam iusticiam in dicto porprisagio predicto frumento et de hoc atornavi eis dictum Ricardum feodi firmarium. Et ego et heredes mei dictis monialibus successive dictam elemosinam contra omnes homines garantizare integre tenemur. Quod ut ratum et stabile teneatur imperpetuum presens scriptum, sigilli mei testimonio roboravi. Actum anno domini M°CC° nono mense Augusti.

25 *Charter of Simon Pevrel granting an annual rent of one mine of wheat from a purpresture of land at Mathieu for the maintenance of a lamp at the altar of St. Lawrence in the abbey of Holy Trinity, Caen.* [August 1229]

Caen, Archives du Calvados, H, Trinité de Caen, *Cartulaire de l'Abbaye Sainte Trinité de Caen*, 67–9, no. 13. [124–5, no. 55, summary].
Original, Charter 20.

Sciant presentes et futuri quod ego Simon Pevrel dedi et concessi pro salute anime mee et antecessorum meorum Deo et luminari altaris Sancti Laurencii martyris in abbatia Sancte Trinitatis Cadomum constituti, scilicet unam minam frumenti percipiendum annuali redditu feodaliter per annum in Septembris ad mensuram de Matonio in uno porprisagio sito ibidem iuxta terram qua fuit Umfridi filii Marie quod Ricardus Pevrel meus avonculus tenet de me feodaliter, tenendam et habendam dicto luminari in puram et perpetuam elemosinam sine reclamatione mei et heredum meorum de cetero. Ita quod dicte moniales poterunt facere feodaliter plenariam iustitiam in dicto porprisagio pro dicto frumento. Et de hoc atornavi dictum Ricardum feodifirmarium et ego et heredes mei dictis moialibus (*sic*) successive dictam elemosinam contra omnes homines garantizare integre tenemur. Quod ut ratum et stabile teneatur imperpetuum presens scriptum sigilli mei testimonio roboravi. Actum anno domini MCCXX nono mense Augusti.

26 *Charter of Richard of Creully granting to the convent of Holy Trinity, Caen, three virgates of land in Mathieu, with its annual rent of two sesters and a half of a quarter of wheat, one hen and fifteen eggs.* [8 October 1221]

Caen, Archives du Calvados, H, Trinité de Caen, *Cartulaire de l'Abbaye Sainte Trinité de Caen*, 69–71, no. 14. [126, no. 58, summary].

Universi (*sic*) Christi fidelibus ad quos presens scriptum pervenerit, Ricardus de Croleio filius Ricardi filii comitis salutem in domino. Noveritis universi me pro salute Willelmi fratris mei et mea et antecessorum nostrorum concessisse et dedisse ecclesie Sancte Trinitatis de Cadomo tres virgatas terre in territorio Maton[ii] iuxta viam de Buevilla quas Willelmus Fere tenebat de me feodaliter et hereditarie reddendo inde michi per annum de se et heredibus suis duos sext[arios] et dimidium quarterium frumenti ad mensuram Maton[ii] et unam gallinam ad Natale et quindecim ova ad Pascha. Quemobrem (*sic*) volo et percipio quatinus ecclesia Sancte Trinitatis abbatissa et conventus habeant et teneant predictas tres virgatas terre libere pacifice et quiete et integre in pura (*sic*) et perpetuam elemosinam, salvo iure et feodo Willelmi Fere et heredum suorum quod habebant in dicta terra de me ita quod reddant annuatim predicte ecclesie Sancte Trinitatis abbatisse et conventui dictos redditus de se et heredibus suis. Et si forte in alicuius defecerint licebit dicte abbatisse et conventui facere iusticiam suam in terra nominata. Ut autem predicta concessio et donatio mea teneat semper stabilis et firma eam mea presenti carta et sigillo meo confirmavi. Actum hoc anno incarnationis dominice M°CC°XX° primo mense Octobris in festo martyrum Sergi et Bachi.

27 *Charter of Georgia, widow, granting an annual rent of 10s. for the maintenance of a lamp at the altar of St. Lawrence in the abbey of Holy Trinity, Caen.* [August 1222]

Caen, Archives du Calvados, H, Trinité de Caen, *Cartulaire de l'Abbaye Sainte Trinité de Caen*, 93–6, no. 27. [131, no. 68, summary].

Universi (*sic*) Christi fidelibus ad quos presens scriptum pervenerit Georgia filia Henrici de Columbiers et quondam Hugonis de Longo Campo uxor, salutem in domino. Sciatis universi quod ego pro salute mea et patris mei et omnium antecessorum meorum, pro salute etiam domini Hugonis mariti mei et heredum nostrorum et omnium amicorum nostrorum concessi et dedi ecclesie et conventui Sancte Trinitatis de Cadomo redditum decem solid[orum] turon[iensium], ad tenendum lampadem unam ante altare Sancti Laurencii qua semper ard[e]at continue per diem et noctem, habendum et tenendum eis libere pacifice et quiete, in perpetuam et puram elemosina (*sic*) ab omni redditu et servitio et omni consuetudine et seculari, videndum [et] recipiendum per manus filiorum Rogeri Ridel presbyteri de Columbiers et heredum fratrum predictorum. Ita quidem quod si predictis (*sic*) fratres et heredes sui predictum redditum deferent usque Cadomum ad altare Sancti Laurencii per singulos annos in festo Sancti Laurencii, ita si quidem quod de abbatia dabitur ei qui predictum debitum profereret conpetens liberatio ad diem transigendum. Si autem predicti fratres aut heredi (*sic*) sui defecerunt (*sic*) de predicto redditu reddendo abbatia Sancte Trinitatis poterit facere iusticiam et distrintionem suam in anglea terre quam ego emi de Jacobo de Alneto, et quam predicti fratres de me tenent hereditarie. Terra sita est in[ter] terram Ranulfi Ridel [ex una parte] et terram Radulfi Pioc ex altera. Hanc autem elemosinam ego et heredes mei tenemur garantizare predictis ecclesie et conventui et si forte non possemus garantizare, nos tenemur ad faciendum eis competens excambium in propria hereditate nostra. Actum est hoc in viduitate mea M°CC° vicesimo secundo mense Augusti. Ut autem predicta donatio mea perpetuam optineat, firmitatem eam mea presenti carta et sigillo meo confirmavi.

GLOSSARY

accipiter	hawk, falcon
aiel for *avus*	grandfather
allecta	herring
alosa	shad, herring
aloers	allodial tenants
ambros	amber (salt measure)
annico	annual rent (from demesne)
annona	grain
annus	yearling
aries	ram
arpennum	vineyard measure
auqua for *auca, auga*	goose
berbix	wether
bidens	ewe
brasciator, brasarius	brewer
brenagium for *bernagium*	contribution to duke's hunting dogs
Brito, Le Bret	Breton
bruerium	heath, wasteland
bucularius	buckler
caducum	escheat (*ex caduco*, without an heir)
campartum, campardum	champart, sharecropping rent
canabis	hemp
carigata	cartload
*carwa**	flax
caternum, catenum	chain (for books), see also *quatenum*
cervus	stag, deer
cobla	fishing net
coisnebelius	son-in-law(?)
contharium	gift(?), from *congiarium* or *contiamium*
coopertura	roof, covering
cortillum	enclosure, curtilage
de reliquo	henceforth
dica	tally
dilacero	destroy

dinoscio	recognise, acknowledge
for *dignoscio*	
disraino	deraign, establish title
ebur	ivory
facticius	baked
fava	bean
folart, fullo	fuller
follus	crazy
fovea	ditch (fish-trap)
fraxinum	ash tree
*frusta, frustrum**	piece of land (of recent cultivation, assart)
fumagium	manure payment
garba, garbagium	tithe
*gravatoria**	jeopardy
grudum	coarse grain
*helmus**	shed
horreum	barn
hostiarius	usher
huellum	hoe
induciis for *indutiis*	stay in proceedings
latrocinium	theft
leignagium, lignagium	timber rights
linum	cloth
linosium	linen
lis	decision (legal)
mediator	sharecropper
mercennarius	hireling
merle	nasty (ironical)
meschinus	young
molta	milling dues, multure
oblicta	grain rent
occupo	conduct a trade
orreum	barn
for *horreum*	
*panerna**	ham, bacon
panifex	baker
parentela	family, kin
parmentarius	tailor
pelliparius	skinner
peschenerius	weaver (?)
pigache	pointed-toe (?)
pitor, pistor	baker

placenta	bread-bun
plaga	country, region
ponter	bridge-keeper, bridge-wright
porpriso	purpresture
porterius	carter
portitor	messenger
postes	wooden posts
preces, precarias	boonworks
preco, precor	crier
presto	retted flax
pulagium	fowl rent
puteus	pit, well (*putei factor*, well-digger)
puteo effundre	casting-pit (?)
quatenum, quaterna	booklet, quire
questio	dispute
recognitio	recognizance, inquest
reperta, repentur	lost or abandoned property, shipwreck
rete	fishery
sabelina	sable fur
saignare	bleed (oxen)
salsa	salt
scaeta for *escaeta*	escheat
sellarius	saddler
sera	lock
summa	load (salt), total (rents)
summagium	carriage service
trabes	timber beams, measure of grain (thrave)
tutrix	guardian, warden
vadimonium	mortgage, security, pledge
varium, vairum	miniver
verece	shipwreck
vinagium	carting of wine
virga, virgata	virgate, quarter-acre
virgutum for *virgultum*	copse, wood
Wasconicus	Gascon

* Holy Trinity context cited in Du Cange, *Glossarium mediae et infimae latinitatis* (new edition ed. L. Favre, 10 vols, Paris, 1883–7).

Addenda and *Corrigenda*

in
Charters and Custumals of the Abbey of Holy Trinity, Caen
edited by Marjorie Chibnall

p. xxxvii l.33 *for* 1224–5 *read* 1223–4

p. xxxviii l.12 *for* 1223–4 *read* 1222–3

p. xxxviii l.13 *for* 1224–5 *read* 1223–4

p. xxxviii n.2 l.1 *for* 1161 *read* 1261

p. xliii n.3 l.1 *for* 1224–5 *read* 1223–4

p. 1 Charter 1, date, *for* 1155×1162 *read* 1155–1158; *and after* Pd. *add* Delisle/Berger I, no. xlv;

p. 1 Charter 2, heading, *after* Pd. *add* Delisle/Berger I, no. xlv note;

p. 105 l.5 *after* Introduction pp. *add* xxxviii-xxxix

Index, p. 154, *under* Spilman *add* Adam

Index of Persons and Places

The principal place names in the Surveys are indicated by capitals and their pages in bold.

Acard, of Luc-sur-Mer, 77
  de Lunda, 79
Acelina, daughter of Acard, 100
Acho *de Humma*, 85
Adam, Anglicus, 96
  crier, 55, 67
  de Quareus, 105
  son of Odo, 61, 63, 69
  son of Roger, 22, 26, 62, 64, 65, 67, 68, 69, 70
Adelaide, of Escanneville, 84
  of Ouistreham, 27, 125
  daughter of Thurstan Haldup, 4, 7, 8, 125 n.
Adèle (*Adeloia*), 86
Adeliz, abbess of Holy Trinity Caen, 29, 35
  abbess of Winchester, 117
  wife of Robert of Calix, 122
Adelold, chamberlain of the bishop of Bayeux, 126, 127
Adeville (Manche), 8 n.
Aelard (*Aelardus, Alardus*), Nepos, 48, 62, 66, 69
  son of Dere, 67
Aelwin (*Aelevinus, Aelevrai*), 64, 70
Agnes, of Ryes, 89
Alan, of Putot-en-Bessin, 112
Albereda, Croclee, 97
  Gallica, 88
  La Rossel, 97
  of Maizet, 132
  daughter of Fulk, 8 n.
  daughter of Oismelin, 86, 87
  wife of Alfred, 65
  wife of Durand, 88
Alberic, nephew of Wiger of St. Mère-Eglise, 120
  son of Mot, 125
Alexander, of Froide Rue, Caen, 131
  of La Valette, 109
Alfred (*Alveredus*), bordar, 76
  fuller, 70
  de Ludreio, 127
  de Scarda, 102

son of Guy, 65
son of Wimond, 64, 70
Alice (*Aelais*) Lubias, 67
Alicia, abbess of Holy Trinity Caen, 3, 29, 35, 132
  abbess of Winchester (?), 117
Amaury (*Amauricus*), of Crouay, 133
AMBLIE (Calvados), 3, 4, 15, 17, 18, 21, 25, **59**, **107–8**
  carting of grain to, by tenants of Villons-les-Buissons, 105–6
  grain measure of, 34, 108
  seneschal of, 44
  tithes of vavassors, 119
Amelina, 73
Amisus, son of Ilbert of Exmes, 117
Andrew, 90
Anffred, 121
Anfrid, cobbler, 67
Anfrida, of La Valette, 109
  daughter of Adam, 88
Angerville (Calvados), 72
Anquetil (*Anschetillus, Ansquitillus, Hanquitillus, Hansquitillus*), 130
  clerk, 37
  of Cambes-en-Plaine, 55
  de Monasterio, 67
  son of Stephen, 84, 85, 86
Ansell', *de Mortune*, 79 n.
Ansgar, 17, 93
Ardenne, Premonstratensian abbey, 29, 35, 40
Argences (Calvados), 7, 10 n., 37, 112, 115, 116, 126
Argentan (Orne), 130
Arnold (*Ernoldus*), de Fonte, 84
Arthur, priest, brother of William, 113, 129
  porter, 120
  serviens, 131
  son of Hermenfred, 119, 124
Ascelin, son of Odo, 67, 68
Ascelina, daughter of Cobla, 106
  daughter of Seyrie, 64, 70
ASNIERES-EN-BESSIN (Calvados), 11, 13, **56**, 127

Attard Acelin, 110
AUBERVILLE-SUR-MER (Calvados), 3, 7, 11, 13, 22, 24, 25, 26, 30, **89–92**, 126, 127
Aubevoye (Eure), 7, 126
Aubin, of Vire, 112, 114
Audulf, 114
Avening (Gloucestershire), 15 n., 76 n.
Avernes-Saint-Gourgon (Orne), 126
Avice (*Avicia*), 93

Baldric, *peregrinus*, 66
of Carpiquet, 61, 62
Baldwin, de Toene, 37
son (unnamed) of, 114
Barbières (Calvados), road of, 118
Barfleur (Manche), 9, 11 n.
Barges (Orne), 4, 6 n., 30, 40, 41, 117
Bartholomew Droc, 133
BAVENT (Calvados), 3, 6, 15, 16, 17, 19, 20, 21, 22, 25, 26, **58, 92–4**
field name, Campum de Mara, 92
Bayeux (Calvados), 6, 9, 13
assize, 79
bishops, see Henry, Odo, Philip, Richard, Robert
mint of, 33
Beatrice, of La Pommeraye, 132
BEAUVOIR (Calvados), 3, 19, 20, 31, 74, 86, **87–9**
Bec, prior of, 119
Benedict, chaplain, 123
of Loches, 113
Bénouville (Calvados), 4, 23
Bény-sur-Mer (Calvados), 34, 38, 44
field name: Gardign', 38, 45
grain measure of, 34, 44
Bernard, 116, 117, 121
clerk, 123
Petite Boche, 64, 70
of Calix, 120–1
de Gardineio, 36
Bertran, of La Valette, 109
of Verdun, 112
Beuville (Calvados), 46, 127
road of, 135
Billeheut, of Bavent, 17, 93
of Ranville, 102
of Vernon, 127
Bitot (Calvados), 72
Blainville (Calvados), 23
Blay (Calvados), 8, 20, 23
BONNEMAISON (Calvados), 53, **57**, 74
Boso, the Breton, 90
of Ouistreham, 3, 121–2
de Fossa, 90, 91

de Monasterio, 90, 91
son of Wimarc, 90
Botart, fee of, 84, 86
BOUGY (Calvados), 3, 15, 19, 25, 26, 34, 49, **59, 89**, 105
grain measure of, 34, 49
Bourg-l'Abbé, 10
Bourg-l'Abbesse, 10, 29, 35
Bourg-le-Roi, 10
Brienz, vavassoriate of, 48
Bures-sur-Dives (Calvados), 6
Burton Abbey, surveys, 12

CAEN (Calvados), arable and meadow in, 4, 6, 9; urban development, 9–10, *see also* Calix, Bourg-le-Roi, Bourg-l'Abbé, Bourg-l'Abbesse; *bailli* of, 47; provostship of, 10; fair of, on octave of Pentecost, 21; foire du pré (October), 94, 100, 101, 105, 106, 114, 131; fishing rights in, 123; castle, 7, 10, 113, 116; dwellings, houses, messuages, 3, 35, 49, 123, 128, 131; mill, 3, 9, 131–2; grain measure of, 34, 104
abbey of Holy Trinity, abbess of, xii, 30, *and see* Adeliz, Alicia, Beatrice de Hugueville, Cecilia, Dametta, Isabella de Crèvecoeur, Johanna, Juliana de Saint-Sernin, Matilda
cartularies of, 1, 2, 10, 27, 28, 32, 133ff
nuns of, 4, 6, 8, 10, 21, 49
altars, of St. Lawrence, 51, 134, 135, 136; of St. Mary, 51–2, 133–4
abbey of St. Stephen, 11 n., 60, 100, 105
collegiate church of the Holy Sepulchre, 41, 46, 47, 133
parish church, of St. George, 7; St. Giles, 6, 23, 39; St. Martin, 7, 21; St. Stephen the Elder, 7, 21
place names, Calix, Froide Rue, Gémare, Vaucelles, Vaugueux
Cairon (Calvados), 20, 23
road of, 103, 117, 118
Calix, in Caen, 3, 6 n., 7, 9, 10, 13, 113, 115, 116, 117, 119, 122, 129
abbess's men at, 120–1, *see* Bernard, Gilbert and Godfrey of Calix
Cambes-en-Plaine (Calvados), 23, 103
Campion Hamel, unidentified, 107
CARPIQUET (Calvados), 3, 4, 7, 15, 18, 20, 21, 22, 24, 25, 26, 34, **54–5, 61–70**, 72, 82, 85, 88, 104, 110, 111
field and place names, Buissinis Abbatisse, 67; Campania, 48, 69; Costillu', 65; Cultura Borgagii, 69; Cultura de

Busmanet, 68; Cultura de Sachet, 66; Hovellenc, 68; Martelet, 48; Pars Fornilli, 65; Puteo Effundre, 4 n., 68; Vinea, 68
advowson of church, 3, 30, 47–8, 65, 129–31
Cauville (Calvados), 4
Cecilia, abbess of Holy Trinity Caen, 3, 8, 9, 14, 119, 121, 122, 123, 131
Cerisy Abbey, 50, 51
Cesny-aux-Vignes (Calvados), 126
Channel Islands, 2, 28, 32, *see also* Jersey and Guernsey
Chauffour (Orne), 4, 6 n., 116
Chouain (Calvados), 7
Christian, 83, 86
Colevile (Calvados), near Grainville-sur-Odon, 82
COLLEVILLE-SUR-ORNE (Calvados), 3, 23, 27, **54**, 113, 114, 121–2
Colombelles (Calvados), 11, 13, 21, 126
Constantine, of Beauvoir, 88
de Insula, 115
Cornières (Calvados), 4, 6
Corsard, 117
Cotentin, 2, 4, 8, 9, 10, 11, 32, 121
Courcy (Calvados), 126, 127
Cuverville (Calvados), 4

Dametta, abbess of Holy Trinity Caen, 3, 14, 29, 35, 36, 61, 76, 94, 122
David, Picot, 106
chaplain, 31, 38
Démouville (Calvados), 4
Diera, *La Cuierdasne*, 97 *see* Richard Cuirdasne
Dinan, of Cairon, 113
Divenses, tenant(s) of Ouistreham, 114
Dives, river, 13, 68
Dives-sur-Mer (Calvados), 6
Divette (Calvados), 19
Doone, Bardulf, 112
Doumesnil (Calvados), 10, 128
Ducy-Sainte-Marguerite (Calvados), 7, 127
Durand, 36
Boisard, 122
the Gascon, 83, 85
Le Gorge, 77
Lenerio, 115
son of Boso, 83, 84, 85
son of Rainbolt, 83, 85, 86
son of Richard, 85, 86
son of Warin, 85

Ecouché (Orne), 6, 21
Elias (*Helias, Helyas*), de Kemino, 24, 80
of La Roche, 97

Elvaston (Derbyshire), 36, 37
Emma, wife of Roger of Tassilly, 97
Engelier, *uxor*, 114
Engelram (*Engerannus, Enguerannus, Enguerram, Hengerrandus, Ingelrannus*), 82, 127
Patric, 112
of Grainville, 81
of Villers, 79 n.
England, 2, 6, 9, 12, 21, 22, 27, 29, 32, 33
ENGLESQUEVILLE-LA-PERCEE (Calvados), 11, 13, 21, **60**, 105, 126
Erenborg, daughter of John, 101
Erengot, miller, 131, 132
Ernulf, 84
ESCANNEVILLE (Calvados), 3, 4, 6 n., 15, 19, 20, 21, 22, 25, 30, 31, 34, **58**, 69, **82–6**, 87, 88, 89, 111, 126, 130
dispute over tithes, 48–9
Étard, 114
Eterville (Calvados), 4
Eudo, smith, 64
of Graye-sur-Mer, 56
de Fontanis, 37
de Morevilla, 108
son of Jocelin, 76
son of Thurstan, 126, 129
Eure, *département*, 6, 11
Evan (*Evainnus*), 128
Evesham Abbey, surveys, 22 n.
Evreux (Eure), 98
wood of, belonging to count of Evreux, 93
Ewald, of Saulques, 70
Eward (*Evardus*), Anglicus, 67
Exmes (Orne), 4, 7

Fagelina, 81
Falaise (Calvados), 3, 4,
churches of, 21, 30, 41, 47, 132
exchequer court at, 47, 132
Falco, 64, 70
Farsit, 118
Fawel, 64, 67, 70
Felsted (Essex), 21, 22, 27, 117
Feugeurolles-sur-Orne (Calvados), 4
Flori, 90, 91
Foulbec (Eure), 4, 11, 13
Froger, bishop of Sées, 29, 30, 35, 36
of Bracqueville, 38
Froide Rue, Caen, 131
Fromund, priest, at Ouistreham, 125
Fulbert (*Fubertus*), of Secqueville-en-Bessin, 122
Fulk (*Fulco*), chamberlain, 119
cook 109

vavassor, of Graye-sur-Mer, 56
Paenel, 133
of Asnières-en-Bessin, 127
of Aunay, 133
of Cambes-en-Plaine, 55
of Canteloup, 133
of Montbouin, 95
of Ouistreham, 114
Fulchered Oger, 35
Fulchod, 116
    queen's chamberlain, 10
Fulchout, 86

Gacé (Orne), 6, 11, 126
Gamul, 9
Gauchier, Le Bort, 96
Gémare, Caen, 131–2
Geoffrey (*Gaufridus, Galfridus*), brewer,
    120
chaplain, 119
monk, 50
Duredent, 112, 129
Faciens Nichil, 110
Fiquet, 112
Goiz, 110
Huelin, 63, 69
Leflac, 95
Mosteil, 110
Rossel, 133
Salomon, 20, 56 n.
Torgis, 110
of Beuville, 113
of Caumont, 124
of Cinglais, vavassoriate of, 48
of Ouistreham, 114
of Repton, 131
de Bosco, 79 n.
de Cortun', *magister*, 133
de Haia, 131
son of Aupais, 73
son of Goie, 67
son of Reginald, 123
son of Wimarc, 90
Georgia, daughter of Henry of Columbiers,
    widow of Hugh of Longchamp, 136
Gerald (*Geraldus, Geroldus, Geroudus,
    Giraldus, Giroldus*), marshall, 120
of Arry, 133
of Les Planches, 107
of Saulques, 71
de Castello, 116
Gerard, of Saulques, 71
Gerelmus, of Ouistreham, 113
Germain (*Germanus*), Florie, 73
Le Clos, 72
Morin, 73

Gersenda, mother of Robert son of
    Ernesius, 120
Gervase, of Coleville, 82
of Escanneville, 85, 97
GIBERVILLE (Calvados), 8, 23, **59**
Gilbert (*Gislebertus*), Caperun, 96
Crispin, 125 n.
firmarius, 63
Le Merle, 94
Pirus, 75
of Argences, 116
of Calix, 120–1, 123
of Chauffour, 116
of Cinglais, 95
of Gournay, 95
of Le Homme. 85
of Sassy, 95
de Aquila, 120
de Foro, 113
de Gorlaio, 95
de Tileriis, 130
son of Godfrey, 88
son of Humphrey, 117
son of Ralph, *firmarius*, 61, 62, 63, 69
Gisla, daughter of Thurstan, 8 n.
Gisleta, 106
Godard, of Sallen, 77
Ferlart, (fuller?), 110
Godfrey (*Godefridus*), abbot of Saint-Sever,
    112
Iuvenis, 9, 116
Lesware, 71
Parvus, 68
of Calix, 116, 117, 121, 123
of Hérouville, 116
of Lion-sur-Mer, 104, 105
of Ouistreham, and mother (unnamed) of,
    125
of Pitot, 71
of St. Aubin d'Arquenay, 114
of Tourlaville, 3, 131
son of Aubrey, 116
son of Aupais, 73
son of Herbert, 124
son of Ralph, 70
son of Robert, 120
Godwin (*Godoinus*), palmer, 61, 64, 69
Goislen, chamberlain, 124
of Ranville, 100
Gondwin (*Gondoinus, Gunduinus*), Brunus,
    106
of Ouistreham, 114
GONNEVILLE (Calvados), 3, 19, 20, 31,
    83, 86, **87**, 88
GRAINVILLE-SUR-ODON (Calvados), 3,
    15, 17, 21, 22, 24, 25, 26, 30, 47, **56–7**,
    79–82, 91, 107, 108, 131
field and place names, Aguillinis, 81;

Belveer, 81; Busco Torq'tel, 81; Campania, 82;.Cortereie, 81, 82; Coutura, 81, 82; Couvert, 81; Duas Culturas, 82; Glaucam Terram, 82; Holegate, 82; Londam, 82; Longam Ream, 82; Magnum Rivum, 81; Petram Mond'r, 82; Pontem Ogeri, 81; Sallebec, 81; Septem Virgas, 82; Tasnerias, 81; Vicos, 82
Grandcamps-les-Bains (Calvados), 11, 12, 13, 127
GRAYE-SUR-MER (Calvados), 3, 15, 16, 20, 21, 24, 25, **56**, **109–11**, 127
field name, La Valette, 109
Great Baddow (Essex), 9
Grente, of Ouistreham, 114
GRENTHEVILLE (Calvados), **60**, 105, 113
Grip, 125
Guare, 123
Gudeman, 102
Guernsey ? (*Guernereio*), 107
Guibray, 4
Guimar, the Breton, 35
Guy (*Wido, Guido*), of Le Manoir, 46
of Saint-Valéry-en-Caux, 62
son of William, 63

H', scribe, 79 n.
Hacol, son of John of Soligny, 38, 44
Haeis, of Escanneville, 84
Hamelin, smith, 107
Corteis, 104, 105
of Orival, 108
of Ouistreham, 114
son of Godfrey, 106
son of Richard, 106
Hamo, butler (*pincerna*), 112, 129, 130
son of Robert *del Maisnil Ursin*, 120
Hardoin, 63
Harvey (*Herveus*), clerk, 106
of Graye-sur-Mer, 16, 56
Hawisa, of Bavent, 17, 93
daughter of Turold Papillon, 119
widow of Robert Marmion, 2, 119
Heldebert, 56
Helto, steward, 20, 56
Helvida, de Sancto Paulo, nun of Holy Trinity Caen, 54, 117
Hénouville (Seine-Maritime), 11, 126
Henry, I, king, 27, 119
II, king, 15, 29, 35, 130
count, 11, 123, 127
bishop of Bayeux, 112
abbot of Fécamp, 112
Graverenc, 110

Lovet, 129
Lupellus, 85, 113
Taillebois, 79 n.
of Saint Denis, 133
of Sainte-Croix-sur-Mer, 111
of Tilly, 112, 128
de Agneaus, 79 n.
de Novo Burgo, count of Auge, 112
son of the priest, 90
son of Ralph, 37
son of William, 122
Herbert, of Les Andelys, canon of Rouen, 50
Anglicus, 96
Perchardus, 102
of Arry, 89
of Bourgeauville, 22, 89, 92
of Escanneville, 84
of Le Hamel, 71
of Vienne-en-Bessin, 76
de Fossa, 90
son of Bernard, 112
son of Dodeman, 119
son of Odo, 93
son of Robert Walter, 83, 85, 87
nephew of Godfrey, 119
Herfast, of Graye-sur-Mer, 56
Herluin, *de Fonteneio*, 120
Herneis, priest, 36
Herold, king's porter, 117
Hérouville (Calvados), 4
Heuta, daughter of Morin, 110
Honoratus, of Sallen, 77
Honorius III, pope, 50
Horosius, house of, 38, 44
Horstead (Norfolk), 15 n.
Hubert, *de Bosco*, 78
Huelina, bordar, of Vaux-sur-Seulles, 76
Hugh, 117
bishop of Coutances, 133
bishop of Lisieux, 4
chaplain, 119
baker, 41–2
mason, 84, 86
miller, wife (unnamed) of, 97
pauper, wife (unnamed) of, 86
reeve (*prepositus*), 100, 101, 102,
Ansgot, 101
Bordel, 123
the Breton, 94, 115, 124
Buschard, 112
Follus, 80
Le Merle, 95
Monacus, 91
Normant, 95
Pagan, 128
Pasturel, 35
Rosel, 40

of Boulon, 88
of Chauffour, 117
of Gruchy, 17, 93
of La Motte, 67
of Le Breuil, 71
of Livet, 112
of Longuevalle, 102
of Ouistreham, 113, 114
of Reviers, 127
of Vercreuil, 77
of Vire, 71
de Bosco, 73
de Bougneio, 133
de Voire, 79
son of Aubrey, 11
son of Gilbert of Chauffour, 116, 117
son of Roger de Mota, 68
son of Warin, 90
son of Wimarc, 90, 91
brother of Osbern of Billy, 116
Humphrey (*Hunfridus, Umfridus,*
    Unfridus), of Adeville, 8
chaplain of bishop of Bayeux, 35
Farsit, 118
Rufus, 65
of Adeville, 8 n.
of Ouistreham, 114, 124
son of Ansgar, 109
son of Gilbert, 84, 86
son of Mary, 51, 52, 134, 135

Inge', wife of Gerald de Castello, daughter
    of Godfrey Iuvenis, 116
Ingouville (Seine-Maritime), 4
Isabella, of Crèvecoeur-en-Auge, abbess of
    Holy Trinity Caen, 115
Ivo, Taillebois, 132
of Amblie, 107
of Ouistreham, 30, 47

James (*Jacobus*), de Alneto, 136
Jersey, 3, 4, 6, 13, 21, 43, 121,
Jocelin (*Gocelinus, Goscelinus*), of
    Ouistreham, 125
of Sallen, 78
de Monasterio, 90, 91
Johanna, abbess of Holy Trinity Caen, 1,
    3, 31, 36, 37, 38, 43, 44, 45, 46, 50, 112,
    128, 131
John, bishop of Evreux, 4
of Eraines, archdeacon of Sées, 130
chaplain, 36, 123
baker, 41–2
brewer, 62, 63, 64, 69

the Breton, 113, 129
Fortis, 102
Goiel, 79 n.
Grossus, 83, 86
Pigace, 130–1
Salmon, 101
of Ouistreham, 113
of Soligny, 37–8, 44, 112
de Grantia, 113
de Hais, 90
de Monte, 101
son of Gerald, 101
son of Godfrey the cook, 123
son of Lucy, 113
son of Norman, 65
son of Ralph, 100
son of Waudri, 62
son of William, 115
Jon, baker, 68
Jordan, bishop of Lisieux, 133
priest of Bavent, 17, 93
dyer, 90
of Grendon, 37
of Trois Monts, 38
de Landa, 112, 129, 130
Julian, Wagel, 110
Wiger, 110
son of Basil, 110
Juliana de Saint-Sernin, abbess of Holy
    Trinity Caen, 13, 29, 31, 45
Jurques (Calvados), 119, 120
JUVIGNY-SUR-SEULLES (Calvados), 3,
    15, 16, 21, 25, 26, 30, 53, **57–8**, **74–5**
field-name, Campania, 16, 75
grain measure of, 34, 75

La Bigne (Calvados), 72
La Boite (Calvados), 120
La Bouette (Calvados), 120
LA FONTENELLE (Calvados), 53, **57**
La Motte, Carpiquet, 61 n.
LA ROUELLE (Calvados), 3, 25, 26, 70,
    72–4, 78
Le Foc (Manche), 21
Le Homme, *see* Sainte-Mère-Eglise
Le Parquet (Calvados), 119, 120
Le Puits (Calvados), 57
Lesceline (*Lescelina*), of Grainville-sur-
    Odon, 81
Les Moutiers-en-Auge (Calvados), 21 n.
Les Moutiers-en-Cinglais (Calvados), 21 n.,
    75 n., 90 n.
Les Moutiers-Hubert (Calvados), 21 n.
Lessay Abbey, 4
Léry (Eure), 7
London, England, 31

Longeau (Calvados), 57
Longues-sur-Mer Abbey, 51
Lucas, *magister*, clerk of Vaux-sur-Seulles, 50
Lucius III, pope, 28, 39

Mainard, son of Vitalis, 104, 105, 106
  Maisnile Urselli, 7
Malfilâtre, family, 43–4
MALON (Calvados), 15, 53, **55**
Malored, of Ouistreham, 125
Manasses, son of Robert Marmion and
  Hawisa, 119, 120
Manche, *département*, 6, 21
Mantes (Eure), 7
Margaret, bordar, 76
  grand-daughter of John of Soligny, 38, 44
Maria, of Le Londel, 97
Martel, nephew of Ranulf, 93
Martin *magister*, of Grainville, 81, 131
  Fouchier, 115
  of Bavent, 93
  of Ouistreham, 114
  de Hosa, 113
Mathieu (Calvados), grain measure of, 34,
  51, 52, 134, 135
  grants of annual rents, 51–2, 133–5
Matilda, empress, 112
Matilda, wife of William I, 4, 6, 7, 8, 9, 96, 130
  abbess of Holy Trinity Caen, 7, 8, 9, 14,
  115, 116, 117, 121
  daughter of Thomas Bardulf, 36–7
Matthew, son of Muriel, 105
  de Scherie, 123
Mauger, 121
  Ferun, 113
  of Rosel, 45, 121
Maurice, 119
Maurilius, archbishop of Rouen, 4
Melida, *de Gaveluiz*, 80
Merville (Calvados), 48, 85
Michael, son of Warin, 113
Milet, gate of, 50
Milo, of Lévis, 133
Minchinhampton (Gloucestershire), 21
Missy (Calvados), 82
Mondrainville (Calvados), 82
MONTBOUIN (Calvados), 3, 10, 11, 14, 15,
  19, 20, 23, 24, 25, 34, **59**, 61, 76,
  94–6, 105, 126, 128
  grain measure of, 34, 94
Montpied (Calvados), Saulques, 72
Mortefemme (Manche), 2, 8, 120
Mue, river, 105 n.

Nicholas, clerk, of Ableville, 79 n.
  clerk, 30, 35–6

Pigace, 130
  of Anisy, 79 n.
  of Vesqueville, 36
Nigel, of Ouistreham, 122
  d'Oilly, 126
  son of Geoffrey, of Ouistreham, 124
Norman, son of Denis, 83, 86
  son (unnamed) of, 70

Odo, bishop of Bayeux, 4, 39,
  count, 65, 68
  chamberlain of Count Henry, 123
  Brun, of Froide Rue, 123, 131
  of Grainville-sur-Odon, 80
  of Hérouville, 118
  of Ouistreham, 114, 125
  de Selles, 116, 120
  son of Avice, 76
  son of Gerald, 68, 69
  son of Ralph, 108
  son of Roche, 85
  son of Thurstan Haldup, 7
  brother of Durand Boisard, 124
  brother of Reginald, son of Anquetil of
  Hérouville, 124
Oger, son of Ingulf, 84
Oielor, of Escanneville, 84
Oismelin (*Huismelinus*), of Ouistreham,
  114
Orderic Vitalis, 22 n., 91 n.
Orne, river, 7, 10, 100, 123
Osanna, of Ouistreham, 102
  of Ranville, 114
Osbern, of Billy, 116
Osbert, chaplain, 37, 130
  priest, 113
  smith, 131
  Anglicus, 109
  Bordon, 67
  Gilbert, baker, 55
  of Ouistreham, 114
  son of Ralph, 61, 63, 69
Osmund, Norman, 64, 70
  the Wise, 108
  of Canville-la-Rocque, 13, 121
  of Carpiquet, 62
  of Longuevalle, 102
  of Ouistreham, 114, 125
  of Verson, 120
  brother of Roger of Sallen, 118
Osulf Heriz, 101
Otoer de Grantia, 123
OUISTREHAM (Calvados), 2, 3, 7, 10, 11,
  21, 27, 30, 31, 47, 48, **53**, 122
  rentals, 113–14, 124–5
  fish-market and shipwreck rights, 115

market and tolls, 123

Parent, 100
Paris, clerk, 37, 112
Périers-sur-le-Dan, tithes of, 23
Peter, of Thillai, *bailli*, 42, 133
   abbot of St. Stephen's Caen, 112
   Ruaud, knight, 42
   of Argentan, 130
   of Loucelles, *magister*, 79 n.
   of Ouistreham, 113, 124
   son of Nigel 118
Philip, de Harcourt, bishop of Bayeux, 35
   Le Bret, procurator (1632), 31
   Suhard, 112
   of Creully, 112
Philippa, of Rosel, 39, 40, 45
Pichot, 68
Pinbury (Gloucestershire), 21
Pinel, of Brieux, 119

Quatrepuits (Calvados), 126
Quettehou (Manche), 9 n., 11 n., 21, 127

Rabellus, 121
Rainer the Mad (*Insanus*), son (unnamed) of, 125
Ralph (*Radulfus*), Taisson, seneschal of Normandy, 40, 112, 128, 130
   vicomte, 112
   of Bayeux, 62
   abbot, 113
   chaplain of Airi, 123–4
   chaplain, 35, 36, 123
   scribe, of Caen, 131
   quidam homo, 121
   baker, 83
   bailiff (*pretoris*) of Villons-les-Buissons, 2, 27, 117
   Vitalis, carpenter, 118–19
   reeve, 122
   Bellus Filius, 85, *alias* Pulcher Filius, 84
   Biset, 75
   Blondus, 80
   Bobert, 80, 81
   Bos, 116, 120
   Briquet, 76
   Canu, 96
   Clinchamp, 112
   Docher, 102
   Durand, 70
   Fatuus Infans, 116

Gaisclun, 85
Le Gros, 97
Lepus, 78
Malpoint, 78
Matefelun, 81
Morel, 76
Muriel, 70, 73
Otto, 102
Pantouf, 65
Peilevilain, 78
Pigache, 25, 91
Pioc, 136
Quatre-pieds, 84
Rufus, 106
Tesard, 78
Tope, 88
Ulfier, 122, 123
Viviani, 77
   the Wise, 109
   of Amblie, 119
   of Bavent, 16
   of Brécy, 112
   of Cagny, 35
   of Cairon, 113
   of Cambes-en-Plaine, 15, 16, 109
   of Crèvecoeur-en-Auge, 98
   of Gonneville, 84
   of Foulbec, 124
   of Hérouville, 36
   of La Valette, 109
   of Lisieux, 130
   of Pitot, 71
   of Quettehou, 109
   of Trois Monts, 132
   of Villons-les-Buissons, 118
   de Cortlandun, 128
   de Fonte, 86
   de Hospicio, 113
   de Wallanomonte, 30, 37, 129, 130
   son of Ansered, 118
   son of Bentie, 131
   son of Brienz, 61, 62, 66
   son of Emma, 80
   son of Eudo, 30, 48, 66, 84, 129, 130
   son of Godfrey, 101, 102
   son of Herbert, 110
   son of Humphrey, 106
   son of Ivo, 118
   son of Osbert, 78
   son of Robert, 108
   son of Sello, 110
   son of Vitalis Caisnel, 98
   son of Wantar, 119
   son of Yvel, 83
   brother of William the priest, 89
Ramsey Abbey, surveys, 12
Ranulf (*Ranulfus, Rannulfus, Rainnolfus*), *vicomte* of Bayeux, 7, 8, 9, 12

Meschin, *vicomte* of Bayeux, 127
ad Nummos, 75
the Breton, 107
moneyer, 9 n.
Malart, 81
Manchu[n], 73
Milet, 78
Ridel, 136
Wiger, 109, 110
of Baugy, 118, 119
of Bavent, 16, 17, 92, 93
of Cairon, 118
of La Valette, 109
of Le Breuil, 71
of Luc-sur-Mer, 79
of Presles, 112, 129
of Villons-les-Buissons, 113
de Bosco, 74
de Fresne, 65
de Grandi Valle, 112
son of Anquetil, 72
son of Godfrey *de atrio Sancti Petri* (St.
Pierre-sur-Dives ?), 116
son of Osbert, 78
son of Ulger, 118, 123
brother of Wiger, 128
nephew of Nigel, 113
RANVILLE (Calvados), 3, 14, 15, 18, 20,
24, 25, 26, **58**, 82, 93, **99–103**, 128
field name, Camoret, 102
Reginald (*Reginaldus, Rainaldus, Ranoldus,
Reignaldus, Reignoldus, Reinaldus,
Reinoldus, Renaldus, Renoldus*), de
Ville-Thierry, *bailli*, 133
chaplain, 117
smith, at Carpiquet, 63, 69
smith, at Villons, 106
Durel, 120
Filius, 84
Flori, 76
Landun, 128
of Amblie, 107
of Le Douet, 112
of Hérouville, 118
of Pierrepont, 108, 119
de Marisco, 85, 86
de Puteo [effundre?], 61, 63, 69
de Roqua, 110
son of Anquetil of Hérouville, 123
son of Sup'licia, 101
son of Yvel, 85
son of Rohais, wife (unnamed) of, 65,
70
Regnar, *de Ros*, 67, 68
Reiner, of Evreux, 98
Richard, I, king, 13, 29
fitz Samson, bishop of Bayeux, 44
clerk, 106

Bel Aeil, 63, 69, alias Pulcher Avus, 61
Bevrel, 112, 130
Bonus Homo, 109
Bordon, 50
Buisun, 113
Carbonel, 133
Cuirdasne, 98, *see* Diera *La Cuierdasne*
Fatuus Infans, 118
the Fleming, 107
Hurtelov, 61
John, 107
Marchie, 98, 99
Painel, 124
Osmund, son of Richard, 70
Palmer, 78
Peilleve, 72
Pevrel, 51, 52, 134, 135
Piquet, 84, 85
Rainoard, 87
Rufus, 55, 120
Le Vavasor, 115
of Argences, 112
of Beaufour, 112
of Cairon, 71
of Cambes-en-Plaine, 105
of Cardiff, 37
of Courcy, 11, 126, 127
of Creully, 135
of Graye-sur-Mer, 56, 111, 112–13, 119,
120
of La Motte, 68
of Le Hamel, 71
of Longueval, 100
of Luc-sur-Mer, 118
of Ouistreham, 114, 125
of Rochester, 111
of Roullours, 8
of Tilly-sur-Seulles, 79 n.
of Ussy, 97, 99
of Vauville, 76
of Vernon, 133
de Aula, 120
de Caigel, 79 n
de Floreio, 133
de Fonten', 133
de Ruello, 94
son of Baldwin, 125 n.
son of Ernald, 100
son of Gifard, 112
son of Godfrey, 70
son of Henry, 113, 129
son of Herluin, 11, 19, 59, 126
son of John, 115
son of Pagan, 111
son of Ruald, 63, 64, 69
brother of Gilbert son of Ralph, 69
gener of Grenton, 116
Richer, clerk, 35

Ricilda, daughter of Restold, 116
Ricof, son of Richard, 106
Ro', Michael, 115
Robert, Curthose, 3, 10, 11, 12, 13, 14, 53, 93, 123, 124, 125
   count of Alençon, 133
   count of Meulan, 112
   de Montfort, 124
   de Mowbray, 126
   seneschal of Courseulles-sur-Mer, 38
   of Pierrefitte, castellan of Pommeraye, 133
   fitz Hamo, 7
   des Ablèges, bishop of Bayeux, 49, 133
   archdeacon of Nottingham, 130
   chaplain, 112
   priest of Barges, 117
   priest of Bavent, 93
   priest of Sallen, 77
   cobbler, 67
   doctor, 115
   dyer, 67
Achu[m], 79
Aculeus, 120
Anglicus, 110
Belet,113, 129
Berout, 73
Bertran, 11, 21, 126
Blanchart, 74
Blondo, 129
Braose, 63, 69
the Breton, 36, 72
Brotin, 124
Cardonnel, 90, 91
Caruel, 78
Cervus, 73
Coisnebeli', 96
Corbi', 89
Gervase, 97
Harel, 74
Harvey, 74
Ivo, 75
Lacaille, 131
Larme sa feme, 64, 70
Le Barbe, 83
Le Chevalier, 99
Le Clos, 73
Le Nevo, 37
Loherenc, 97
Loste, 97, 98
Mainard, 104
Marmion, 2, 119, 120
Mauger, 110
Nigra Capa, 109
Pantulf, 126
Popel, 73
Puhel, priest, 79 n.
Rex, 100
Rollant, 91

Sochun, 73
Tirel, 77
Torquetil, 108
Wimunt, 73
of Angerville, 72
of Assy, 95
of Bernay, 130
of Bonnebosq, 126
of Brucourt, 112
of Cairon, 79 n.
of Calix, 3, 122–3
of Colleville-sur-Orne, 114
of Cormolain, 43
of Corsout, 122, 123
of Creully, 79 n.
of Cully, 112, 129
of Gonneville, 83, 86, 87
of Harcourt, 130
of Les Dunes, 84, 86
of Les Loges, 78
of Livet, 112, 129
of Longvillers, 112
of Luc-sur-Mer, 113
of Ouistreham, 113, 114
of Pied Taillis, 71
of Saint-Aubin-d'Arquenay, 84, 114
of Saint-Martin, 79
of Ussy, 97
of Vaux-sur-Seulles, 133
of Villers, 80
de Corsout, 123
de Cortwandun, 74
de Cruis, 133
de Fontaneis, 119
de Fossa, 90, 91
de Freschen', 133
de Genz, 128
de Guz, 128
de Manerio, 112, 129
de Meisnill', 133
de Pontisara, royal bailli, 79 n.
de Uz, 126
de [ ]villa, 133
de Warda, 65, 67, 68, 69, 70
son of Anquetil, 86
son of Ase, 78
son of Baldwin, 124
son of Bernard, 35
son of the Breton, 82
son of Erphast, 122
son of Hamo, 7
son of Herneis, 133
son of John, 74
son of Reginald, 36, 129
son of Restoud, 109
son of Richard, 108
son of Richard de Scrotonia, 112
son of Robert son of Ernesius, 120

son of Roger, 79
son of Sello, 110
brother of Adam son of Roger, 68
Roche, 83
Roger (*Rogerus, Rogerius*), 37, 117
  Mala Corona, dispensator, 123, 124, 126
  constable, 9
  Anglicus, 110
  monacus prior of Bec (?), 119
  buckler, 89, 129 n.
  custodian of fugitives, 107
  vavassor, 99
  Alis, 122, 123
  Alis, sister (unnamed) of, 122
  Auber, 107
  Brundos, 67
  Constan'e, 115
  Folquered, 80
  Herbert, 110
  Le Heir, 72
  Loherenc, 97
  Malesperun, 107
  Nepos, 80
  Pescheneiro', 133
  Poignant, 123
  Restold, 102
  Rex, 73
  Ridel, priest of Columbiers, sons
    (unnamed) of, 136
  Tolem', 94
  of Arry, 37, 112, 129, 130
  of Auberville-sur-Mer, 90
  of Avernes, 126
  of Cambes-en-Plaine, 106
  of Candos, 11, 126
  of Carpiquet, 118
  of Courcelles, 124
  of La Motte, 61, 67, 68
  of Le Hamel, 71
  of Les Dunes, 84, 86
  of Les Moutiers, 55
  of Ouistreham, 114, 125
  of Pitot, 71
  of Saint-Aubin-d'Arquenay, 114
  of Sallen, 118
  de Moeio, 120
  de Monasterio, 75
  de Scutella, 126
  son of Aubrey, 11
  son of Erphast, 122
  son of Landric, 113
  son of Rainfred, 54
  son of Reginald, 106
  son of Yvel, 83
Rohais, wife of Thomas Bardulf, 36,
  37
Rohard, 131
Rosel (Calvados), 8, 39, 40, 45

field names, Campum de Viis Furcatis,
  Campum de Sirecamp', Campum de
  Villeta, Campum de Virgatis, Campum
  de Valle, Campum de Colle, 40, 45
grain measure of, 34, 45
Rouen (Seine-Maritime), 7, 9, 11
  mint of, 33
  currency of, 126
Rouvres (Calvados), 128
Roza, nun of Holy Trinity Caen, 117
Rucqueville (Calvados), 4, 6

Saffred, 92
  Le Chevalier, 94
Saillehache, 85
Saint-Agnan-le-Malherbe (Calvados), 74
SAINT-AUBIN-D'ARQUENAY
  (Calvados), 27, 53, **54**, 84, 113, 114, 117
Sainte-Croix-sur-Mer (Calvados), 15, 56
Saint-Georges-d' Aunay (Calvados) 70, 71,
  72, 119, 120
Saint Giles, church, Caen 6, 23, 39
Saint Lawrence, altar of, at Holy Trinity
  Caen, 51, 134, 135, 136
Saint Martin, church, Caen, 7, 21
Saint Martin, church, Bonnemaison, 57
Saint Mary, altar of, at Holy Trinity Caen,
  51-2, 133-4
Saint Sever, abbot of, 102, 112
Saint Stephen, abbey of, 11 n., 60, 100, 105
Saint Stephen the Elder, church of, Caen, 7,
  21
Saint Vigor, abbey, 51
Sainte-Marie, port of, 114
Sainte-Mère-Eglise (Manche) 2, 9, 10, 120,
  127
SALLEN (Calvados), 2, 3, 4, 6 n., 7, 10, 11,
  13, 23, 25, 26, 30, 34, 72, **77-9**, 118
  grain measure of, 34, 79
  wood of, 128
Salomon, saddler, 131
Samson (*Samson, Sanson*), of Avesneles,
  clerk, 40, 41
  of Ouistreham, 125
  of Sallen, 78
Sanxon, of Cortwald', 74
SAULQUES (Calvados), 3, 25, 31, 36,
  70-2, 73, 82, 111
Savary, son of Cane, 123, 124
Saxony, duke of, 113
Seher de Quincy, constable of Nonancourt,
  130
Sello, of Beauvoir, 88
  of Ouistreham, 115
  de Monasterio, 75
  son of Hubert, 104

son of Humphrey, 105
Sepulchre, collegiate church at Caen, 41, 46, 47, 133
Serlo, 53, 121
  Torel, 122
  son of Goi, 67, 68
Seulles, River, 7, 13
Shaftesbury Abbey, surveys, 12
Silvester, bishop of Sées, 30, 40, 41, 133
Simon (*Simon, Symon*), dyer, 90
  Pevrel, 51, 52, 133, 134, 135
  of Camilly, 123, 124
  of Felsted, 22, 27, 117
  brother of Osmund of Longuevalle, 102
Stephen, king, 12, 22
  Oain, 88
  Rosceli', 95
  of Ouistreham, 114

Tarrant Launceston (Dorset), 21
TASSILLY (Calvados), 3, 10, 11, 13, 28, 31, **96–9**, 126
  presentment of church, 29–30, 35–6, 98
Techa, of Auberville-sur-Mer, 92
Theobald (*Theboldus*), of Saulques, 71
Thiéville (Calvados), 10, 127
Thomas, *firmarius*, 100
  messenger, 113
  Bardulf, 20, 29, 36, 37
  of Auberville, 24, 91
  of Bouttemont, 112, 129
  of Carpiquet, 67
  of Cinglais, 95
  of Evrecy, 49
  son of Roger, 65, 70
Thurstan (*Tustinus, Turstenus, Turstinus*), 121
  Haldup, 4, 7, 8, 125
  priest, 116
  haste vilani, 117
  Malet, 119
  of Juvigny-sur-Seulles, 74
  son of Godfrey *de atrio Sancti Petri* (St Pierre-sur-Dives ?), 116
  son of Osmund, 63, 67, 69
  son of Turold (possibly Turold Papillon), 107
  son of William, 116
  nephew of Osbern of Billy, 116
Tilshead (Wiltshire), 15 n., 53
Tinchebray, battle of, 14, 53
Torald, hosteler (*hostiarius*), 123
Torgis, son of Godfrey, 76
  Boenpain, 115
Turold (*Turoldus, Toroudus*), Papillon, 2, 119
  nephew of Osbern of Billy, 116

Ulric (*Hulricus, Ulricus*), 117
  of Ouistreham, 114
Umberleigh (Devon), 9
Urse, sons (unnamed) of, 89

Varaville (Calvados), 19, 31, 34, 86, 93
Vaucelles (Calvados), 4, 21
Vaugueux, Caen, 10, 123
Vauville (Calvados), 76
VAUX-SUR-SEULLES (Calvados), 3, 4, 6, 14, 15, 18, 19, 23, 25, 30, 42–3, 50–1, **55**, 61, 63, **75–7**, 82, 111, 115, 117
Vernon (Eure), 7, 11, 127
Vienne-en-Bessin (Calvados), 76
Vigolent, of Saint-Aubin-d'Arquenay, 54
VILLONS-LES-BUISSONS (Calvados), 2, 3, 15, 17, 21, 22, 24, 25, 27, 34, 46–7, **59**, 64, **103–7**, 108, 112–3, 117–8
  field and place names, Cultura, 118; Fornas/Furnas, 117, 118; Foseta, 104; Fossa, 103; Fossa Grimete, 104, 117–18; Fossa Levodel, 104; Hortolatio, 118; Les Genetets, 104, 118; Longum Boel, 103, 118; Longum Estrac, 104, 118; Macerias, 103, 118; Marete/Marches, 104, 118; Mesler, 104; Miricent, 103; Muce Lupum, 118; Muchelov, 103; Muta Gerof, 118; Nigras Terras, 104; Picois, 104; Plani, 103, 118; Quadratos, 117; Runcerium, 117; Sevet/Seviet, 104, 117; Vetus Busonem, 117; Wendic', 104
  grain measure of, 34, 107
Vitalis, *prefectus abbatisse*, 118
  prepositus, 120
  Caisnel, 97, 98
  Stephen, 122
  of Escanneville, 84
  son of carpenter, 118–19
  son of Nigel, 104

Waleran, son of Ranulf, moneyer, 9
Walter (*Walterus, Walterius, Galterus, Gualterus, Gualterius*), king's chamberlain, 133
  Anglicus, 67
  Ausent, 97
  the Breton, 94, 95
  Lesbaht, 83, 85
  Le Tros, 72
  of Brionne, 112
  of Ranville, 100
  of Silly, 79 n.
  de Meduana, 124

son of Goi, 70
son of Quintin, 85
gener, 64
Waquelin, de Ferrers, 112
Warin (*Warinus, Garinus, Guarinus*), bishop
    of Senlis, 133
  priest, 22, 92
  Coillart, 83
  of Auberville-sur-Mer, 89
  of Cinglais, 48, 62, 66
  of Colleville-sur-Mer, 114
  of Neuilly, 133
Widelin, 116
Wiger, 2, 110, 120
  of Sainte-Mère-Eglise, 120
  nephew of Wiger of Ste-Mère-Eglise, 120
Wiguen, the Breton, 128
Wigen, of Caen, 123
William, 116
  I, king 3, 4, 6, 9, 39, 56, 96, 123
  II, king, 9, 12
  fitz Ralph, seneschal of Normandy, 37,
    130
  du Hommet, constable of Normandy, 14,
    102, 133
  count of Evreux, 19, 86, 126
  seneschal of Amblie, 44, 45
  de Mara, *vicomte* of Sainte-Mère-Eglise,
    129, 130, 133
  de Mara, of Graye-sur-Mer, 15, 16, 109
  bishop of Avranches, 133
  canon, 115, *see* W. Thomas, canon of
    Bayeux
  de Semilly, dean of chapter of Bayeux, 49
  Acarin, dean, founder of collegiate church
    of the Sepulchre, Caen, 41, 47, 133
  chamberlain, 124
  chamberlain of Tancarville, 112
  chamberlain, son of Roger of Candos, 11,
    126
  priest, brother of Arthur, 113, 129
  priest, of Bougy, 89
  priest of Bourgeauville, 92
  clerk of Argences (?), 37
  Aboveville, 100
  bridge-keeper, 75
  dyer, 69
  fuller, 71
  miller, 76
  parmenter, 119
  skinner, 118
  Aelard, vavassoriate of, 48
  Arrabi, 80
  Bacco, 8
  Baudric, vavassoriate of, 48
  Belet, 113
  Bernard, 78
  Bertran, 11, 126, 127

Boet, 78
Canu, 69, 95
Canute, 63, 69
Caperun, 69
Carbonel, 133
Cat, 73
Coillart, 96
Fawel, 64, 67, 70
Fere, 136
Fleming, 101
Fochoi', 73
Fortis, 91
Gernun, 128
Godelent, 67, 68
Graverenc, 109
Guy, 97
Harviel, 74
Hefovache, 102
Hurtelov, 63, 69
Judas, 126
Julina, 109
Lachor', 38
Le Chevalier, 97, 99
Leflac, 94
Le Merle, 95
Le Meschin, 101, 102
Le Prior, 98
Leterier, 115
Loe, and wife (unnamed) of, 46
Magnus, 68
Maincoir, 65
Marmion, 120
Moltun, Montun, 22, 90, 92
Nepos, of La Rouelle, 74
Patric, 9
Peregrinus, 61, 63, 69
Pingui, 112
Rainoard, 111
Reigecel, 80
Rex, 90
Pantulf, of Almenèches, 98
Salmon, 102
Samson, 115
Silvan, 112
Walter, 85
  of Aisy, 97
  of Anisy, knight, 79 n.
  of Auberville-sur-Mer, 91
  of Bretteville, 79 n.
  of Cairon, 107
  of Calix, 37, 113, 129, 130
  of Calix, wife (unnamed) of, 129
  of Creully, 79
  of Ecorcheville, 113
  of Giberville, relative (unnamed) of, 8 n.
  of Graye-sur-Mer, 38
  of La Bigne, 72
  of Longuevalle, 100

of Magny-en-Bessin, 76
of Mondrainville, 82
of Mortemer, 133
of Ouistreham, 30, 47, 113
of Percy, 69
of Rupierre, 127, 128
of Sallenelles, knight, 43
of Sainte-Croix-sur-Mer, 15, 56
of Saint John, 128
of Sallenelles, knight, 43, 44
of Vaux-sur-Seulles, 42, 43, 123
of Vieux-Pont, 127
of Villers, 79 n.
de Aspres, 120
de Cruce, 78
de Gardigno, 97
de Grania, 115
de Logevilla, 39
de Maletot, 131
de Manerio, 112
de Mariscis, 79 n.
de Merula, 112
de Pirou, 90
de Ulfieres, 120
son of Abbot, 103
son of Aubert, 105
son of Bence, 78

son of Geoffrey, 77
son of John, at Ranville, 99
son of John, at Saulques, 71
son of Hermenent, 91
son of Humphrey, 103, 104
son of Ivo, 104, 107
son of Pagan, 63, 69
son of Reginald, 62, 64, 69
son of Restoud, 80
son of Robert Walter, 83
son of Roger, 35
son of Stephen, 132
son of William, 115
brother of Herbert Walter, 87
brother of Richard of Creully, 135
uncle of Robert, son of the Breton,
    82
Wimond (*Wimondus, Wimundus*), 116, 117,
    122
Hurtelov, 67
of Calix, 119
of Grainville, 24, 80
of Sallen, 78
of Villons-les-Buissons, 106
son of Adam, 62
W., Thomas, canon of Bayeux, 48–9 *see*
    William, canon

Index of Subjects

acres, size of, 33
administration, of the estates, 20–3
advowson, church of Auberville-sur-Mer, 30, 92
  church of Barges, 40–1
  church of Carpiquet, 3, 30, 47–8, 65, 129–31
  church of Falaise (St. Gervase), 41
  church of Grainville-sur-Odon, 30, 81
  church of Juvigny, 30, 75
  church of Sallen, 30, 79
  church of Tassilly, 29–30, 35–6, 98
  church of Vaux-sur-Seulles, 30, 55, 77
aid, of vavassors, 75, 80
allod, 127
  in suo burgo, 116
allodial tenants (*aloers*), 23, 53
almoner, 23
almonry, allocations to, 17, 19–21, 23, 59 n., 65, 96
  grain measure of, 34, 96, 105
  ground corn transported to, 105
alms, 49–50, 58, 81
alms, grants in free and perpetual, 36, 37, 38, 40, 42, 49, 50, 51, 52, 134, 135, 136
altars, gifts for maintainence of, 28, 51–2, 133–7
  gift offered on, 113, 118, 119, 120, 122, 129
ambers, of salt, 19, 34, 58
aquets, asquez, of salt, 34
arpents, vineyard 'acres', 7, 116, 117, 126, 127
assart (*frusta*), 22 n., 27, 117, 118
assize, at Bayeux, 79
  at Caen, 42, 112–13, 128, 129–30
  at Falaise, 132

bacons, hams (*panernas*), 21, 92
baker (*furnarius, panifex, pistor, pitor*), 41–2, 55, 68, 83, 85, *see* IPP, Hugh, John, Osbert Gilbert, Ralph
bailiff (*pretor*), 22, 27, 103, 117
barley, 16–19, 28, 53 *et passim*
barn (*horreum, orreum*), 22, 56, 57; *see also* granary
beans, 127
beer, 131
black earth (*nigras terras*), 49, 104

bleeding, of oxen, 3, 131
boonworks (*precarias, preces, precaturas*), 16, 18, 24, 26, 62, 63, 76, 80, 81, 92, 96, 98–101, 103, 105, 108, 111
bordage tenure, 15, 18, 25–6 *et passim*
borough (*burgum*), 9, 10, 127
  Bourg-le-Roi, 10
  Bourg-l'Abbesse, 10, 29, 35
  Bourg-l'Abbé, 10
bread, 10, 16, 24, 46, 62 *et passim*
brewer (*brasarius, brasciator*), 62, 63, 64, 69, 120, *see* IPP, Geoffrey, John
bridge-keeper (*ponter*), 75, *see* IPP, William
buckler (*bucularius*), 89, 129 n., *see* IPP, Roger
buildings, demesne, 22, 62
burgage tenure, 9 n., 18, 29, 61, 65 n., 69

chamberlains, 10, 11, 112, 119, 124, 126, 127. *See* IPP, Adelofdus, Fulchod, Fulk, Goislenus, Odo, Walter, William
candles, rent, 18, 55, 77, 104
canons, attached to abbey of Holy Trinity, 23
capons, 18, 24, 25, 26, 53 *et passim*
carpenter, 119, *see* IPP, Vitalis
carting services (*summagium, cariagium*), 16, 18, 19, 24–6, 34, 62, *et passim*
castle, at Caen, 10, 116, 123
  castle church of St. George, 7
censarii, 15, 17, 18, 22, 23, 27, 56, 57, 58, 80, 114
champart, 16, 18, 25–6, 54 *et passim*
chaplains, *see* IPP, Benedict, David, Hugh, Humphrey, John, Osbert, Ralph, Reinald, Robert
cheeses, tithe, 21
clerk (*clericus*), 55, 56, and *see* IPP, Anquetil, Bernard, Hervey, Lucas of Vaux, Nicholas, Nicholas of Ableville, Paris, Richard, Richer, Samson of Avesneles, William Acarin, William of Argences (?)
cloth (*pannos*), 113; of silk (*pannos sericos*), 115
cobbler (*sutor*), 67, 68, *see* IPP, Anfrid, Robert
cook (*cocus, coquus*), 109, 123, *see* IPP, Fulk, John son of Godfrey

corn, ground (*farina*), 105
corvées, 16, 18, 25, 56, 57, 59, 63, 84, 100, 101, 105
cottage (*cotagium*), 109
court, duty to attend, 56–7, 93, 95, 118
cowherd (*vacarium*), 58
crier (*preco, precor*), 18, 23, 55, 67
crops, *see* barley, beans, legumes, oats, rye, vetch, wheat
currency, relative values, 33
change in value of, 121
curtilage, 26, 73
custodian of fugitives (*tutrix fugitivorum*), 107, *see* IPP, Roger

darrein presentment, to church of Carpiquet, 30, 129–31, *see* advowson
demesne, 16, 17, 18, 19, 22, 26, 27, 31, 66–9, 74, 75, 79, 81–2, 85, 88, 89–90, 92, 94, 102, 103, 117
dispossession, 10–12, 13, 43–4, 125–8
ditch, repair of, 105
doctor (*medicus*), 115, *see* IPP, Robert
dogs, 115, 128, *see* bernagium in Glossary
Domesday Book, 23
dormitory, 21
dowry (*maritagio*), 98
dyer (*textor, tinctor*), 67, 69, 90 *see* IPP, Jordan, Robert, Simon, William

eels, 18, 76, 79, 114
eggs, 18, 19, 24, 25, 26, 53 *et passim*
enclosure (*clausum, clausulum*), 26, 73, 76, 94
encroachment (*porprestura, porprisagium, porprisum*), 17, 26, 51, 52, 65, 66, 81, 82, 83, 91, 95, 106, 133, 134, 135
escheat (*scaeta, escaeta, ex caduco*), 36, 37, 64, 92, 93, 95, 99
exchanges of property, 20, 37
exchequer, held at Caen, 40, 47, 129–31
at Falaise, 3, 132

fair, of the Meadow (*feriam prati*), at Caen, 94, 100, 101, 105, 106, 114, 131
of St. Giles at Saulques, 72
falcons, 115
farm, of estates in England, 21, 22
of Auberville-sur-Mer, 22, 92
of Carpiquet, 22, 62
of property in Jersey, 3, 13, 121
of Mâlon, 15, 55

farm, carting of, 94
farmers (*firmarii*), 16, 50, 58, 63, 100 *see also* IPP, Gilbert, Thomas
fee-farm, 17, 18, 24, 25 *et passim*
field names, *see* IPP principal place names
fish, tithe of, 6
fishery, 53
for whales, at Graye-sur-Mer, 109
fishing rights, at Caen, 10, 123
fish-market, at Ouistreham, 2, 115
flax, 48, 105
forester (*forestarius*), unnamed, 18, 23, 55
fuller (*fullo, folart*), 70, 71, *see* IPP Alfred, William

gardens, 53, 57, 118
gates, 22, 62
geese, 19, 54, 57, 63, 66, 75, 80, 84, 86, 88, 89, 90, 91, 95, 96, 97, 105, 106
grain (*annona*), 58, 59, 127, 128
mixed (*bladum tercionarium*), 65, 66, 69, 75, 76, 89, 92, 94, 107, 108
measures, 33–4
granary (*grangia, granchia, granarium*), 62, 63, 84, 87, 88, 100, 101, 105
measure of, 75, 79
grout, mash (*grudum*), 63, 66

harrowing (*herciare, herciatura*), 53, 55, 63, 92
haymaking (*falcare, fenagium*), 92, 93, 100, 105
heathland (*bruerie*), 92
hemp, 48–9, 105
hens, 16, 19, 24, 26, 54 *et passim*
herbage, pasturage payment (*herbagium*), 103, 107
herring, 53, 115
horses, loss of, 126, 127, 128
hospital (*maladeriam*) of St. Thomas Becket, 129
hosteler (*hostiarius*), 123
house, grant of, 3, 9, 129
household servants (*famuli*), 6, 115

infirmary, 21
inheritance, *see also* escheat, relief
abbess designated as heir to property at Grainville-sur-Odon, 80; land of Roger of Sallen, 118–19; land in Calix, 122–3
agreement of first-born (*primogeniti*) to quitclaim, 43

inquiries, concerning tenurial conditions (*inquirendum est*) in Survey B, 15, 72, 81, 89, 107, 108

jurisdiction, exemption from episcopal, 6
jurors, of Carpiquet, 15 n., 61–2, 64
  of La Rouelle, 74
  of Ouistreham, 115

lamp, grain rents for maintenance of, 51, 52, 133, 134, 135, 136
lampreys, 115
lazar-house, *see* hospital
leases, of demesne, 18, 19, 22, 66–9, 102
legumes, 85, 86, 88
leper, 129
linen, cloth (*linum, linosium*), 105
livestock, losses, 10, 126–8
locks, 22, 62

malt-grain, 53, 54, 56, 57, 58, 59, 63 (*vel grudi*), 66 (*et avene*), 80, 105, 106
manure, payments for (*fumagium*), 54, 63
market, at Ouistreham, 10, 123
marriage payment (*extra vilanagium*), 63
marshland, 109 n.
mason (*cementarius*), *see* IPP Hugh, 84, 86
meadow, 4, 6, 7, 10, 18, 42–3, 59, 63, 76 n., 81 n., 90, 93, 99, 102
messuage (*mansio, mansura, masagium, masiagium, masuagium*), 3, 9, 15, 17, 26, 27 *et passim*
  vacant (*vacue*), 57, 75
métayer (*mediator*), 17, 18, 23, 58, 59
mill, 3, 6, 7, 22
  at Amblie, 17, 18, 21, 59, 106, 108; at Caen, 9, 131–2; at *La Hoiste*, 120; at Ouistreham, 114; at Ranville, 58, 102; at Sallen, 79; at Saulques, 72; at Vaux-sur-Seulles, 18, 55, 75; unnamed, 124
  Thomas Bardulf's at Elvaston (Derbyshire), 29, 36–7
  multure (*moltam, moutura*), 106, 107, 132
  repairs, 3, 132
  stones (*molas*), 107
tithe, 10, 21
miller (*molendarius, molonarius, de molino*), 76, 97, 131, 132, *see* IPP Erengot, Hugh, William
mortgages (*in vadimonio*), 54, 56

names, occupational, *see* baker, brewer, buckler, carpenter, cook, cowherd, crier, doctor, dyer, forester, fuller, mason, miller, oxherd, palmer, parmenter, porter, reeve, saddler, scribe, skinner, smith, swineherd
nuns, maintenance of (*ad victum sanctimonialium*), 10, 21
  social origins of, 4, 8
  see IPP, Helvida de sancto Paulo, Roza

oats, 53 *et passim*
ovens, 10, 56, 110, 122
oxen, 10, 24, 62–5, 99, 100, 126–8
  bleeding of, 3, 131
oxherd (*bubulcus*), unnamed, 18, 23, 54

palfrey, 57, 122
palmer (*palmarius, palmarus*), 61, 64, 69, 78, *see* IPP, Godwin, Richard
pannage (*pasnagium*), 25, 63, 93
parmenter (*parmentarius*), 119, 120, *see* IPP, William
parceners, co-tenants (*participes*), 55, 88
pasturage, for oxen, 99
pepper rent, 3, 131
pesella, salt measure, 34, 83
pigs, 10, 127, *see also* swineherd
porcagium, payment for grazing, 53, 54, 105
pit-maker, wife of (*femina putei factoris*), 55
pleas, attendance at abbess's, 93, 95
ploughing (*aratura*), 63, 92, 101
ploughlands, 5, 9 n., 18, 33, 55, 56, 57, 58, 59
ploughs, maintenance and repair of, 16, 54, 56
poor, the, 23
porpoises (*porpedes*), 115
porter (*portarius, portitor*), 113, 117, 120, *see* IPP, Arthur, Herold, Thomas
postes, wooden posts, 92
presentation, to churches, *see* advowson
priest (listed in survey), 55, 57, 77, 81, 89, 92, 93, 106
pulagium, fowl rent, 57, 58
purchases, 9–10, 115–17
  of wheat rents in 13th c., 28 n.
purprestures, *see* encroachment

quarry, 105

reeve (*prepositus, prefectus*), 100, 101, 102, 118, 120, 122 *see also* baliff (*pretor*)
regarda, dues of bread, poultry and eggs 24, 25, 26, 63, 66, 89, 91, 104, 129
relief, payment of, 24, 74, 77, 80
rental, of Ouistreham, 2, 27, 113
repairs, to mill, 3, 132
  to manorial buildings, ditches, 22, 64, 105
roads, Froide Rue (*Frigidum Vicum*), Caen, 131
  in Caen (unnamed), 10
  Barbières road (*via de Barberes*), Villons-les-Buissons, 118
  Beuville (*via de Beuvilla*), 135
  Cairon road (*vicum de Carun, via de Caron*), 103, 118
  in curceria vie de Cortiseign', 38, 45
  in Carpiquet (*Keminum*), 65
  Church road (*via Monasterii*), Villons-les-Buissons, 103
  of the Hebrew (*Keminum Hebreceii*), Grainville-sur-Odon, 82
  via de puce fondre, Carpiquet, 48
  Missy road (*via Misseii*), Grainville-sur-Odon, 82
roofwork (*coopertura*), 105
rustici, 66, 69–70, 84, 95, 124–5
rye, 89

sheep, 10, 11, 19, 126, 128
  ewes (*bidentes*), 19, 66, 84, 92
  wethers (*berbices*), 54, 58
  yearlings (*anni*), 66
sheepfold (*bercariam*), 55
shepherd (*bercarius*), 16, 23, 56
shipwreck, right of (*verece, reliqua repertorum*), 2, 92, 115
skinner (*pelliparius*), 118, *see* IPP, William
smallholders, 17, 18, 25, 26, 73, 84
smith (*faber*), 16, 23, 56, 63, 64, 69, 106, 131, *see* IPP, Eudo, Hamelin, Odo, Osbert, Reginald
  tenement of (*mansura fabri*), 74
sower (*seminator*), 16, 23, 56
swineherd (*porcarius*), unnamed, 108

tally (*dica*), 132
tallage, 38
thraves (*trabes*), measures of corn, 92
timber, 115, 128, *see also* woodland
  for mill repairs, 3, 132
tithe-collectors, peasant, 20–1, 23
tithes, 30 *et passim, see* sheaves
tolls, 6, 10, 21, 123, 127 (*pedagium*)

sacristan, cartulary, of, 28, 133
sacristy, 21
saddler (*sellarius*), 131 *see* IPP, Salomon
salmon, 115
salt, tithe of, 6
  Escanneville, 19, 34, 58, 85–86, 89
  measures, 34
saltpits, saltworks, 11, 19, 58, 126
salt-rent, 82 (at Grainville-sur-Odon), 83 n., 85–6 (at Escanneville)
scribe (*scriptor, scriba, qui . . . scribebat*), 79 n., 131, 133, *see* IPP, H', Ralph, William Acarin
sepulture, 6, 21
serjeant (*serviens*), 17, 58, 93
serjeanty (*in sergantia*), 16, 110
silk cloth, 115
service, with horse (*servicium equi*), 17, 24, 25, 62, 71, 72, 73, 80, 88, 89, 91, 94, 99, 100, 104, 107, 110
service, by foot (*servicium peditis*), 17, 24, 64, 104
sharecropping, *see* champart
sheaves of grain, as tithe (*garba, garbagium*), 42, 48, 55, 57, 58, 59, 60, 66, 72, 75, 79, 80, 81, 84, 85, 89, 92, 96, 98, 99, 105, 107, 108 *see also* tithes

urban property, 2, 9–10, 13, *see also* IPP, Caen, Calix

vavassoriate (*vavasoria, vavassoria*), 43, 44, 46, 48, 71, 93, 94
vavassors, 11, 15, 16, 17, 18, 19, 22, 23, 24, 25, 27, 32 *et passim*
villeinage tenure, 23, 25 *et passim*
vinagium, payment for carting wine, 24, 62, 63, 64, 65, 74, 75, 79, 80, 81, 83, 84, 87, 88, 93, 99, 100
viticulture, 2, 3, 7, 10 n., 11, 48, 68, 115–17, 126

whale fishery, 109
whales, tithe of, 6
wheat, 8, 16, 17, 18, 19, 26, 39 *et passim*
widowhood, 136–7
women, 4, 8
woodland, 6, 7, 10, 11, 22, 62, 72, 74, 93, 103, 118
wool, tithe of, 21

RECORDS OF SOCIAL AND ECONOMIC HISTORY
(New Series)

I. *Charters of the Honour of Mowbray 1107-1191.* D. E. Greenway. 1972

II. *The Lay Subsidy of 1334.* R. E. Glasscock. 1975

III. *The Diary of Ralph Josselin, 1616-1683.* A. MacFarlane. 1976

IV. *Warwickshire Grazier and London Skinner, 1532-1555. The Account Book of Peter Temple and Thomas Heritage.* N. W. Alcock. 1981

V. *Charters and Custumals of the Abbey of Holy Trinity, Caen.* M. Chibnall. 1982

VI. *The Cartulary of the Knights of St. John of Jerusalem in England, Secunda Camera, Essex.* M. Gervers. 1982

VII. *The Correspondence of Sir John Lowther of Whitehaven, 1693-1698.* D. R. Hainsworth. 1983

VIII. *The Farming and Memorandum Books of Henry Best of Elmswell, 1642.* D. Woodward. 1984

IX. *The Making of King's Lynn.* D. M. Owen. 1984

X. *The Compton Census of 1676. A Critical Edition.* A. Whiteman. 1986

XI. *The Early Records of Medieval Coventry.* P. R. Coss. 1986

XII. *Markets and Merchants of the Late Seventeenth Century. The Marescoe-David Letters, 1668-1680.* H. Roseveare. 1987

XIII. *The Diary of Bulstrode Whitelocke, 1605-1675.* R. Spalding. 1990

XIV. *Contemporaries of Bulstrode Whitelocke, 1605-1675. Biographies, Illustrated by Letters and other Documents.* R. Spalding. 1990

XV. *The Account Book of Richard Latham, 1724-1767.* L. Weatherill. 1990

XVI. *An American Quaker in the British Isles. The Travel Journals of Jabez Maud Fisher, 1775-1779.* K. Morgan. 1992

XVII. *Household Accounts from Medieval England, Part 1.* C. M. Woolgar. 1992

XVIII. *Household Accounts from Medieval England, Part 2.* C. M. Woolgar. 1993

XIX. *The Warwickshire Hundred Rolls of 1279-80: Stoneleigh and Kineton Hundreds.* T. John. 1992

XX. *Lordship and Landscape in Norfolk, 1250-1350. The Early Records of Holkam.* W. Hassall & J. Beauroy. 1993

21. *The Books of Assumption of Scottish Benefices, c. 1562.* J Kirk. Due 1995